The Anato
by Mic

Some of the people in this book have had their names changed to protect their identities.

For information, write to thelifeadrift@gmail.com

First Edition
Paperback print edition ISBN: 9781980806172
Edited by Julia at https://edit911.com/
Cover Design by Cal Sharp at https://www.caligraphics.net/

For Rosie

Table of Contents

Introduction

From a passion for the natural world, the natural world of which we are all an interdependent part, came my desire to stop destroying it. The economic, political, and social conditions that most of us live in today do precisely that: destroy it. We live on a finite planet where everything is ecologically connected, and yet our systems and individual behaviours do not reflect this. This becomes clearer with each passing year as we see record extinction rates with depleted and polluted forests, oceans, and all those things we depend on to live a good life. None of this made any sense to me. These systems are our creations, but they are working against humanity and the other living beings of the earth, not for them. Why are our systems like that then? How did we get here? What assumptions about our world do we take to be facts when they are actually only misguided and destructive beliefs? In examining these questions and uncovering some fundamental truths arose my imperative to escape from this framework. I discuss this in Part 1.

Scattered across twenty years, living primarily in Australia, I executed a series of clumsy attempts to escape from systems and indeed a way of life that seemed contrary to promoting well-being and longevity of ourselves and our habitat. Across those years and with each successive escape attempt, I came to understand two things. First, I cannot change the nature of these systems, at least, not in any meaningful or significant way. Second, there can be a process of escaping from those systems. In Parts 2 and 3, I explain much of what I have learned.

Eventually, after much reflection, self-education, and practice, I earned my black belt in escape. I learned how to live a good life, which for the most part is free from the contradictions of those systems. By doing away with many standards and conventions that we have come to assume are true, I worked out how to be healthy, prosperous, and happy without having a strong relationship with things like work, money, and material possessions. The resultant lifestyle, taking this introduction full circle, promotes the persistence of a habitable and healthy planet. Part 4 is all about this way of living. It is about escapee life.

You might be thinking that by abandoning ship in this way, I am being selfish, and you would be right in some ways. I selfishly want to lead a life well lived. But as I discovered and as I retell in this story, a good life is difficult to find in isolation. I want as many people as possible to undermine the systems that so patently are harming us and our planet. And I have come to realise that one of the best ways to do that, one of the best ways to withdraw support for them, is to leave them and live with new systems that support a good life.

This brings me to why I wrote this book. I want to expose the unfortunate realities of the incumbent systems and how to escape them and to paint a realistic picture of what escapee life can look like and what a good life can be.

This is not a guide to getting rich quick, escaping to a far-flung paradise, and living in luxury. Neither is it a blueprint for how to live with nothing at all. This book is not on that spectrum as I aim to define and live a good life, as much as possible, outside of the old-world parameters of money and material belongings. But I do not ignore such things. While this escape plan can be executed with little or no funding, as I will explain, I make no secret of the fact that I did start with some resources. I am also well aware that seeking and living such a life might seem a heck of a lot easier for an unmarried man without children, such as myself, than for family folks, for example. But even though I write through my own view of the world, I am sure that much of this book is relevant to other than my own demographic.

In any case, I have not written a "how to live" book. These can be boring and vain, and besides, they are very '80s. Instead, I have written a story, a memoir perhaps, narrated through the lens of a year of escapee life in Southeast Asia, starting from around October, 2016. Throughout that, I reflect back across two decades on my own escape process, both mental and physical, that led up to that year. The result is the tale of two related journeys revealing in my experiences many useful bits of knowledge if you decide to do something similar, or it can just be material for you to chuckle at if you prefer.

Some of the writing here has appeared in previous essays and articles of mine, but most is appearing for the first time. You can read the previously printed material on my website, thelifeadrift.com.

Part 1: ESCAPE?

1. Evolve

DISSECTING FAILURE

"Mike, she finish," he says. His voice is barely audible and downbeat as it always is, but now it also carries a note of disbelief. I knew that he meant she was dead, but not knowing what to say and needing to say something, I respond over the scratchy mobile connection, "What? Daniel, what do you mean?"

"Elvira. She dead. She stop breathing. We go home to village now. I go. Funeral in two days."

Daniel, a local man from the single street village behind and up the hill from Sorake Beach, was Elvira's father. He keeps a house up in the village, but his family spends most of their days at a wooden, one-room hut about fifty metres back from the famous Indonesian surf beach. In front of that on the beachfront, he had constructed accommodations for tourists for whom his family cooked and cleaned.

I am not one of those tourists. I choose instead to live in a converted bus I call Rosie a little further along the beachfront in a hotel car park.

A few weeks before that terrible phone call, I met Daniel and his family. I had followed his faded surfboard repair signs which led me to his clunky and clumsily built front door. After a few minutes of talking to him about the needed fin repair, I abandoned any thoughts of negotiation. His price was fair, and I could tell he was not in the rip-off game. I chose to respect his price and inadvertently him as well. I met his wife and two daughters during that first encounter. All three of them cautiously emerged from the tiny earthen floored abode to observe what they thought was another tourist.

After that first day, I saw Daniel, his modest and loyal wife, and his daughters every day. They'd be milling about their tourist bungalows attending to this or that. His wife, Mamma Martin, was usually withdrawn but always threw me a genuine smile, perhaps appreciative that I brought them some business with my board or maybe just because I seemed to be sticking around longer than most of the other surfing folk. Sometimes in the afternoon, I'd stop in at their house and share a beer with Daniel. His wife would always sit in silence somewhere nearby. Elvira, the brains of the family, would be diligently doing her schoolwork, and Tata, the younger of the two, would be flitting about the place. She would come in and out of sight, showing off her mastery of English with me, even though I preferred to speak in Indonesian as even though Daniel spoke some English, Mamma Martin spoke none.

Those days passed in a pleasant lack of hurry. Nobody was in a rush to do anything in particular; there was little to do except surf and cater to surfers. Island life was what it was; a tourist needing a fin fixed was considered a notable event; a tourist popping in for a social visit was cause for celebration. In some ways, I would have liked there to be no more events of note, but that didn't happen.

Walking back from an afternoon surf, across the barnacled and exposed part of the reef, one such event began to unfold. When Daniel's bungalows and his beaten-up old beach shack came into view, I could see him standing on his front porch. He saw me at the same time and hurried from his lookout to meet me.

"Mike. Mike, I need your bus. Can you drive us to the big town?" he asked nervously.

"Of course, why, what's up?" I said as I came down from my surfing high.

"Elvira, she very sick."

He led me inside, and I realised how genuinely tiny this dwelling was. It was one room with two mosquito-netted beds. Elvira was on the one closest to the entryway. There was nothing else in the house except a small table with a gas cooker on it and some pots and pans hanging off hooks on the rough timber wall behind it. A curtain covering the front of the table probably hid plates and glasses and the like. I wondered where they bathed or even went to the toilet.

Daniel pulled back the netting and Elvira, whose eyes and mouth would typically smile and who usually would have something to say, didn't even roll her eyes towards me. In her underwear, her eleven-year-old body was shining with a greenish sweat. Her eyes, open but misty and vacant, wearily looked up to some uneventful space above her. She did not react at all to our presence or when we spoke. I struggled to comprehend that this was the same girl who only a few days earlier seemed so healthy. I stared at her, afraid to look at her parents for what I might see there.

"She need go to hospital," Daniel said. "She very sick; she been like this two days."

8

"What is it? What's wrong with her?" I asked.

"I don't know. I think black magic," he responded as Mamma Martin bowed her head in agreement with the diagnosis.

"Black Magic? What are you talking about, has she got fever, diarrhoea?"

"It's black magic, Mike. She very sick."

He explained that she was having troubles with her classmates. She was a smart kid, and it was generating a lot of jealousy and in some cases hatred amongst the other students. Daniel told me more about it as we drove to the big town, Telukdalam, the second largest on the Sumatran island of Nias. Elvira and Mamma Martin bounced around in the back of the bus on my bed, Elvira more so as she was unable to control her weak body when I trundled in and out of giant potholes.

Mamma Martin tried to steady her, but her hands, controlling their clothing, bedding, food and cooking equipment that they would need in the hospital, were full already. They would all stay there overnight on the floor if there were no bed. Daniel went on to tell me that he wasn't sure how, but somehow as a result of this hatred against his daughter one of the other families from the school had conspired to cast a spell over Elvira. He was sure that the doctor at the big town's hospital would agree.

We arrived at the hospital in the big town after about half an hour and at about the same time that the electricity cut out. Another of the frequent Nias blackouts had hit almost as if in collusion with the black magic, and everything except life support systems, which would run off the generator, were dead.

Two hospital staff emerged as we parked in the emergency bay. They wore white coats, which gave me some assurance, and with Daniel carried Elvira's limp body inside. Mamma Martin asked if I could go out again and find some candles and some fried rice as it would be challenging to cook now that the power was out. Taking note of this and a few other bits and pieces she needed for a night in the hospital with no power, I was hit by the sadness, the defeat in Mamma Martin's face. Her eyes confessed that they had seen many misfortunes such as these in a place that has so little of the things that I would take for granted. Despite her dreadful sorrow, she remained functional; she had to be, for her daughter.

When I returned, Daniel came out to meet me and took the plastic bag of supplies.

"Don't have proper doctor here; they do what they can, give her medicines. They think she has blood poisons. They say like me. Is black magic. She need good doctor in Medan."

Medan is the closest reasonably sized city. It is perhaps two hours of driving and then an hour's flight away from where we were. I could detect a pleading in his voice, inviting me to offer to pay for an excursion to Medan.

"What can I do, Daniel? What can I do now to help?" Selfishly, I hoped he didn't hit me up for the cost of airfares to and accommodation in Medan. It would have been an inconvenience, but unlike Daniel, I could have afforded it.

He paused for a few tense seconds, and then as if reading my mind, he said, "It's OK, Mike. You go now. I call you tomorrow."

We hugged "OK. Call me for anything you need, Daniel."

That was yesterday. And now he has called me. But he needs nothing. His daughter is dead. He hangs up the phone. Aside from the shock, the shock that this illness—or black magic as he called it—was so severe and the deterioration of Elvira so quick, I think about his voice. There was that something different about his voice. Then I realise that it wasn't disbelief that I heard in his voice. It was failure. I detected in his voice that he felt he had failed, failed Elvira, and failed as a father.

His daughter has just died, and I respect that he will be a mess now and for some time to come. But I hope he ultimately realises that he did not fail her in any way. Folks tend to resort to that conclusion, that they have failed or that they are a failure far too commonly. Perhaps we could argue that the economic, social, or medical system failed them as they did nothing to prevent little Elvira from having such a short life. Perhaps it was I who had failed them all. Had I responded to Daniel's guarded plea to go to Medan, maybe things would have been different. I would carry this guilt for a while but would eventually convince myself that at the time I didn't consider that death was a possibility.

Daniel and Mamma Martin did not fail Elvira. They were devoted and affectionate parents and for her eleven years all the way to the unhappy end; they gave all that they knew how to give. Neither was Elvira's life itself a failure; it just ended. The experience of being a father and the life of his child had no element of failure just because she died at eleven. There is no mandate to live until the age of eighty and die peacefully in your sleep for a life to be a successful one. Neither is this required to demonstrate that he had been a good father. This concept of failure too often refers to the very end point of something and ignores all that came before it.

We like to say that something has failed and someone is a failure in doing something if the end result, the very distinct and finite thing at the end of the experience, does not go as planned. If failure or the lack of success is defined by not "having the correct or desired result", as in the dictionary, then failure does not just have negative connotations.

Failure can be a positive thing because at least someone started something. A specified end result is often there just to pull us through an experience from beginning to end. It is the journey as much as the destination that is desired.

I'll venture further and say that failure often turns out to be a good thing. If I only did things that I knew had a good chance of achieving the desired end, I wouldn't take many risks in my life, and I probably wouldn't attain much personal growth. Even by attempting things that come with a guarantee of failure, I am learning and getting one step closer to success.

I see my life as just a series of experiments or games. I sit around and ponder what might be an interesting experiment or a fun game to play, and then that becomes my purpose. I don't see one overarching life purpose; I see many, and I am the creator of them. I usually have no clue about the chance of success in terms of any end goal I might set, but I set one anyway and then play the game.

Often this involves an element of risk, but usually that risk is not real. For instance, one of my experiments as I write today is an experiment in escape. In this experiment, which started in June 2015, I decided to leave work and consumer society and live a simple, nomadic life. There were plenty of perceived risks with leaving a substantial income and the stability and security that come with it. But what was the worst-case scenario? It was the life I was already living, working sixty-hour weeks under fluorescent lights, highly stressed, and unhappy. The experiment, it seemed, had no downside. So, I gave it the green light. And so far, so good.

Without being conscious of doing it, I have been living a life of mostly failed experiments that have been rewarding and crucial to my growth and happiness. In the years before my current experiment in escape, which I deem a success already on many levels, I undertook four prior escape attempts. All of these failed in terms of their final result because their conclusion involved a return to work in the West, but they were a heck of a lot of fun. Each one of those four experiments resulted in about a year of living as an escapee in Latin America. For different reasons that I will discuss below, the system recaptured me, and it was back to the fluorescent lights.

Even though I was re-apprehended—well, it was more a case of turning myself in—each one of those attempts brought me closer to a successful escape, even though at their conclusion I returned to my worst-case scenario. I lost nothing; I just returned to where I was with another ridiculous experiment under my belt. Aside from inching closer to a successful escape, each attempt was worthwhile in and of itself. Each one was full of adventure, friendship, and growth.

Where would I be today if I hadn't run those absurd experiments? Well, I would have spent those four years living in my worst-case scenario where I miserably worked my butt off as the human equivalent of a battery hen. I wouldn't have shared amazing experiences with so many people who still are my closest friends. I wouldn't be able to speak Spanish. I wouldn't have discovered the many eye-opening places in Latin America that I know I will return to one day. I would not have grown as an individual in my acceptance and understanding of other ways of living and come to appreciate and be grateful for what I have. I would not have written this book. Thinking back now, when planning and executing those escapes, I didn't concern myself with failure. Those four failed escapes, I now see, were some of my finest achievements to date.

My friend Daniel may not have consciously decided to bring Elvira into the world, but even so he took that risk, and he had a fantastic daughter, whose life, albeit short, was full of joy.

So, don't get caught up in the end result. Don't let the prospect of failure get in the way of experience. Life is the lab, and each of us is our own mad scientists. In the face of possible or even probable failure, go forth and experiment!

13

YOUR SPECIES NEEDS YOU!

It is the morning of the second day since Elvira's death. I have just returned to my bus from the morning surf, and I have a missed call from Daniel. Dammit. I didn't want him to think I needed reminding. Sitting on an upholstered storage box inside my four-or-five-cubic-metre-home, I return his call.

Through a cacophony of loud male voices, I squint to hear Daniel asking where I am, for the funeral had started. I had lost track of time, but I say I am on my way, that I'll be there soon. I put some hot water on for a coffee and think about what's ahead. I am surprised to feel nervous. Knowing I'll be the only white person doesn't normally bother me as I'm usually the only white person anywhere I go in Sumatra. I've become accustomed to the confused and curious stares. I am used to the rock star-like existence, although some days I feel a bit more like a human oddity or sideshow freak. Usually, I don't mind the attention, but not today. I don't want to draw any attention on this occasion.

I look around me and put on my best clothes, which unfortunately are the same as my worst clothes, only cleaner. Today is the first day in a long time that I wish I had footwear other than flip-flops.

Before the water comes to a boil, I sprinkle two large tablespoons of coffee from my two-kilogram bag into the pot, stir it, and pour a mug full. Too full. Coffee splashes on my t-shirt, but it remains the cleanest thing I have, so it stays on. I gulp it down, pour the rest of the hot water into the thermos flask, and secure the back section of the bus for motion.

I drive out of Sorake Beach and turn left and up the hill towards the village. I've only been there once before. It's the kind of place that's interesting to see only once. It consists of a 200-metre-long strip, with traditional houses on either side, and the "jumping stone" positioned in the centre. As a rite of passage into

14

manhood, the boys of the village have to jump this stone. It is high. Maybe my height of six feet.

As Rosie struggles up the hill slow enough for first gear, groups of people join me on either side and walk in the same direction. They form something like a motorcade's indigenous secret service. They must be coming from other villages. They are chatting and laughing and look as though they have dressed for church, but it's not Sunday. I park the bus fifty metres before the village starts to avoid attention, and as I walk through the entry archway I wonder how I'll find Daniel's house. I start to ask some well-dressed villagers as they filter through the archway, but before I finish asking I know where his house is. The commotion there gives it away. I listen to their responses and thank them.

Villages in Nias hold funeral ceremonies outside the house of the deceased's family. As I approach Daniel's house I see the enormous marquee is in fact a patchwork of smaller tarpaulins stitched together. Under it, are about a hundred men in colourful, traditional clothing seated in a three-sided square, the open side facing the house. The three sides of the square are each about four or five rows deep. I can see one man standing with his hands aloft and yelling at a panel of five or so men dressed in white outfits with the traditional headdress. Of those five men facing the open square, one is Daniel. I also recognise his brother sitting next to him, but I don't see Mamma Martin. In fact, I see no women.

Pulling with me the stares of several heads dumbfounded by my whiteness, I walk around the far side of the square behind the panel to where Daniel is receiving the tirade from the shouting man. I am not sure if it is my place to approach him, but I do anyway. It turns out to be appropriate as Daniel stands and turns with a smile, takes a few steps, grabs me by the arms, pulls me towards him, pushes his nose into my cheek, and then again into the other.

15

OK. So this is how it rolls. I don't say anything. Instead, I press my hand over my heart, communicating with telling eyes how I feel and then hug him. Words would have poorly expressed my feelings. He turns back to his shouter, and I turn and walk further behind the panel to the buildings where it seemed the less important folks are hovering.

Slumped like a drunkard in a chair against Daniel's concrete house, one of the few untraditional buildings in the village, is Cobba. I know Cobba from the beach strip; he's a local surfing legend and has been called Cobba for so long by his Australian surfing counterparts that it has stuck with him. After some small talk, he tells me I should go and see Elvira and Mamma Martin and directs me to one of the two open concrete doorways facing the square of men outside.

My heart rate accelerates. I've never seen a dead body before. I have no idea what I am supposed to do in there. As I pass through the doorway, aside from the elderly woman fanning flies off of Elvira's body now two days' dead, what hits my senses most and causes an involuntary gulp is the smell. The waft of her decaying flesh seems so ugly, so inappropriate to be coming from this beautiful little girl. Elvira is laid out in her Sunday-best clothing, but this strikes me less than the greyish colour of her skin and the cotton blood-stained gauze protruding from one nostril.

I scan to her right and stop at Mamma Martin, listless and looking into her hands as if holding a baby. The instant she looks up I lock eyes with her. As if to confirm my association with her daughter's death, her shoulders drop, her head tilts back, and her wail now joins her tears. I can't get to her because of the other women in the room and Elvira's raised dais. I don't know if it would be appropriate, so I just put my hands together as if in prayer and nod my head to her in silent acknowledgement.

16

She gets my intention and nods back at me and resumes her wailing. She is comforted by several women close to her, and I think about how tight this community seems. I stay there and look at Elvira's lifeless body and try to feel as much as I can about what this death thing is all about. She looks so much like a living human, something that contains life, but it doesn't; it is just early-stage dirt. Life is finished here. I look once more at Mamma Martin and leave the room.

Outside, a different man is now yelling and invoking the energy and supporting cheers of the others. It seems each man has his turn to stand up and shout, maybe about the injustice of death; I don't know. Up here in the village, only the Nias dialect is spoken, not Indonesian, so to me, he sounds no different from the boisterous street vendors in Telukdalam.

Several hours pass like this. The sun is now high above the centre strip of the village, and my perch next to Cobba is too hot for me. I move around the square and sit in the back row in a vacated seat, protected from the sun by the tarpaulins. The men now seated around me spin their attention to me and start asking, thankfully in Indonesian, "Where are you from?" and "Why are you here?" and the like. I answer the first few inquiries but then fake my attention on the shouting man to deflect their interest. This seems to do the trick.

Soon after I sit down, the pace changes. Elvira is carried out on a sheet of triplex by a few able men and put into a white casket that I only now can see. So many people play a significant role in the funeral. A man who seems to be the master of ceremonies enters the scene through a newly created gap in the crowd to my left. Trailing him is a group of about ten school children, Elvira's classmates. They enter the "ring" and sing a melodic and happy-sounding song to honour her. I can't help but see the irony here in that supposedly it was these kids who were behind the black magic that ended her life. Still, it is beautiful to listen to.

17

Following them are at least ten other troupes, including other schoolchildren, adults, church groups, and groups from other villages. Surely not all of these people knew her.

An hour of this passes, and now a man dressed in a priest's garb is having his say. He has a lot to say, but as he finishes, everyone but me seems to know what to do. Those still sitting, stand and slowly start walking up the main strip away from the beach end of the village. I join them, and as we walk I am surrounded by villagers again asking all manner of questions about me.

We all walk to the burial ground, which I soon see is only fifty metres away from the top of the village. This procession is surprisingly jovial and social. Although many here are from other villages, everyone mingles as if they are one community.

We arrive at the grave in drips and drabs. Somehow, the priest and the casket are already in position; I must have dawdled. By the time that I am close enough to the pit to make sure that Daniel sees me there in support, the priest seems to be concluding. Three cemetery folk, distinguished by their filthy attire, start wrestling with the casket. There are no ropes or pulleys, just three fellows dragging it in from the long end of the pit. I think to myself: I wouldn't want to be the guy in the hole.

After a while, everyone is back at Daniel's house, and there is talk of a luncheon feast. Several of the villagers invite me, but I politely refuse with a believable lie. It's not that they made me feel unwelcome in any way, but I don't want any attention, and I know I will get plenty of it if I stay.

Daniel and his brother take their seats. Mamma Martin is next to Daniel this time. I walk over to them and tell them I thought it was a beautiful ceremony without knowing if that is considered a good thing or not and excuse myself, repeating my lie. Daniel noses me as he did before. I take his brother's hand and press it to my forehead and do the same with Mamma Martin. I have no idea if this is custom here, but I've seen it around in Sumatra as a respectful way to address an elder. I know they know I am clueless, and Mamma Martin gives me a teary half-smile. I walk back down the hill to Rosie and drive back to the beach.

Since the day of Daniel's phone call when I first learnt of Elvira's death, I'd struggled to organise, and indeed even find my thoughts and emotions about it. When I did, aside from sorrow, I found guilt. First, there was guilt that I didn't know how to react to her death, then the guilt that I come from a country where this needn't have ended like this and finally guilt that I could have done something about it and didn't.

It seemed so cruel and unfair. Everything about it and the subsequent events were based on something entirely tragic. But the funeral provided an unexpected consolation, not in what it commemorated, but in how it was. It was not like any funeral I'd ever heard of in Australia. What was so special about it? I think it was the sense that 'we're all in this together'. So many people came and contributed, from the impassioned shouting men to the young singing troupes. Not all of them knew Elvira. They went out of respect for a member of their broader community. Even I was welcomed as if I were family.

In that way, the villagers had a particular kind of richness different from that which we have or seek in Australia. Here there was very little display of monetary wealth. Doing that might have seemed garish, even obscene. Doing that may also have been difficult given there was very little monetary wealth to display. I generally refer to monetary wealth as including money or currency itself, valuable possessions, property, resources or other riches.

The wealth in the village was mostly non-monetary. Their wealth was in the priority to and fullness of their human community. There was wealth in their connection to nature; it added to their quality of life. The surfers, fishermen, and farmers treated their natural world with respect; they were fully aware that they were an integral part of it. They had aspects of wealth which perhaps might be deficient in places like Australia.

I am not suggesting that the largely subsistence lifestyle in the village is somehow better than, say, my life in Australia. The people of the village certainly would benefit from more of the things monetary wealth could buy, such as more health and education. If Elvira had been in Australia, she may have lived longer than eleven years. Theirs is not a perfect life. But there is still a lot we can learn from the village.

Success up there in the village seems to be measured by the strength and solidarity of human and natural communities, their greater selves. It got me thinking not only about the subjectivity of success for different peoples but also the interdependency of success between those people and their communities. Universally, the success and the survival of any individual depends on the success of the species of which it is a part, so it would again be easy to see a funeral as a failure.

So let me leave the funeral for a moment to talk about another member of the natural world, the mouse-like *antechinus*. This very excitable Australian marsupial mates itself to death. At maturity at one year of age, the male of the species becomes obsessed with sex. He stops eating and resting and does nothing but sleep around with as many partners as he can. He loses most of his vital proteins and shuts down his immune system to generate the metabolic energy for his heroic sexual marathon. He exhausts himself so thoroughly that he starts to disintegrate physically. His fur falls off, he bleeds internally, and without a functioning immune system he invites infection and becomes riddled with gangrene. Within a few weeks of non-stop debauchery, he is dead. His dedication to the survival of his species is unbeaten in the animal kingdom.

Thinking about the character of Elvira's funeral, the generosity of the villagers and their devotion to their community as much if not more than to themselves, is how I came across that selfless, furry little sex god and his devotion his to species. I wondered about how we, in Australia for example, think about our communities and further, about our species. What behavioural traits and other qualities do we value that lend themselves to success and the survival of a community or species?

How we define success seems like an excellent next step. I like the dictionary definition of success because within its two explanations we are given not only the meaning of the word but also some clues about its changing nature. The first denotation is 'having the correct or desired result', and the second is 'having gotten or achieved wealth, respect, fame'. The definitions could be referring to two completely different terms. But if I venture beyond the print and look into history, I can see that many moons ago they both faithfully described the same thing. Further, if I take the subjects of life and reproduction, since I am on it anyway, the applied definition of success over the course of history becomes fascinating indeed.

'Having the correct or desired result' seems to be the more objective explanation. Aside from my earlier qualification that success occurs along the way as well as at the definitive end of an experience, this definition rings true across many different contexts and throughout history. With life on earth, the many species or communities of a species, individual creatures, or even at the level of microscopic male reproductive cells, spermatozoon, this definition is consistent with the idea of survival.

The process of reproduction in most mammals involves a winner-takes-all swimming competition for around 100 million sperm cells racing towards the coveted and usually singular female egg. Amongst fellow sperm, the strongest and most talented one-time swimmer is considered a success. It is its roughly 750 megabytes of DNA data that merge in the soup of creation with the data of the prized egg to form the basis of new life, or 'the desired result'. Interestingly, as the average human ejaculate contains about 180 million sperm cells, it can carry approximately 13,500 terabytes of data, which is comparable to the hard disk space of 135,000 laptops of the type I am writing on now. I wonder if I should get ahead of the Silicon Valley boffins and patent ejaculate-based storage media.

Not only at this microscopic level, where amongst its peers the victorious sperm cell is considered a success, but reproduction, the event itself, is deemed to be successful. Then, the individual male creature that delivers his payload to his female counterpart is viewed as a success amongst fellow herd, mob, or clansmen. His genes help perpetuate life. As the most aquatically able sperm from the fittest male creates life together with the most desirable female(s), the species itself, according to Darwin's survival of the fittest, achieves 'the desired result'. The community and the species survive as they evolve with the incremental advantages that the champion sperm and those complicit creatures bring to the act.

This definition of success I find hard to fault. Success and having achieved the desired result mean the same thing in this case: survival. This holds whether referring to the sperm and egg, the individual creatures, the community, and the species. Success (and the desired result) may well be achieved by acting out of self-interest, consciously or unconsciously, but undoubtedly also instinctively to perpetuate the species. This priority of species over individual makes sense, for the former can survive without the latter, but not vice versa. The end even for the sex-crazed antechinus justifies the means.

The second, human-centric definition is more interesting and is both subjective across different peoples and contentious as its

22

meaning and recent application had evolved from a time when a very different set of circumstances were in place and its validity could be understood. Is 'having gotten or achieved wealth, respect, fame' a valid definition of success today? Are those characteristics conducive to survival? Or does this second definition expose a wrong turn somewhere back in our history? We need to roll back the clock to see what happened there.

The hominoids back in Neolithic times got along just as every other animal did and evolved according to the rules of natural selection and survival of the fittest. Accidental, advantageous traits that bolstered one individual's ability to survive over another would result in reproductive success for that animal through the perpetuation of his and her genes, evolution, and a higher chance of success for the species. I can see the lineage between prehistoric competitive traits, drawn into existence because of the threat of not surviving back then, and our modern-day behavioural traits of seeking wealth, respect, and fame. For instance, one's wealth derives from displaying an ability to provide sufficiently for one's offspring to ensure their survival. Respect has early beginnings in a male or female seeking acceptance of their dominance within a tribe, perhaps. And fame, I suspect, evolved out of the need for attention to attract a mate. The modern definition evolved from competitive qualities once required for reproduction, evolution, and survival. Competitive, individualistic behaviour and qualities resulting in the success of the individual and the species were then perpetuated, and so it goes.

Fast-forward to today's version of man. Is competitive survival of the fittest behaviour still relevant for human beings' survival? Is it still improving our chances in the long run? This is where it gets a bit prickly.

I would venture that up until a certain point in our evolutionary history, being a faster, stronger, smarter, and more

23

competitive hominoid meant that you had a better chance of attracting a mate and reproducing which would have enhanced those same characteristics within the gene pool and subsequently improved the survival chances of the species. It would have improved the fitness of our species to what we were trying to fit, our environment. This 'fitness' involves two players, both of which are in a constant state of flux. Player one, is the human species, which in the grand scale of cosmic history, evolved or adapted very quickly. Player 2, is our environment, our planet which historically has changed at a vastly slower rate.

But what if during our evolution, we reached a point in our development when, as a species, we had developed sufficient mastery over other beasts and dominion over the natural world that long-term survival was no longer in question? I concede that I am generalising as there are many individuals struggling to survive because of inequitable wealth distribution, famine and wars. But I could argue that these are man-made or at least are within man's ability to prevent. On that basis, I will ignore that sad reality and posit that at some point in our relatively recent past as a species we did reach the point of almost assured long-term survival. I say almost assured because both players in the 'fitness' game are constantly changing, so we could never in practice reach 100% assurance, but I shall use the term assurance for this argument.

The problem was that these competitive behavioural traits continued to develop after the imperative of survival had left us. These days, it is expected that we should display competitive, individualistic behaviour as a means for success if we can, so much so that this idea has become part of the dictionary definition. But why are we further evolving traits that are no longer necessary? And beside their being unnecessary, they are now actually getting in the way of our survival as a species.

The pointless pursuit of monetary wealth in particular increasingly leverages both human and natural resources. As it is primarily an individual endeavour, man's separation from both his fellow humans and the natural world continues to become more pronounced. This being *apart*, as against *a part* of the human communities and the natural world has made it easy for this leverage to go from use to abuse and even exploitation of these resources as people seek individual success while unmindful of the success of the species or the planet on which their lives depend. Even at the individual level, this separation often underpins much unhappiness and poor health; so, all around it's hardly what I would call a successful evolutionary trait. Perhaps we could learn something from species that have taken the opposite approach. Some species of ants have survived relatively unchanged for ninety million years.[1] It has been suggested that their social organisation and their prioritising the colony over the individual has had a lot to do with this.

The success of an individual depends on the success of the species, and the species needs somewhere habitable to live. Even after survival became assured, chasing monetary wealth at the expense of nature was not a big deal with a relatively small global population. But we have grown in number and in our ability to adversely affect our habitat. That which we had evolved to fit so perfectly, is becoming less of a good fit, not because we are changing, but because we are changing it. Environmental destruction and habitat loss is no news flash, but as it is the first time in our evolutionary history that it has been possible to annihilate our habitat, I can understand how we have ignored the threat.

With the indefinite growth of our populations and economies, environmental depletion will only get worse. Now we are faced with the ultimate irony in that the same individual traits that were once beneficial for survival as a species, these 'means', unabated, have become a means to a very different end, namely, the end of our species. Without corrective action, we will soon join the ninety percent of all species that have ever lived, in extinction.[2]

We have been living in a way that falsely underpins our survival as a species since the day so many moons ago when survival became assured. Humans are arguably unique, though, in the extent to which we can reflect on the past and hypothesise about the future. We can think about past mistakes and what would have happened if we had done things differently and we can imagine the future outcomes of actions we might take today. Possibly more so than any other animal, we can make conscious choices that affect our survival. We can take evolutionary steps by redefining success such that it does not prohibit the survival of the species and the living planet. We need a new definition that favours cooperation with the human and natural community instead of competition against it. Instead of encouraging behavioural traits associated with survival, the new definition would focus on what it is to lead a good life. Then we could move away from the idea that working for most of our lives to individually accumulate monetary wealth is 'successful'.

2. Rebel

The Dalai Lama, when asked what surprised him most about humanity, answered, "Man because he sacrifices his health in order to make money. Then he sacrifices money to recuperate his health. And then he is so anxious about the future that he does not enjoy the present; the result being that he does not live in the present or the future; he lives as if he is never going to die, and then dies having never really lived."

RETHINKING WORK

For about twenty years of my life, from my last day on the university campus, I would wake up each morning with the bleak prospect that for yet another precious day I would sell my time and my soul to the highest bidder in this grand farce called work. For those two long decades, excluding four of those years when I was tangled up in failed escape attempts, work was something I did consistently, obediently, and for the most part unconsciously.

These days, however, I wake to no such prospect. It is an hour before the sun will send its first rays of today through the palm tree army lined up on the far side of the bay. It is several days after Elvira's funeral and the last day of my current stay here in Sorake Beach.

It's almost light enough outside to navigate the barnacle walk out to behind where the waves break and paddle into position for the last perfect waves I will ride for a while. I crawl out of bed, collect my yoga mat, and unravel it just outside the bus on the gravel that signifies the start of my one compulsory daily ritual. My own mad scientist's concoction of Qi Gong, Pilates, and yoga wears away the gristle and grinding in my bones and muscles. A rooster, maybe two, announce that it could be any time at all.

I finish limbering up, swap my mat for my surfboard, and plaster my face in bright white zinc cream. The clown mask serves as sun protection, but I wear it mostly because the smell reminds me of something, perhaps my untroubled childhood days at the beach. I walk across the car park and to the start of the saw-toothed and rocky shelf that separates me from the bobbing black outlines of the few surfers who have already staked their claim in the line-up. I hopscotch across the not-yet-clearly lit rock steps that will take me to the deep water behind the breakers. I can make out three surfers. They are all foreigners. The local surfers don't tend to paddle out early; they take their time, as they do with most things they do.

Not just the surfers, but all of the local villagers avoid hurry; they avoid busyness. This is noticeable most when it comes to working. The idea of working all day, every day has not established a foothold here. The prevailing mentality is that work is done to ensure that enough food and basics are available across the community, and then beyond that work is a bit pointless. The remainder of the day is spent eating, napping, chatting, and gossiping. Some kids go to school for a few hours a day, depending on the surf conditions. Other folks like to go to church, and most have minor daily chores. I accept that I am simplifying things a bit. It is true that there are periods when

28

work is more onerous, such as the high season for tourism and certain times during the rice growing cycle, but in general this is not the case.

Two hours have passed in the water, and I can feel the skin on my back is considering its future as crackling. I paddle back to the shoreline. I can make out the shape of Billy waiting with the barnacles; none of them is a competent swimmer, preferring to stick to the rocks. Billy is Cobba's twelve-year-old son and my faithful attaché here in the bay. He likes to follow me wherever I go and tell me stories of his surfing prowess, which I know to be untrue because they are the legendary tales of his father. His English is broken but decipherable.

I reach the rock shelf as I hear his regular morning greeting, "Hi, Miss, good afterning." I like the way he says this and so have never corrected him. In any case, his English is better than most kids' here. We walk across the barnacles together back to Mamma Naya's hotel car park and the bus. Still, there is very little human activity. It's about 9 am.

I don't expect to see much activity here for a while either. Mamma Naya's staff are hard to identify because they do about the same amount of work as non-staff, not much. After several weeks of being here, I have no idea who is on the payroll, or even if there is a payroll. Suspected staff like to collect around the car park to chat with me or each other. There always seems to be plenty to discuss.

Mama Naya is diminutive but still a formidable force around the car park. She stands out from everyone and perhaps everything in Sorake Beach because of her grumpy and officious demeanour. She seems always to be brandishing some large kitchen utensil or animal part and wears a constipated scowl that quite possibly frightened all of this gravel from its granite at some point. So, when she needs something done, it seems that

29

whoever is within earshot of her, staff or not, fearfully gets to the task. Some work is a necessity, but it is minor.

Work has always been a necessity for humans to some degree. Before the Industrial Revolution (1760-1830), human toil was needed to produce food, shelter, and clothing. The desire for a more comfortable life drove the need for and the quantity of work. A combination of both societal and individual expectations determined the benchmarks of a comfortable life.

With the advent of the steam engine and other production breakthroughs, without raising the comfort benchmark, theoretically, humans should have been able to work less. Today, only minimal human work would be necessary to produce enough for humanity. This idea seems to have caught on at Sorake Beach and in many other places that I have come across in my travels.

But this is not the case elsewhere where many still work themselves to the bone. Why? They do this because two things happened.

First, the spoils resulting from increased production from the steam engine, other breakthroughs in mass production, and more recent technological advances were not equitably distributed. Many inventions and discoveries, if not conceived by, were seized by the holders of capital, and the benefit from the resulting production increment concentrated their monetary wealth and power while often not affecting the standard of living of the vast majority. In fact, throughout the late 1700s and early 1800s in England, for example, the standard of living was reduced for many people. In *The Forgotten Slaves: Whites in Servitude in Early America and Industrial Britain*, Michael A. Hoffman II doesn't argue that progress was good for everyone. He writes:

In the 18th century in Britain and America, the Industrial Revolution spawned the factory system whose first labourers were miserably oppressed white children as young as six years of age. They were locked in the factories for sixteen hours a day and mangled by the primitive machinery. Hands and arms were regularly ripped to pieces. Little girls often had their hair caught in the machinery and were scalped from their foreheads to the back of their necks.[3]

Nice huh?

This increased production could not have benefitted the industrialists and the elite had there been no consumers. As production grew, they needed consumption to grow with it, so the second factor was the dawn of widespread consumerism. Since then, post-industrial nations have single-mindedly focussed on production and sales and its noxious counterpart consumerism. The beneficiaries of consumerism continued to develop economic, political, and social systems and standards that persuaded consumers that they need more. This left those consumers shackled in debt and wage slavery to pay for it.

Companies in all manner of industries have substantial vested interests in ensuring people continue to spend carelessly. Financial profit is their number one measurement of success, and this depends on consumption. To better encourage consumers to consume, retaining as many people as possible inside the forty-hour work week is a top priority, as this is just enough time to leave little for much else. The lack of free time exacerbates our spending on conveniences, and we ignore things that are free such as walking, reading, sports, and hobbies because the time is just not available.

The government is also dependent on a nation of obedient worker-consumers, as their yardstick of success aligns with that of corporations - consumer spending. Regardless of the quality of the spending, all expenditure contributes to the gross domestic product (GDP). George Monbiot, a British writer known for his environmental and political activism and the author of *Feral: Rewilding the Land, the Sea and Human Life*, fittingly surmises:

Governments are deemed to succeed or fail by how well they make money go around, regardless of whether it serves any useful purpose. They regard it as a sacred duty to encourage the country's most revolting spectacle: the annual feeding frenzy in which shoppers queue all night, then stampede into the shops, elbow, trample and sometimes fight to be the first to carry off some designer junk which will go into landfill before the sales next year. The madder the orgy, the greater the triumph of economic management.[4]

This systemic conditioning now has us playing the roles of workers and consumers mostly without question, so much so that in much economic and political dialogue, instead of being referred to as people or citizens, we are referred to as *workers* and *consumers*.

The conditioning starts from when we are quite young. When I was a boy, I was bundled off to my first day of school in my grey uniform to begin my indoctrination into standard education. As a five-year-old, I did not have the intellect to question why this was necessary, why I had to spend between six and eight hours for five days a week under my first set of fluorescent lights. Seated in rows to receive my programming, it never occurred to me that there could be anything else. My days of running wild and exploration were reduced from seven a week to two.

With high school I started the standard eight-hour day, the type of day that would continue for just under thirty more years.

My new masters imposed rules and regulations including wearing a tie, a blazer, and high socks held up by garters. Those things messed with my circulation.

Why? They told me that I needed discipline; I had to learn to obey and to follow the rules. But why? Because if I couldn't follow the rules, how would I be a good worker? Why do I want to be a good worker? Remind me? It was so I could get and keep a good job, spend my able years climbing a corporate hierarchy, and retire with enough money to take me through my remaining days.

Right. Got it.

By the time they finished processing me, I was churned out as a mostly obedient, well-finished, work-ready, standardised human unit. I was primed to be plugged into the work-consume-die program. I was allocated a two-day weekend and allowed four weeks a year to recover from the other forty-eight to make sure I'd be able to go the distance until retirement when my real life would then be permitted to start. It sounds like a sentence for a crime, doesn't it? It would be almost twenty years before I would begin to see through this disturbing charade and ask myself, "Is this really a good life, or am I being conned?"

Without the advent and systemic promotion of consumerism, resulting in our endless pursuit of more, so much of our goods and services would be unnecessary. Products would be more durable; planned obsolescence would itself become obsolete; continually upgrading possessions would seem silly, and folks would be satisfied with enough. Entire industries would disappear. Junk food and other wasteful and useless products, advertising and marketing, sales, and all the other sectors that are used primarily just to keep consumers consuming would no longer be needed. As a result, much less work would be required. We would need to develop a better system of wealth distribution, but I am convinced that creating and selling useless, wasteful, and even destructive products just to distribute wealth via employment is not the best we can do.

This brings me to an important distinction I must make about the term *work* as I refer to it in this book. Just like in Sorake Beach, some work is necessary. But as there would be so little of it in a nonconsumerist system, we would each need to do less. We could do only the work we chose to do, the work we enjoy, or that we find worthwhile. Many of us do just that, and with that, I see no problem. But many more of us do work that we find mundane, unproductive, uninspiring, but often necessary, at least in part brought about because of inequitable wealth distribution and consumerism. This is the type of work I am concerned with in this book.

***

Billy likes to hover around the bus in the mornings because, although he has already had breakfast with Cobba, he eats a second breakfast with me and sometimes a third with Mamma Naya on the other side of the car park. I'm not sure if he likes my sardines and eggs. It's possible he just eats it to be courteous. I know he doesn't appreciate the absence of rice.

"What are you up to today, Billy?" I ask, knowing that he's up to whatever I'm up to.

He shrugs. "Don't know; school maybe."

School seems to be a voluntary occupation amongst the kids here. It also seems a bit optional amongst the teachers. I've seen some of the material they use for English class, and it is amusingly full of spelling and grammatical errors. Students and teachers alike learn English by talking to the surfers. Perhaps they are better off not in school.

"Do you want to come visiting with me? We can take the Frisbee."

"Yes, why not?" he answers, as he unilaterally cancels school.

Although he is an appallingly inadequate Frisbee partner, he is the best I have, and it means I can keep him at least twenty meters away from me and only periodically have to listen to his fake surfing stories. Walking along the beach, we hurl the disc to each other. I tell him I'm leaving the island for a couple of weeks to visit my parents, to which he seems genuinely dismayed. I add that I'll be back in a few weeks with my brother. This ends his disappointment, and probably better suits his belief that I am here on a permanent basis, even though I am not.

We stop in on many of the folks I have come to know over the last few weeks. Most of them are leisurely undertaking something that only very loosely could be called work. Some are already napping on their porch. All of them, if conscious, call us over for a chat.

I see over and again that life here is simple. I see only smiling people. I recognise that my absence from work and consumerism is making me a more uncomplicated and more frequently smiling person. I know that people here may see us foreigners and covet what we have with all our 'comforts', but I also know that they don't quite comprehend some of the more human things that we have lost along the way.

THE 3-LEGGED-STOOL

Some people enjoy work. I have no beef with work that is optional and enjoyable. But it is one of the most dehumanising falsehoods of modern times, that in developed countries, work as we know it is still necessary and noble. Historical necessity embedded this into our psyche. As the genuine need for work

35

diminished, our elected governments and created corporations ramped up a covert economic and psychological assault. They conspired to keep us at work to meet goals of their own, which were not consistent with the well-being of individuals, communities, and life in general. Infinite growth fed by consumerism became their economic weapon of choice. Monetary wealth and materialism became the backbone of their propaganda machine.

To support these audacious suppositions, I must first introduce you to my three-legged stool analogy, upon which the greatest lie of our times does sit.

Picture a three-legged stool. One leg is consumerism. Consumerism is an economic theory that increased consumption and spending lots of money on goods and services is beneficial to a nation's economy in the long run. The second leg is excessive monetary wealth. Monetary wealth is excessive when it exceeds what I refer to later as *enough*. The third and final leg is materialism, or a desire to buy excessive items and to accumulate ever more tangible goods. The seat of the stool represents the need for work. Remember my clarification earlier about the type of work I am concerned with. It is the work that would be less necessary in the absence of consumerism, materialism and the seeking of excessive monetary wealth, which I believe would be a very large proportion of it. So, the need for work is propped up by materialism, consumerism, and excessive monetary wealth without which the stool would cease to be a stool and the need for work would fall into a heap. And it is no accident that I choose for my analogy the stool. It also acts as an appropriate metaphor for what I am describing if you contemplate another meaning of *stool*.

Why do I think that this stool, upon which our need for work fraudulently supports itself, is so malevolent? Am I saying that we need to scrap these fundamental economic ideas and start again? Maybe.

We do need to have a realistic and grown-up conversation (i.e. not driven by political or short-term goals) about the stool's design and potentially refurbish it; we could change the bits that don't work, adjust or replace the legs, and replace the seat for a smaller, more ergonomic one. As it sits today, there is no question in my mind that this dangerous item of furniture is behind much personal, societal, and environmental damage and dysfunction.

First, let's look at the harm done to individuals. The actual work day (as distinct from the legislated work day) in Australia is getting longer, even as we automate our world.[5] Wasn't automation supposed to bring about more leisure time? Folks are spending more hours at work as they progress through their careers and as their responsibilities grow. We often see employees starting out working eight hours per day, only to work ten as a manager and then get rewarded with twelve hours a day as the head honcho. Not only are we working all these hours to support our spending habits, but because we have so little time otherwise, we also need to purchase even more in the form of convenience. Talk about double-duped!

And then all this working and spending does nothing but take time away from things that make us happy such as our relationships. Is that a triple-dupe?

For much of my life, I have slaved away the years while plonked upon the three-legged stool. But I remember an earlier time when this was not the case. I consider my days at university to be some of the simplest and most enjoyable of my life. My friends and I worked part-time jobs to provide for our frugal student lifestyles. None of us earned very much, but it was sufficient to cover accommodation, albeit in a communal situation, food, albeit mostly beans and tuna, and wine, albeit served in a four-litre box.

It was enough to afford a good life. All of us were healthy and unencumbered by debt, stress, and as it happens, ambition. We lived simple, happy, and healthy lives. We owned, admittedly on account of our financial limitations, only those things that were necessary or brought us joy. We had plenty of time for family and enjoyed much of the proverbial wine, women, and song.

As we graduated and ventured out into what some call the real world, for the first time in our lives we encountered the three-legged stool. We all quickly found jobs in our chosen professions although this was not so much chosen as it was expected.

Life changed in the rat race. Work hours skyrocketed as our jobs transmuted from a minor sideshow to the most significant activity of our days. The extra money that I earned I, applied to one of the legs of the three-legged stool: excessive materialism. I replaced my reliable old Volkswagen Beetle with a fancy Japanese sports car. My shared accommodation partners gradually moved on as I moved into a comparatively extravagant flat on my own. Communal living was hardly appropriate for a professional. New bills materialised for services and subscriptions, phone plans, car insurance, home contents insurance, cable channels, and credit card interest. After all was said and done, I was retaining the same amount of money that I had been saving at university (i.e. none).

With so much work I saw less of my friends and family. I spent my weekends winding down from the last work week and winding up for the next one until, eventually, I was working from home on weekends to stay afloat. I could see that there was more luxury in my life, but even though I was not someone who appreciated that kind of thing, I accumulated it anyway in accordance with my programming.

After about two years of this, I figured I should be saving some money. After all, why the hell was I doing this? I hadn't saved a brass razoo in the preceding two years, so I figured a night job in a bar would help me get there. And indeed, it did; money started to accumulate. I shifted my weight onto one of the other legs of the stool, seeking excessive monetary wealth.

Five days and six nights a week started to take its toll on more than just my available free time. I started drinking coffee for the first time in my life to stay awake during the day after my long nights in the bar. It didn't help that the fairly liberal bar actively encouraged drinking with the patrons during a shift. While I don't regret anything about discovering drugs in those nights at the bar, I do see that I was using amphetamines just to manage, rather than as entertainment. With the coffee, the alcohol, and the drugs affecting my physical and mental state, stress showed up for the first time, and I suspect this encouraged my weekend binge drinking, which would prove to be problematic for another twenty years to come.

I was lucky not to accumulate many other common ailments associated with long work hours and work-related stress. These include depression, obesity, cardiovascular complications, and eyestrain. I wasn't lucky enough to escape sleep disorders. To this day, I suffer from insomnia, which only recently have I traced back to those crazy days of accumulation. I had become an unhappy, mindless money-making machine for reasons that at the time I was not entirely sure of but today know it to be at the directive of the three-legged stool. I'd lost sight of the joy in everyday life and instead was living to work and working for some time in the future when . . . I wasn't sure what.

While not always as intense, this work madness would go on for much of the next twenty years before I would finally realise that what I wanted was just to live a simple, happy, and healthy life, to own only those things that were necessary or brought me

39

joy, to have plenty of time for family, and to enjoy that wine, women, and song with my friends as I had done before. This realisation pulled the stool right out from under me. All those years of what was essentially self-harm were in so many ways, unnecessary.

Harm is experienced both by individuals and our communities as well. I realise this as I pass through the hedonistic island of Bali. I'm on my way back to Australia to visit my parents, from my most recent home in Sumatra, Indonesia. There, I lived a life similar in some ways to mine at university. It was a life I enjoyed. It was mostly absent from consumer society. Being here in Bali now reminds me of the extent of the harm caused to communities by the three-legged stool.

This morning I woke up early, as I usually do, and am walking to the beachfront to a seaside public park surrounded by frangipanis where I plan to do my morning exercise. It is light, but the sun is not up yet. I arrive at the place where a park with an expansive view of the ocean once provided a space for locals and tourists to hang out. It was a public space. It was free.

But today I see no frangipanis; only a fraction of the park remains. The larger section of the park is now a construction site, the perimeter boarded up with particle board. I feel a familiar anger at seeing a beautiful public place replaced by the undertakings of private enterprise.

I walk around the boundary walls, and I see flyers stapled to the particle board every two metres or so. What is worse than having yet another public space sold and commercialised is the propaganda on the flyer. It tells the reader that they can now enjoy 'the lawn', as it is known, without having to sit on the grass and without having to bring their own food and beer.

Did I really read that? The three-legged stool strikes again, and the community, the residents, the surfers, and the sun bakers who went there because it was a free public place where they could sit around on the grass, enjoy the view, each other, and perhaps a few beers, can no longer do so.

Irritated, I walk past the building materials to the beach to exercise. I think about the many ways this is such a perfect example of the harm to communities that our economic reality causes. Not only is the right to a good life being monetised, such that we can have a good life provided we have the money to pay for it, but these beautiful public spaces where people gather just to spend time with each other are being eaten up. People are being corralled into commercial establishments, hooked up, and milked of their money. The have-nots will have to go elsewhere, and I assure you that the majority of local people who frequented the lawn fit that description.

The three-legged stool harms communities in other ways as well. I've now landed in Brisbane, Australia. My parents are giving me a ride from the airport to their home. We drive past a new housing complex of low- and medium-rise housing units. I see no common areas, only restrictive glass, concrete, and pavement. This structure leaves absolutely no space or opportunity for community, for knowing one's neighbours, or for just loafing about and gasbagging. I contrast it to my Sumatran home where there were no walls or fences between abodes. In many cases, there weren't even any doors, and folks there were loath to spend any time indoors when they could be outside in the square or the park mixing it up with the community.

As we become more monetarily wealthy, we seem to insulate ourselves from others and fortify our assets, and thus shield our lives against them.

The other thing I see is the way that the three-legged stool functions to restrict choices. I noticed when I arrived at the airport a short time ago that since my last visit here, perhaps a year ago, most if not all of the water fountains have been removed. With the privatisation of the airport in 1997, it has been gradually transformed from a public service facility to a commercial venture.

Why should the public drink free water when they can buy it? I also took note of how ridiculously maze-like the duty-free shops were. They were no longer shops that we could choose to walk past and ignore. They have been redesigned so that people must walk through them to get out. They were designed to ensure people spend as much time in there as possible. So even if I chose to ignore the junk that they sell in these places, I was forced to walk at length through the whole store; the retailer hoped that I would crack with the passage of time and buy something.

And then there is the environmental impact. The glaring contradiction of modern economics in the pursuit of infinite growth is a world that does not recognize that resources are finite. In treating resources as unlimited, much of the environmental cost of the extraction, production, transportation, and disposal of goods is externalised (i.e. it is not factored into the price of a product).

As consumers, we don't see the cost of human exploitation, forest destruction and depletion, pollution of the air and waterways, and species extinction. As such, we find ourselves separated from the reality of what our consumer choices are doing to the world's natural and human resources. In some ways, we are forced into ignoring reality.

Paradoxically, while the supply side accounts for resources as if they are infinitely available and exploitable, the demand side of consumer society stresses the opposite (i.e. shortage over abundance). Shortages underpin competition over cooperation and result in increased individualism. This belief that the self is so separate from others and the environment encourages us to consume and accumulate stuff to bolster the boundaries of self against everything that is other than the self. And further, we feel immune to what we are doing to other beings in the process.

Our inveterate conquest and exploitation of nature to reinforce ourselves against the not-self has another more acute impact. The quest for more does not satisfy us. It is endless, and we live and work for some time in the future where we think we might be satisfied and where the impossible will be possible. If we look perpetually to the future, we cannot live in the present where life happens.

Throughout our education, we prepare for the future. Then comes work. Then, when we are too old to work, we can finally enjoy life. But until then, life is geared towards the future when we are too old to work and often are too old to do a lot of things. All we can do is kick back, put our feet up on our three-legged stool, and ponder the years that it took from us.

REJECT THE PARADIGM

The three-legged-stool depicts a failing economic system. Excessive monetary wealth, consumerism, and materialism only lead to work and individual and planetary ruin. They do not support what I would call a good life or how I define success. When our human systems, whether agricultural, energy oriented, social, political, or economic, are not serving us anymore, we need to question our systems or risk a demise like that of the early Polynesian inhabitants of Easter Island.

What transpired on that lonely island was an instructive beta test for our entire lonely planet. There, the island's ecosystem once provided for its human inhabitants' needs. The vegetation of the island provided food for the population and homes for birds and the other animals, which in turn sometimes became food for the people there. The trees also provided timber to make their houses and the enormous rollers that transported the iconic, stone Moai statues around the island.

Then something happened. As the population grew unchecked, the forests shrunk. The people asked no questions and made no adjustments until one day they all looked up and saw that no trees or vegetation remained. Naturally, the fruit disappeared with it, the animals and birdlife either perished or left, and then just as the lights went on and they realised that they needed to question their human systems, they too had to vacate the island.

How foolish were they not to see this coming? And how foolish would we be today not to learn from their mistake?

I'm all for living in the present moment, but I don't mind keeping an occasional eye on my forward trajectory. Such an approach might have saved our Polynesian friends. They might have made observations about problematic symptoms, such as 'There's not much food about'. Then they might have had an informed, open discussion to identify the underlying cause of those symptoms. Perhaps they would have concluded that 'too many people are chopping down too many trees'. Then they could have had an inclusive and creative debate, free from individual and political bias, leading to the right solutions, having considered all known collateral and future impacts. Solutions might have included 'We need to have fewer people', or, 'We need to stop moving these statues around the island'. Both solutions would have ruffled many political, religious, and social feathers. Johnny Woodchopper also would have been upset. But the implementation of that change would have instigated the beneficial evolution of their systems, and while there may have been fewer of those giant stone statues, they needn't have looked so sullen.

We do see variations of this approach, although not as well-structured and not always free from bias in many of our systems. Our agricultural systems evolved with technology, innovation, and economies of scale, moving us away from systems that consist of mostly small holdings and community farming towards mass agriculture.

In ever-growing numbers, we see people questioning this approach and deciding that monoculture farming, which uses significant amounts of toxic and unhealthy chemicals leading to widespread health issues, no longer serves them as they return to a more local and organic food system. We also see discussions about our energy systems and the consensus that fossil fuel-based energy should be phased out and replaced by cleaner, renewable sources of energy. Social systems are under review as people choose the types of communities they want to build and inhabit. Some prefer a suburban lifestyle, others self-organise and create rural communities, and some just pick up their belongings and go in search of a social system that suits them. And while political systems themselves are slow to change, in democracies constituents can at least vote for their representatives and through this mechanism have a voice and initialise change. There is an argument that democracies in some countries are no longer representative, but in general the discussion around policy and political systems is not taboo.

Such steps leading to meaningful progress are hard to find, however, in our modern economic system. Discussing the sustainability of the prevailing economic system in many countries is off-limits. Many Australians believe their mostly unobstructed version of capitalism no longer serves the majority of people or the environment on which we all depend to survive. But identifying capitalism as the source of undesirable symptoms and having a discussion about tweaking it or even replacing it with something else is considered somewhat insane. Why is discussing the economic system so unthinkable?

One explanation of why we don't examine the fundamentals of our economic system comes out of the concept of a paradigm. Unregulated capitalism is one name we could give to our economic paradigm, or framework. The underlying, unseen, and unquestioned assumptions include the idea that money is wealth and that infinite growth is both possible and essential. These assumptions are so intrinsic in our mental processes that they are often confused with a demonstrable truth.

If our mental framework assumes that economic growth is an unchangeable fact of life, we restrict the scope of our solutions as we look to work around that supposed fact and protect it at all costs. Sometimes those costs are human and natural ruination. We tend to seek alternate and often ineffectual solutions because we cannot challenge what we perceive to be the truth.

However, if we can step outside of this paradigm and reach a place where we can be critically objective in evaluating the assumptions, we would greatly expand the problem-solving options available to us.

We also don't question the economic system because there are potent forces at work to either keep the paradigm concealed or—if it is exposed—to encourage us not to question it. Corporations have a tremendous vested interest in maintaining the status quo. They were born out of and evolved with capitalism. They are the perfect product of this paradigm and as such have built-in protection against changes that might upset their profits and their power. These entities have no interest in a conversation about moderating capitalism or growth. Why should they? Whether through lobbying, corporate propaganda, or product advertising, their message is clear: we need to consume more and continue to grow, interminably. Mainstream media are on board as well, being owned and controlled by the same structure. Their message is full of often fear-based disinformation that serves to re-enforce the paradigm as a fact.

***

This morning, I am sitting on the porch at my parents' house in suburban Brisbane. My father is cooking his version of eggs benedict for me, his customary 'welcome home' dish. An integral part of my nomadic life is returning to Australia once a year or so to visit friends and family. I have returned this time to do just that. For about a decade my father, a retired accountant, has been the lord of the kitchen, and my mother and I are made well aware of that. At seventy, she continues to work as a nurse and is quite happy for him to be the master of household affairs.

On the porch, we begin the download of our lives' happenings over the previous year. My father appears and disappears, setting the table and lastly bringing out his creation of which we both know he is very proud and I am very fond. He places the folded newspaper next to his plate, knowing that once the eating is finished, there will be a scrimmage while I am at the table for the tastiest sections of the journal of creative fact. But I can already glean from a front-page headline an article that reinforces the ostensible message that economic growth is not negotiable.

Despite the paradigm and my family's living within it for most of their adult lives, it is not taboo to debate its assumptions such as the imperative of economic growth at this table. We finish eating, and in amongst the conversation we have about our lives and adventures, with the flipping of each page comes the sputtering outbursts from my father usually starting with, "Ah, bullshit."

He is reading the financial pages. I am impressed by this man who, given his professional background and immersion in this world of finance and economics, can see the paradigm for what it is and is quite vocal about it. He has noticeably mellowed in his retirement, but this is one topic on which he becomes quite animated. His outbursts are an expression of his frustration because, even though he recognises the paradigm, he feels helpless to act against it.

The conversation now centres on the front-page article's content, and without either of us explicitly saying so, we are questioning the paradigm. As I chime in on the matter, I am also impressed by the way he can lift his head to look over his glasses at me while they stay focussed on the newspaper. It is as if they are impatiently waiting for him to return to his scorn of the article.

My mother tends to say more with less. She is working through the word games section, but I know she is listening, at least partially, because she has a way of refereeing my father and me and bringing the rowdiness down with a few correctional statements. Sometimes I think she has always known the truth about the paradigm, but like my father, she felt that there was not a great deal that they could do about it. I love these mornings, which is fortunate because I will have another two weeks just like this before returning to Sumatra.

Aside from corporations and the pro-paradigm elements of the media, government's involvement in this psychological assault is most insidious. Initially designed to represent the voters, though it increasingly represents lobbyists, the representative government seems increasingly at war with its constituents.

Do you ever feel that as citizens, we are increasingly pleading and protesting our government to stop destroying our communities, selling our public assets, and endangering our living planet at the behest of the economic system? In Australia, environmental protection laws get changed to allow otherwise illegal mining operations to proceed. Public utilities and services are sold to multinationals who then sell those services back to the citizens. In Africa it is arguably a lot worse. There we see foreign corporations corrupting officials to rob resources, usually without much enduring benefit if any for citizens and often doing so while a country is in crisis. From unscrupulous mining companies' ravaging poverty-stricken failed states to international food and beverage companies commandeering desperately needed public water supplies, the list of inequities is a long one.[6]

But it's not just big, scary corporations, government, and the media that have a vested interest in the paradigm. Almost all non-aboriginal individuals in Australia have lived their entire lives within this model. It stands to reason that everyone would try to make the most of our situation and prosper within and from it. With much time and effort invested in adapting to and benefiting from a particular economic system, people will tend to resist any talk about change. Few would be happy if the very foundation of what they have built a satisfactory existence on is under debate.

And further, this has fostered the use of labels. Capitalism is one such label. But it is only a theoretical term. No country hosts a purely capitalist economy, as every country has at least some social services, which makes them, at least, a socialist-capitalist hybrid.

Paradigmatic diehards use labels as self-defence mechanisms. Anyone's so much as suggesting ideas that could be conceived as for the social or environmental good is called a socialist, a tree-hugger, or worse, a commie or a hippie. Labels are useless except that they are alarmist. They have the effect of shutting down conversations that could otherwise be constructive.

49

Let me demonstrate how unhelpful labels are. I tend to keep my head shaved bald. In at least one sense, it would not be incorrect to call me a skinhead. But I do not flit about calling myself a skinhead, because that label has other connotations that might conjure up images related to the skinhead subculture of the 1960's in London, England. These don't really apply to me, and that is the danger of dealing with labels instead of people's actual character or characteristics. Labels get in the way of mature and progressive conversations.

As individuals in our communities, we need to identify the economic assumptions such as that money is wealth and that infinite growth is necessary, as paradigms, not facts. We need to discuss this openly and without ridicule, intimidation, or castigation. And finally, we need to be able to have the discussion free from being labelled one thing or another.

The first supposition that we need to talk about is whether money is a valid measurement of wealth today. Frequently in the past money itself had intrinsic value. Shells, gold and sacks of flour were all valued either because they were rare, pretty or could be eaten. In some specific circumstances today, such as cigarettes in prisons, money still has an intrinsic value. In addition, these forms of money were valuable in facilitating trade because they were usually able to be standardised and often were not big and clunky, so commodities could be easily exchanged through that medium.

In modern times, gold, silver and other precious metals became coins, still holding their intrinsic value and making trade even easier due to their transportability. Gradually, the precious metals in coins gave way to less valuable metals and the coins started taking on a more symbolic representation of value. Next, money was printed on paper, which intrinsically had almost no value and these days, money is not even printed; it exists only in electronic systems.

In general, today, money itself has no intrinsic value. Money, or currency's only value comes about when we dispose of it, when we trade it for those goods and services that do have value. Money is indeed a measurement but not of wealth. It is a measure of the ability and capacity to trade.

Thus, money is only a means to an end. I broadly define an end that has value as one that contributes to a good life and one that improves genuine well-being. Of course, we do need some money, a lot less than most of us think, to trade for the things that we need to live a good life. But if we treat it for what it is, a middleman that stores the product of our working days until it is assigned to the purchase of something, then inversely and in the words of Henry David Thoreau, "The price of anything is the amount of life you exchange for it." It's a kind of literary algebra that exposes money's real purpose as a means of exchange for a good life.

This algebra, crude as it is, was not something I could fathom back in my first few years out of university. In 1995, at twenty-three, I had been working two full-time jobs for over a year and was treating the means, money, as an end in itself. I was chasing money for money's sake and didn't realise that the legitimate end that all this money was originally designed to be applied to, a good life, I already had found without any such money when I was a student.

Absurdly, all this chasing of money had prevented the attainment of well-being and happiness. I failed to recognise that once I had enough, once my basic needs had been met, more money was not making me any happier, but was instead causing high levels of stress, poor health, and unhappiness.

In that year, despite showing symptoms of treating money as an end, I came across the idea to move overseas. I had heard about the vast sums of money other Australians were making at my age with only slightly embellished resumes. I may have been starting to question money, but I was still hungry for it. I was asleep at the wheel as my well-being deteriorated. Money was still king for me, and from that year I would chase it even more fervently, earn even more of it, as I watched my well-being decline in London for two years.

Using money as a measurement of wealth doesn't truly serve anyone. We cannot measure non-numerical qualities with a numerical measurement. How do we measure a good life or the quality of our communities and our relationships, which over and again have been proven to be far more important to happiness than financial wealth? How do we measure liberty, freedom of speech, security, the quality of education, and the amount of free time we have to pursue our interests?

The second assumption of the economic paradigm that we generally accept as fact is that infinite growth is both possible and desirable. Sure, there was a time when growth was advantageous and using it as an indicator of how well we were doing was appropriate. Perhaps as recently as a century ago when our population was but a small fraction of what it is today and when we still had abundant resources, the growth model succeeded in bringing us housing, energy, and food. But it is no longer a good thing, or even truly possible. We must respect the planet's very real limits.

Science proves that we are not respecting these boundaries. For instance, our human population is currently consuming 1.6 planets' worth of resources, and this is not evenly distributed. If every person consumed the same as the average Australian, we would need 4.8 Earth's to compensate.[7]

How are we making up for these deficits? There are two primary sources. The first is the future. As we further outgrow the earth's limits and overconsume non-renewable resources, we are borrowing on a non-repayable loan from future generations. Won't those future generations look at their bare

52

and polluted planet, scratch their heads, and wonder why on earth we did this? Won't they look back at us with rage and disgust that we would knowingly do this? The second is by plundering other nations through questionable financial arrangements, political persuasion and corruption, or straight-up military invasion.

These inter-generational and inter-geographical plunders are merely collateral damage because under the infinite growth dogma of our economic system, the more we produce and consume the better we are doing. And that is why the GDP is a nation's benchmark of success. GDP accounts for wealth by the velocity at which money moves through an economy. So, we are compounding an already inept measurement of wealth by capturing the rate at which it moves. This is insanity squared and possibly cubed when we look at what we include and exclude in this measurement.

First, included in the GDP is consumer spending and business investment. So, we include spending on food, clothing and housing, which may be seen as contributing to the national wealth. Some spending by business also can be seen as a positive thing. Government spending is also included. We include the cost of beneficial services provided throughout the economy such as water and electricity. I can't fault that either. But if the number of prisoners in our jails increases or the incidence of chemical spills and other environmental disasters increases, we include the cost of managing this in the GDP. According to the statistic, this is considered a beautiful thing.

We should not be patting ourselves on the back about the latter examples. The GDP doesn't factor in what a money movement was about; it just factors in that it moved, and the more movement, economists consider, the better.

This is nonsensical if we are calling GDP a measure of wealth. It's like a company's taking all of its income and, instead of subtracting expenses, just adding them together. The company could be losing money hand over fist, but as long as the number is big, that's all that would matter to the shareholders.

Equally as silly is what we exclude from our evaluation of the GDP. Based only on money, the GDP does not take into account important elements of wealth that have no relationship with money. It can't account for an increase in community and individual happiness, the strength of family bonds, or improved quality of life. It doesn't account for negative instances such as ecological or social costs, either now or in the future, associated with extracting, producing, and disposing of those items that do feature in GDP. Neither does it account for the cost to those countries or species that get in the way of so-called progress. This measurement is inadequate and misleading as a measure of success.

Notwithstanding all that I have said thus far, money is a widely accepted measurement of monetary wealth. That is to say, money is a good measure of money. But monetary wealth is, if anything, just one element of overall wealth. What I call overall wealth includes factors that contribute to quality of life that are non-monetary. This includes items from Maslow's Hierarchy of Needs. Some of these can be affected by monetary wealth, such as health, security and safety. But other elements might be unrelated, less related or adversely affected by monetary wealth, such as love, belonging and other psychological factors. To avoid confusion, I will use the term *prosperity* to refer to *overall wealth,* which includes non-monetary wealth and considers other quality of life factors. I will use *wealth* to refer to monetary wealth.

Modifying the way that we think about prosperity at the individual level is part psychological and part practical, but it all starts by questioning our thoughts and changing the conversation. At the nation-state level, it's an enormous task to

54

change the way we measure prosperity and therefore how we go about it. But this too starts with questioning ourselves. We have to accept the fact that the current methods both individually and system-wide contradict maintaining the very basis for life: an ecologically functioning and sustaining biosphere. We rely on it to live, so what could be a higher priority?

It is not easy to have this conversation; we have not had to do so in the past while our population and lifestyle were within what the earth could sustain. But we have outgrown that now. Because of the paradigm and the forces of self-interest that stifle the conversation, we avoid so much as talking about it.

And even if those forces tell us that such a change will cause catastrophic economic collapse or adjustments that are at best uncomfortable, it is still nowhere near the scale of what will happen if we don't change. Remember Easter Island? Whether we need to change is not in question. The question is, do we change now, or do we first make the earth even less habitable and then try to change?

These forces of resistance to even having a grown-up conversation respond with things like, "What about jobs?" and, "But the economy will crash." Maybe, but neither jobs nor the economy are reasons not to have a conversation. Perhaps these lost jobs are in industries contributing the problem. The sooner we discuss it, the better we can plan for job migrations for people in those industries. Why have entire industries producing useless rubbish just so that consumers can buy that rubbish and then throw it in a landfill, all to keep somebody in work? No value is added to the system.

Would it not be better to remove the production and consumption of those products and redeploy the labour into something beneficial? What about redeploying labour from extraction and depletion to conservation and renewal? Or we could all just work less and investigate better alternatives for wealth distribution. Spare time can be used for something useful and creative. This idea that we must all be fully employed is archaic as it creates jobs that quite simply are wasteful and, worse, destructive.

Some countries are having the conversation, and hints of change can be seen. In Bhutan, they have another measurement of success called gross national happiness (GNH). In Sweden, they address the human cost of an endless pursuit of wealth by restricting weekly work hours. The French are exploring the impact of a neutral growth policy, whereby quality, specifically the quality of life, is considered as well as quantity. Several other northern European countries are exploring a civilian wage option, which would acknowledge that everybody has a right to a basic wage and allow folks to work or not as they see fit. This is another possibility to better distribute wealth. I'm not saying any of these are the solution, but at least they are having the conversation. These countries can see the economic paradigm. They consider capitalism and variants thereof as just options. Taboos do not restrict them. They are free to progress. They can see that the manic extract-produce-consume-dispose-at-all-costs cycle is not sustainable. They know that it is only logical to dismantle and rebuild part or all of it in a way that is consistent with persevering life.

In Australia and many other developed nations, any change coming from the top down will at best be at a glacial pace because discussing the very basis of our economic system is not taken seriously by politicians. As such, the government is unlikely to evolve, adjust, and improve as all successful systems should do. I see it getting worse before it gets better.

But who wants to wait? While I will continue to protest against my government's destroying my world, in essence for money, I will also heed the words of the famous stoic Epictetus, "Some things are up to us, and some are not up to us." So instead of witnessing my world's slow and probable death (with me in it), I have escaped and started living in a new system not based on the three-legged stool. The new system defines success as having a good life of genuine well-being. It values health, community, connection, and respect for nature and her limitations. It does its best to get away from the crazy idea that consumerism and a life-long pursuit of money will somehow bring us happiness.

How this new world takes shape will be different for everyone; we all have different circumstances. For myself, it meant leaving it geographically. But we can make meaningful changes without changing our location. By seeing the paradigm, asking the big questions, and abandoning the assumptions that are so patently incorrect and unsustainable, we can withdraw our support and make a new way.

Part 2: ESCAPE PREPARATIONS

3.   A Good Life

REDEFINING SUCCESS

I have now befouled many of the modern-day ideas that we hold onto around work and success. I've concluded that success is not about wealth, respect, and fame, as per the dictionary. Neither is it found sitting on the three-legged stool as this just leads to more work. So, what is success? To redefine success, we need to abandon the dictionary, get up off the three-legged stool, and focus on what it means to have a good life.

When I contemplate the essence of a good life, the philosophy of the ancient stoics comes to mind. They emphasised the importance of a life well lived, which is free, happy, and prosperous. They used the term *free* to refer to liberty from desire and attachment, which I affiliate, at least in part, with modern-day minimalism and the idea of being satisfied with enough.

Not only were they interested in freedom *from* such things, but they also claimed that freedom *for* something was equally if not more important. They stressed the importance of freedom for the pursuit of one's interests and of a life consciously chosen to bring fulfilment, which contributes to happiness. *Prosperity* I will now further refine to mean overall wealth, tempered by the idea of enough. Thus, a good life is all about happiness and prosperity.

This is not unlike our modern-day definition of well-being: "a state characterised by health, happiness and prosperity."[8] Having good health is tantamount to having a good life. So, updating the stoics' definition, which presumably they would not be attached to, success is having a good life, which I now conclude is one of health, prosperity, and happiness. All three elements are crucial and subjective.

The subjectivity of a good life's elements is multidimensional. Not only does every person have their own ideas about them, but each has their unique ideas develop with the passage of time at the hands of experience, awareness, and retrospection. It was all three of these essentials that nudged my turgid arrogance towards an awakening during my first official escape attempt sometime back in 1997.

Back then, I did not have a clear understanding of money and the difference between wealth and prosperity, but I knew I wanted one or the other or both, and that meant that I had to work. For two years, I did just that in the United Kingdom and amassed my then-self's idea of a sizeable fortune. I bundled that loot into high-risk and high-yielding investments, keeping both eyes on the return and neither on the risk. My optimistic financial forecast ignored any possible, and in retrospect probable, downside. I figured that I had a quantity of money such that I wouldn't have to work again. Then, with my undeveloped understanding of what is a good life, I said to myself, "Bluey, you are set for life." I bought a one-way ticket to Venezuela for what was to be an escape only from what a good life was not.

I was twenty-five. I travelled alone throughout Venezuela for two months before reaching the western border with Colombia somewhere near Lake Maracaibo. There, masked locals were aggressively protesting the lack of water in their town. A tyre and furniture blockade was in flames as protesters and projectiles emerged from and disappeared into the grey-black toxic fog that obscured the border I was hoping to cross. The public bus could go no further. This was Colombia. Back then it was a narcotics and leftist guerrilla stronghold; it had a reputation as a place you didn't want to visit.

My first port of call beyond the border mess was to be a small coastal town where I would meet my best friend and flatmate from London, Tyrone. But that didn't look like it would happen anytime soon. The bedlam of the blockade was like a vortex sucking in everyone from around it including the Colombian customs officials. I wandered around unimpeded except for the smoke and the odd airborne bottle or lump of wood, probably crossing the border and back more than once without knowing it. I struggled to find someone who could stamp my passport. When I finally did, they were so disinterested; they were almost annoyed that I was taking them away from this hive of lawlessness. Had I been interested in smuggling back in those days, this would have been a big green light to a small fortune, but I wasn't. In fact, before Tyrone and I left London, we made a promise that we would stay the hell away from cocaine. Such was the reputation of Colombia.

It was slow going, sweaty, and tiring to get transport away from that border town; it seemed everyone was in a convoy towards it as if it were some vast festival, headlined by fire and violence. I did eventually arrive in Santa Marta, the meeting point, after a bumpy four-hour ride in the back of a pickup. When I located Tyrone amongst a huddle of foreigners in the designated hotel courtyard, I thought we would meet and trade travel stories. I had anticipated earning some traveller's recognition, maybe even sympathy for my arduous day. My disappointment in receiving neither quickly left my thoughts, passing on the way out, the inbound rush, from Tyrone's then apparent broken promise. The opening ceremony of what would be a debauched and extravagant year of narco-tourism had begun.

We spent several months in Colombia and accumulated fellow travellers in search of good times, often with the same illicit intentions. We travelled to the eastern rebel-held area of the Putumayo and shared some life-changing experiences with the Cofán Indians, where we learned from the Ayahuasca medicine with the shamans there amongst the jungle and coca plantations. Ayahuasca is used as a medicine to treat the spirit amongst other things. We formed a posse that I still refer to as *The Cactus Crew* because of those adventures and others ingesting mescaline from the San Pedro cactus in the same region. The San Pedro juice is used by indigenous peoples and these days folks all over the world for medicinal, and in some cases recreational purposes. They became life-long friends.

Sure, some would view those experiences as just haplessly taking drugs, and perhaps there was that side to it. But there was an immense amount of bonding, education, and expansion associated with those experiences. I would have thought to myself back then that this is why one travels. Experiences like those, littered along the road behind us, were the seeds that would sprout some months later and form the understory for my distinction between good times and a good life.

Almost everyone was on a shoestring budget back then except me. I usually lived to the same low level of luxury but not out of necessity. I had my pot of gold. Any extravagance was dealt with swiftly like a dirty little secret as there was a kind of pride in being able to live with fewer things and less money; it was almost competitive.

It's telling how in that naïve time of our young lives we unwittingly sought to live with less. I had kicked any notion of materialism, not consciously but on account of the limited space of a backpack, but I still subscribed to the school of consumerism. I didn't spare a thought for shelling out hard-earned pesos on wasteful things. I spent money spontaneously. I consumed without considering the impact of my choices. In this, I don't think I was alone. It wouldn't be until my third escape attempt to this region six years later that I would see a new breed of traveller, the conscientious eco-tourist, emerge.

After Colombia, we travelled south to Ecuador and rented an apartment in Quito, the capital. Our days revolved around the Spanish language school. At night we partied. We accumulated a sizeable clan there. Many were attending school or working as volunteers, and many of those had the same ideas about having a good time. It was hedonistic. But we were doing something constructive in the learning of language. This fact along with the continued abuse of narcotics kept me from any 'deep-diving', any questioning as to where my life was going.

Perhaps I was shielded from these thoughts more than many of my friends in Quito because I had financial means. I didn't worry about where my money would come from in the future. I was twenty-five and retired. What could possibly go wrong?

We continued south through Peru and Bolivia as the journeys of many of the people we met came to an end. Almost always this was on account of their funds' drying up. I started to see that if this were now my life, I would have to get used to people coming and going.

It was around this time that I started to wonder if this were a viable life for me, not on account of money, but in regard to purpose. What the hell was I doing here? Is travel for travel's sake enough? Drifting with Tyrone, in his eternal ebullience, kept most of these thoughts at bay. It wasn't until we separated in Southern Bolivia some six months into the journey that questions began to return.

From Bolivia and onwards, I travelled alone again. I drifted from the north to the south of Chile by bus, boat, taxi, pickup, and once in a refrigerated chicken truck. I still wonder why that driver stopped to pick me up when he had me sit in the back with the cold and dreary frozen chickens. Don't drivers pick up hitchhikers for the company?

In Chile I met mostly older, short-term, and package tourists, perhaps because Chile was more expensive. The lack of substantial human connections, be it Tyrone or others from our like-minded clan, the long hours on transport and the decisive action to stop taking cocaine for a while, it's addictive qualities having started to set in, left me alone with my thoughts. And after the expansionary times and visions of the ayahuasca and the mescaline, they were eager to get some airplay.

Those months in Chile were not always happy ones. Whenever I sat myself down and asked tough questions, I got tougher answers back. I realised that while on the face of it not needing to work or worry about money should have led to nothing but good times, there was still something missing. I realised that I was alone, possibly even lonely. I didn't envisage this life would be like this. It was like breaking out of prison only to find that my careless tunnel had surfaced inside the solitary confinement wing. I was missing connections to people, old friends, and family.

Many of the other folks that I met on that trip had more on their plate and more on their minds besides just travel. I started to suspect I had miscalculated. What was the point of all this money and time, if it were only me? It was like some scary truth lay dormant waiting to be exposed and turn my victorious escape into defeat.

By the time I had reached the southern tip of Chile, about nine months into the trip, I had had a few realisations, which were by no means as organised as my account to you now. I realised that I had built my supposed successful escape by eradicating all of those things that I thought a good life was not. I was free from work and free from financial concerns and material possessions, but I had spared no thought to what I wanted that freedom for or what I might find fulfilling. And I certainly didn't use that freedom for my health as both physically and mentally it had deteriorated ever since that first day in Colombia. Somehow my freedom wasn't making me happy. I realised my mistake was being so geared to escaping from something that I neglected to consider to what I was escaping.

I was at a dead end, both in my mind and continentally. Where does one go from here? As it happened, I went physically to Antarctica on a navy ice-breaker, but mentally I continued down the path of self-doubt.

When I returned to the South American continent not long afterwards, some Norwegian friends from the Quito days popped up on the radar. They were in Venezuela. I thought to myself, "To hell with geography," and to hell with this self-reflection. I bee-lined it to the opposite end of the continent and engrossed myself in the company of the Norwegian girls, Ane and A9, skydiving, debauchery and as if in some act of rebellion against my own mind, more cocaine. What could be a better remedy to the loneliness and hopelessness? And it worked! Well, it worked until it didn't work.

For the next few months life, or rather, the times seemed good again. By then I had concluded that human connections were vital to happiness. The Norwegian girls, together with the adrenaline of skydiving and boosted by less natural stimulants just in case, was all the remedy I needed.

I lived a less frugal life in those months. I was spending more than my investments allowed for, but I could not have cared less. And then in the space of a few days, it all imploded.

One drunken night, returning from a remote village on the Caribbean coast to the drop zone where we would sleep, my stagger disturbed a moonlighting *Mapanare* snake, whose venom is usually lethal. Its defensive bite rapidly sent me into convulsive fits and unwelcome hallucinations as I crumpled and collapsed onto the muddy road. A9, who was my drinking partner that night and romantic interest on others, struck by panic but level-headed as Norwegians are, enlisted the help of some nearby villagers, also drunk, to get me into the back of a pickup and take me to the village clinic.

A chaotic and painful triage process left me knocking in my venom-inspired trip on death's door. The nurse had naively given me pethidine for pain, and when the doctor finally appeared with the antivenin from a neighbouring village, he could not administer it because of the opiates in my blood. The doctor waited as long as possible for the painkiller to subside, and then gave me the shot of life. I survived, as I am writing this now, but not before my lower right leg began its deterioration into necrosis. It worsened over the next few days until the doctor said that they could do no more. My treatment options were to stay there and have the leg amputated at around about the knee, or travel to England for treatment and probably save it. It was not a tough choice.

What has all this got to do with a good life? Manifestly, not much. What happened next does, though. The Norwegian girls and I made our way back to the capital, Caracas, to organise a flight to England for me. Over the telephone, the booking agent informed me that my credit card had no available funds. Of course, this could not have been the case. I was retired and had an endless source of money. I checked the card in a teller machine in the street, as we did not have online banking in those days. I didn't even have email. And the machine did not lie. It resolved my confusion and confirmed my dilemma.

My bank statements at that time were forwarded to my parent's address in Australia, so I put a call in to them. I hadn't spoken to them for months as I had been self-absorbed in my own life for too long by that time. My credit card had bounced with such enthusiasm that it wiped out all of the debit balance plus $20,000 that was not mine to be wiped. My father explained that they had been trying to reach me, or rather hoping that I would contact them, so I could act when they discovered that my so-called investments were in nothing more than an elaborate Ponzi scheme. By the time of my phone call, it had collapsed and taken my retirement with it.

I went into shock. A possible leg amputation and slipping from retired wealthy, to worse than broke in the space of a few days were not ordinarily things to celebrate. But it would be only a week from that phone call when I would discover that, in fact, this was a positive life-changing experience.

I said goodbye to Ane and A9, and thanks to some borrowed money teased out of my parents, I flew to London where doctors were able to treat my necrosis and save my leg. There, a conversation in a smoky pub in London with Tyrone, who had beaten me back to England, would right the course of my life. It was a conversation that snapped me out of my funk and exposed the error in my vision of freedom. It was a conversation that enabled me to start plotting a new escape, hopefully with the benefit of experience, awareness, and retrospect. I was one step closer to knowing what it was, to lead a life well lived.

***

It is the end of October 2016, amidst my fifth and final escape. I've just returned to Sumatra after a fortnight with my parents in orderly and comfortable Brisbane, Australia. I cannot say that the sweltering pandemonium that is the Sumatran capital, Medan, is a breath of fresh air. The dusty and polluted streets force many folks to wear face masks as they hop between the sewer openings on the pavement to the road and back again. They avoid the ambivalent tide of the traffic as if everyone had rehearsed their role a thousand times before. But it does provide an unlikely canvas on which to start sketching the outline of a good life because, evidently, it would seem one is hard to see here.

I'm waiting for my brother, Paul, at the Medan airport, an oasis of cleanliness, air conditioning, and free purified water fountains. He is arriving any time now to live in my life for the next two weeks and to provide the inspiration for what you are about to read. He lives a different life from mine in many ways, but at the foundation we have a lot of similarities. I am older than he is by four years, and it's been in that time that I have put into practice much of the theory about which we mostly agree.

If you asked him, he would agree that money facilitates happiness, but only up to a point. In his accountant's way, he would say that the law of diminishing returns applies to money and stuff. Secretly, as I have not entirely evicted my accountant's thought processes, I would think the same thing.

Even beyond stuff, things like status, both social and professional, and accolades don't provide lasting happiness, and the reason is that just like stuff, these things are external to yourself. External things do not generate happiness. Happiness is an intrinsic quality, so it must be derived internally. The same applies to situations and places. You've heard the saying that the grass is always greener on the other side of the fence. Well, you know it isn't of course? Worry about your own grass. Grass is lush and green not because of where it is, but because it is watered and nurtured. Changing situations or locations may give a fleeting boost to happiness, but because you have brought yourself with you to the other side of the fence, you have also brought your internal condition with you. So, unless you are somewhere like Mogadishu in 1993, where even if there were any grass, it would likely be greener everywhere else but there, just water your own grass.

I see my brother emerge through the sliding one-way glass doors like a contestant being introduced on a game show who has somehow already won the three-piece matching luggage set. In fact, his luggage is quite minimal, and that reminds me that we have been talking a lot more of late, obliquely, about what it means to be happy. He has recently retired from the corporate world as well, and while he may go back to it, he sees work and money as just a means to an end. I think he does enjoy some aspects of work though, those elements that generate fulfilment. Perhaps it's also on an intellectual level because he is learning something or because he is creating or contributing to something. I suspect that he generates more happiness from these intrinsic rewards than from the money.

I could be wrong. But I am right in that he has decided to pursue things that interest him such as his latest obsession, cycling about the globe. In a way, he leap-frogged the premise of my first escape attempt and very much had the idea of freedom for something as opposed to freedom from it, and perhaps that is why his first escape has thrived so far.

We hug each other, and in the initial excitement we run rapid-fire through our usual small talk about the status of our hair loss, beards, and bellies. It's been perhaps a year since I have seen him. We usually meet on neutral territory at another family member's house, but now it is in a place where I feel very much at home. It's where I have grown into a self with which I am very comfortable.

It's not like I expected him to say, "My, haven't you grown!" But in many ways, I had, and I was keen to showcase both my new home and my new life. In my bus on the Island of Nias, where we were now heading, life can get a bit isolated and having my brother with me, at least for a short time, would eliminate that issue.

We wheel through the airport and find the domestic gate for our flight to Nias. It's a short trip on a propeller plane to the capital, Gunungsitoli. There, one of my friends from Sorake Beach, where Rosie has been moping alone for the last few weeks in Mamma Naya's hotel car park, meets us. The journey from the airport passes palm-lined bays on one side and intermittent thickets of jungle on the other. The mood and excitement level in the car seem to ebb and flow directly in proportion to the density and variety of nature's offerings along the way. Nature is a natural stimulant.

We pull into the car park, and I'm surprised to see two things. Mamma Naya, now marching across the car park, seems to have gone from being slim to heavily pregnant in only a few weeks, and Rosie is still where I parked it, unlocked. There is minimal crime here, but perhaps because I had just been in Australia where we lock cars and houses I was expecting worse. I introduce my brother to Rosie, and then to Mamma Naya, who reminds us that not everyone is happy in the tropics. Her greeting is as warm as the bowl of coleslaw she's breathlessly scooping through as if trying to catch up to her runaway pregnancy. I've been away for three weeks, but it was as if I'd just been to the shop to buy some cigarettes. She wastes no time and few words on account of her face being full of cold cabbage and hands me the key to our room.

For Paul and me, it may be the first time in maybe a decade that we have shared a room and possibly as long since we have had unhurried time together. That's not to say we don't hurry about waxing boards and heading out into the swell. After three weeks of being away from the ocean, and away from almost anything natural for that matter, the contrast injects me with more than the usual amount of giddy eagerness as we walk along the beach to the barnacle shelf. I point out the take-off spots as I try to work out why there are so few surfers out. He follows me out along the crunchy crustacean-covered rocks. His high tip-toeing gives away that his feet have seen no hardship for much longer than my three weeks. He declares that this fortnight's objective is to cultivate tougher feet.

Aside from happiness, health is the second of the three factors that lead to a good life. After a couple of hours in the ocean, we declare the opening session a success and head back to the shore to unwind any health advantage we may have gained by slipping into a few bottles of cold lager. The beer would only deplete the obvious and physical aspects of health though, namely fitness and diet. But there's a lot more to a healthy life out here. Just like happiness, good health feeds on nature. In this natural environment, we are relatively free from contaminants in the environment and in what we put into our bodies. The simple connection with nature is good for the mind, for energy, and at the risk of getting too abstract, the soul. It is where we come from, and so connecting with it can only be good for us.

***

It is just before the sunrise on our second day as we paddle out into the bay ahead of any potential crowd. In position, rocking with the waves as if we were riding the world's gentlest and

72

surely first oceanic mechanical bulls, we wait for the first set to come through.

In some way, I like this calm as much as surfing itself, particularly at sunrise. And now I am reminded why that is as the first sunbeams puncture the horizon, and then almost as if choreographed, the set comes through. The magic of the solitude continues for over an hour before another body joins us in the water. Today and yesterday would be the only days un-crowded like this, but they are enough, and I'm happy to share the waves from now on.

Most of our days there for about a week start like this. They are days of lazy simplicity. We surf, eat, chat, read books, surf again, and take random walks up and down the seaside strip. Other than food and beverages, we need for nothing, and there is nothing at all to buy anyway, so we spend very little.

I suspect even if there were something to buy, it would go unnoticed because this lifestyle revolves around experiences instead of material possessions. The idea of consumerism here is as alien as the idea of meeting someone who surfs worse than I do. There are no unmet desires regarding stuff. Because we have as much as we need and indeed want, we are prosperous. That prosperity together with our health and happiness, is all that we require to lead a good life.

REPOSSES YOUR HEALTH

Your weekly trek through scores of colourful and glossy supermarket aisles ends at #24—Health Food. Don't you ever wonder, if this seemingly token section is explicitly labelled *health food*, then what the heck came from the other twenty-three aisles now filling your trolley?

Isn't food supposed to be healthy? Shouldn't twenty-three of those corridors of consumption host healthy food and just one outlier aisle, perhaps signposted *Unhealthy*, contain the shiny processed junk food that today fills the other twenty-three? Then it could also serve as the designated area where lost children, drawn to the sugary glow, could go to meet their parents.

Not only is the food that is healthy for you segregated like some rare, dietary aberration, but its exclusivity demands a premium, as if healthy food is reserved for special occasions. The health factor, one of the three key ingredients to a good life, has been removed from our food so that it can be sold separately back to us.

This unpalatable situation applies to other aspects of health as well. Physical strength, fitness, and flexibility should and once did just happen in the course of everyday life. As hunters and gatherers, people needed physical health for survival. And aside from survival time, I'd wager that cavemen didn't spend a lot of their leisure time sitting around playing with Nintendo's primitive ancestors. How things have changed. Particularly in urban societies, physical activity as an embedded part of life has petered out as we spend more and more time as hirelings and otherwise in sedentary activities. Be it through lifestyle change over the years or darker forces at work which I will discuss, we now explicitly need to do exercise to stay fit.

Mental health, including health of the soul and spirit, is now also something that does not come as naturally as it once did, especially in the developed west. As time wore on, and we became increasingly work-bound, we reduced our dependence on natural solutions to mental health, like sufficient leisure time, time spent in nature, or time at home with families and communities. These were all too time-consuming. To pills and potions, those stealthy agents of addiction, we surrendered not only the responsibility for mental health but any knowledge about the natural predecessors they replaced. We outsourced this aspect of health to doctors and drug companies.

Energetically, we aren't in control of things either. Leveraging diet to optimise our energy was almost a lost art until its recent revival. Additionally, we don't get sufficient sleep, and with a few exceptions, the idea of taking a nanna-nap in the middle of the day to re-energise is not acceptable. We barely understand the flow of energy within our bodies as it too is subcontracted, this time to stimulants and drugs like sugar, caffeine, energy drinks, and prescription drugs.

And finally, for many of us when we get sick, we are so separated from our condition that we are often not able to understand the causes and diagnose ourselves. For the same reasons, we are unable to self-remediate. Without the time, the knowledge, or the notion, we tend to put this task into someone else's hands. Sometimes this is the appropriate course of action, and I am respectful of medical practitioners, but with less separation from our health, we might be able to deal with more ailments on our own. With less separation we might be able to prevent many ailments in the first place.

This unnatural separation of our health from our self-awareness has come about because of the socially accepted notion that a good life is a busy life. The lack of time to personally tend to our health has laid bare a ripe opportunity for those seeking to capitalise on our need for convenience.

This happens in two ways. First, we consensually pay for conveniences with our health. We buy food in supermarkets because it's all there in one place, and it's cheap. We don't have time to go to farmers markets or grow our own food. We pay for gym memberships and fitness classes because on the surface they guarantee health and fitness, and as we have paid so much for the membership, we are motivated to attend. We don't have the time or energy remaining after our workday to be creative about natural solutions or to even get to a natural environment. We take cars, buses, taxis, and trains to and from work, as we don't have time to walk or ride, or we work too far away from where we live.

Our mental health is conveniently taken care of by the pharmaceutical industry. There is a pill for every imaginable condition, some of which exist only in the imaginations of industry advertising departments. There is no end to the range of energy drinks and supplements, and it sure is a lot quicker, although more expensive, to pop a pill or drain a can of Red Bull than to manage your energy naturally. Almost every conceivable area of our health has been commoditised; we just need to buy it.

Accepting these conveniences leads us to the second, more disturbing side of externalising our health. Commercial health enterprises rely on the separation of our self-awareness from our health. And to continue to grow, which is a legal obligation of companies to their shareholders, they must continue to find ways to widen this gap and exploit it. They need to become ever more inventive and sometimes deceptive to gain our buy-in. They'll often orchestrate discrediting campaigns against the natural and sometimes freely available alternatives to draw our business.

76

This is often done with the help of our own government's health authorities, who act more like the large pharmaceutical companies' henchmen than voter representatives. This is consumerism and capitalism at work. To support never-ending growth, they need never-ending consumption, for which they need never-ending new markets and products. It is a case of, "We have a product; now let's create a need."

Allowing our health to be separated from our awareness and then repurchasing it fits nicely into the work-consume-die cycle and as such works against the other aspects of a good life, namely, happiness and prosperity. Consumerism and buying more stuff, including health products, does not make us happy, and when we do get that temporary bump from buying stuff, it steals from our prosperity by thinning our wallet.

Folks, we need to narrow the gap and take actions such that we live in a way that doesn't require us to buy our health back. And further, we need to live in a way that reduces the need to 'do health' because in living in such a way, we 'are healthy'. When we are healthy, we are best kitted out to enjoy life thoroughly.

In a way, nomadic life forced me down this better path. I identified all those elements of my health that I bought and replaced them with something I could do or make myself. I then integrated those things in such a way that they happened as just a side effect of daily life. Nomadic life is active and variable, so I can never be sure I'll do something for my physical health every day, whether for strength, fitness, or flexibility. And so, based on my understanding of a healthy life, I still had some gaps.

So, I cultivated my own inviolable daily wake-up ritual, which captures those elements of health. It's a ritual I sleepwalk into just after waking, almost as if it's just the last phase of my sleep.

And I have now just finished this ritual on the balcony of Daniel's beachfront bungalow to which we have recently relocated. It takes one hour and progresses from passive to active movements, mimicking the very act of waking up. The very act my brother, whom I can hear snoring through the thin timber slat wall that cordons off the bedroom behind me, is yet to play out. The sun will be up soon, and we both want to be in the water before sunrise on our last day at Sorake Beach.

Paul finally wakes up and steps out onto the balcony. It's 6 a.m. It's light enough to see the spray off the back of the waves now, but it's hard to get an idea of how big they are without someone in the water to gauge them against. I can just hear them crashing, which is not typical from Daniel's bungalows.

We throw a few guesses at each other as Paul makes us both cold coffee. The bungalows have no kitchen to boil water. He sits down next to me and checks the swell forecast app on his phone.

"Seven to eight feet," he says.

We both know at that height not only will the competition for waves be fierce, but to get any waves you have to get them early and closer to the shallow part of the reef, perhaps no more than two feet deep when it breaks. We both know our limitations. We both know we've had good surf all week. He looks at me, and I know he's having a mental debate as to whether to head out or not.

"I can take it or leave it," I say.

We leave it and then spend a while telling ourselves that we are not scaredy-cats and that we have plenty of other things to do today on our last day here. I go downstairs under the bungalow between the pylons where Rosie is parked and fire up her gas stove to cook breakfast for us both. After ten minutes, I am back upstairs with two plates of eggs poached in the fried contents of a can of sardines in tomato sauce. By the look on Paul's face, he now realises we needn't have had the coffee cold.

I prepare my own food as much as possible. I know I'm eating well if I make it myself, and except for my guilty pleasure, canned sardines, I know nothing has come from a supermarket. To take control of my dietary health, before I came to Sumatra I did a lot of research and self-experimentation to determine what food I should be putting in my body. I ended up writing a book, _The Consumption Cleanse,_ about my experience and findings.[9]

The point here is that I stopped consuming certain foods intentionally, according to my findings and my self-inflicted rules of the experiment, for one year. As a result, habits formed around this, and those habits are mostly still in force today. In fact, my entire dietary regime is a result of habits that came out of that year of experimentation.

After Paul finishes patronising me about my culinary ability, we talk about the day ahead. I enjoy planning the day with him as he also gravitates towards physical activity. It's fun, and fun doesn't require effort, habit, or ritual. Fitness is an accidental outcome of positioning your life such that the nearest and easiest source of fun and entertainment is outdoor physical activities.

We decide to take the Frisbee and snorkel masks for a walk along the beachside rock pools and out to the headland to check out another break there. It's often bigger and deadlier than the home break, and no doubt it will vindicate our decision to stay on land today.

As we walk and flick the Frisbee, we talk about what's coming up in our lives. He speaks of a triathlon event he has coming up and suggests we head inland to an unused road he found the previous day. It's a steep climb and according to him ideal for hill sprints. I'm not much of a sprinter or even a runner, but I have a reflex action to say yes to physicality, another habit that supports health. However, after a lazy snorkel and some half-hearted Frisbee play by the beach, this particular activity would not turn out to be effortless.

Around here, without time restrictions, I usually opt for the more manual, physical path instead of the convenient one. I take the long way when I can walk instead of drive and make things instead of buying them. This approach might take longer, but in that extra time I'm looking after my physical health. Taking a long way off the road, away from civilisation, along jungle tracks or the beach plays into mental health as well. I can't define what the soul is or how spirit works, but I know that spending time wandering around amongst trees and by the ocean, I am doing both of those things a favour.

With some thought, some planning, and some change, we can be healthy without explicitly doing or buying anything, thereby making the living of a good life that much easier.

PROSPERITY IS JUST ALGEBRA

Because I believe that the path to prosperity is a logical one, I will use an exact and logical science to map it out, mathematics. Now, draw back that exhaled sigh and refocus those glazed over eyes because I'm not referring to differential calculus or trigonometric equations; I am talking about simple algebra. For instance, to denote the story so far, in algebraic terms, I've said that a good life is a combination of health, prosperity, and happiness.

$$G_L = H_L + P_R + H_P$$

Remember that prosperity is not the same as wealth. I see wealth as a by-product of the mentality of excess, whereas prosperity is a by-product of the mindset of enough. Not only that, the pursuit of wealth is futile as governed by excess; it is infinite. It's why so many are trapped in the work-consume-die cycle. Prosperity, however, is a more rational and achievable objective because it is finite and the result of our personal ideas about enough.

Kurt Vonnegut articulates the distinction between excess and enough in his poem in *The New Yorker* in May of 2005, reprinted in John C. Bogle's *Enough: True Measures of Money, Business, and Life:*[10]

JOE HELLER

True story, Word of Honor:

Joseph Heller, an important and funny writer

now dead,

and I were at a party given by a billionaire

on Shelter Island.

I said, "Joe, how does it make you feel

to know that our host only yesterday

may have made more money

than your novel 'Catch-22'

has earned in its entire history?"

And Joe said, "I've got something he can never have."

And I said, "What on earth could that be, Joe?"

And Joe said, "The knowledge that I've got enough."

Not bad! Rest in peace!

We are prosperous when we have enough to meet our expectations. The point of prosperity is reached when our actual situation exceeds our expectations:

$$P_R = A_C - E_X$$

Our actual situation (A_C), focusing on its tangible aspects, includes things like our assets, debts, income, and our spending profile.

Staying with the maths, our actual situation (A_C), is a function of our financial position (Chapter 7), depleted by our propensity for consumerism and enhanced by our inclination towards minimalism (Chapter 5).

$$A_C = \$_S - C_N \text{ (Consumerism)} + M_N \text{ (Minimalism)}$$

Reducing our level of consumerism has many personal and global advantages, but of relevance here is that we just spend less. The practice of minimalism suggests moving towards owning only those things that have utility or that bring us joy. The extent to which we exercise this positively affects our prosperity because we acquire fewer things, own fewer things, and need to maintain fewer things, all of which leads to less spending. Consumerism and minimalism are a product of our mind-set, but they are outwardly represented by physical things, by stuff.

So, to achieve or increase prosperity, one option is to enhance our actual situation (A_C). We can work more and earn more money ($\$_S$); we can reduce our consumerism (C_N) or practice minimalism (M_N). But these are all more difficult than working with our expectations (E_X) because expectations are mostly a mental construct.

This logic is something I failed to recognise some time back in 1998 when I returned to Australia with my tail between my legs and my ears drooping after failing in my first escape attempt. By the end of that adventure, I had managed to figure out that there was something not quite right with my relationship with work and with money, but my thoughts were still very much governed by the idea of wealth without limit. I returned to Brisbane, Australia, and in the vacuum of understanding about prosperity, I maintained allegiance to the incomplete formula that $P_R = \$_S$. At least half a decade would need to pass before I consciously considered consumerism and minimalism, and I spared no thought for the concept of expectations, let alone the idea of enough.

Expectations are not as rigid as our actual situation. Expectations are made of needs and wants, the latter being more flexible than the former.

$$(E_X) = (N_D) + (W_N)$$

In *Letters from a Stoic*, Seneca asks: "Do you ask what is the proper limit to wealth? It is, first, to have what is necessary, and second, to have what is enough." [11] When he talks about a proper limit to wealth, he is referring to being prosperous. To have enough is to have our expectations, our needs and wants, met.

Needs are the more unyielding of the two and are similar for all people. There are some variations for people in different situations, but compared to wants they are more homogenous. According to Maslow's hierarchy of needs, the basic needs are food, water, warmth, rest, security, and safety.[12] I throw in medicine and education for good measure. If these basic needs are not met, it's likely that we do not have enough, and more of something will contribute to our prosperity. Greater access to medical services would no doubt contribute to the prosperity of the village at Sorake Beach.

I'm not suggesting that we all live just on the bare essentials required for survival. I don't want just to survive; I want to live a good life. And this is where wants come into the equation. After my needs are met, I'll seek to have my wants met so that all my expectations are met. This is the most flexible and easiest ingredient to address in my now fully developed formula for prosperity.

$$P_R = A_C(\$_S\text{-}\underline{C_N}+\underline{M_N}) - E_X(N_D+\underline{W_N})$$

For the algebra police, ignore my use of brackets; it's more a depiction thing than a multiplication thing. I've underlined those elements of the formula that represent the low-hanging fruit that have the most scope for change.

The key to prosperity once your basic needs have been met is managing your wants, which are psychological. They are subjective and based mostly on societal and economic conditioning.

Returning to Brisbane all those years ago, that same conditioning hit me like the blast of the tarmac-cooked hot air that you get you when you exit an aeroplane during a Brisbane summer. In contrast to that year away, in Australia I found the messaging about work, ambition, success, money, consumption, and wealth was far and wide. On billboards, on television, in conversation, it was everywhere. Couple that with the cost of living, which contrasted just as much, and the fact that I was worse than broke, I didn't need much persuasion to move to Sydney and seek a high-paying job.

Had I learnt nothing from my first escape? How easy it is to forget when surrounded by so much persuasion. No more than a month had passed in Australia before I found myself back in the machine, working long hours, making lots of money, and consuming lots of stuff. I was never much of an accumulator of stuff, so I was a minimalist by accident, but regarding consumables, my wants were excessive.

So how do we manage our wants? There is a lot of research out there that concludes that once basic needs have been met, more stuff does not make you any happier.[13] You may have read or heard this, but it's another thing to believe it and yet another to act accordingly.

We are bombarded from all angles with messaging to consume more and more. But what about just enjoying what we already have? We experience so much throughput of stuff that enjoyment is short-lived and seems to be focused on the getting of stuff less than on the having of it. If we are incapable of enjoying what we already have, why do we think additional stuff is going to satisfy us?

We only need to look around at the many powerful and wealthy people who spend their waking lives slaving away on the corporate treadmill without the slightest notion of what it is to enjoy themselves. Subsequently, they tend just to want more and more. We need to enjoy each other and experiences and not things. This is the fast track to prosperity.

In some ways, when I moved to Sydney I was one of those wealthy men, except that I had no money yet. I just needed to keep working. I suppose I also differed from them in that I knew how to enjoy people. I moved into a party house in the centre of Bondi Beach where the inmate population ebbed and flowed with visiting friends from my recent journey, and enjoyment was the number one game in town. My bank balance seemed to follow the opposite tidal chart, but it didn't matter; cash flow was good. It was the accumulation of wealth that was somewhat retarded.

Aside from my travelling friends, amongst the inmates of that madhouse was a girl who unwittingly was living the life that I was aspiring to without having gone through the process that I seemed to think was inevitable. Lorena was a professional beach bum in those days, although when I think about it now, while I admire that use of time, I'm not sure there is much profession about it.

Each day I would trudge off to my office early. As I would leave the house with a suit, tie, and briefcase, I would see her in her sarong, bikini top, beach hat, and sunglasses walking out the front door. She'd make a point of informing me where she was going.

"I'm off to the office now; have a great day," she'd say, knowing how that it frustrated me that she could live so easily.

She managed to make ends meet, spuriously or not, but the thing that impressed me most was that while she may have had her own concerns and worries about where her money was going to come from, she had an outstandingly fun life. She was healthy and usually seemed quite happy. We shared a fondness for the party scene, so we forged a friendship initially around that. There were occasional differences of opinion between us, but never any that lasted, and they usually revolved around the timing and delivery of household bills, which were always eventually paid but sometimes under threat of pulling fingernails.

I don't think we understood each other's way of living. I'm sure she wondered why I would work so much. Admittedly I would shake my head at her existence and how irresponsible it was. I wondered how she could not be more concerned with her future and all those grown-up type considerations. But I was secretly jealous of her. I had no idea that one day I would look back at her unintentional existence as one of someone liberated—enlightened even.

After a year in that house, a solution to my accumulation woes presented itself in the form of my next escape attempt, which was even more poorly thought out than the first. This attempt would be all about money. All of my earlier lessons about work, money, and human connection be damned. I had tracked down work in Guadalajara, Mexico that came with an outrageous pay check attached. I calculated that if I completed that six-month project and then the next one in São Paulo, Brazil of the same length, I would be well on my way to infinity, in terms of wealth.

As that year came to a close, I had indeed hoarded a lot of money. But more important, in my lonely nights in five-star hotels, I finally learnt of the pointlessness of chasing wealth. Each night in the hotel restaurant in São Paulo, tables set for one were occupied by single men reading newspapers or journals, filling their oversized bellies, and on occasion the bellies of the prostitutes pretending to listen to their half-drunken, endless blather.

These men were wealthy; that much was clear, but when I thought about the word prosperity, I did not see that at all. For all their money and all the excess including their call girls that they displayed, I only saw sadness, despair, and a lack of any genuine cheer. The guests, consumed by their own monologues, wouldn't have noticed if the piano player slit his wrists out of boredom and bled out right there on the stage.

It was in the hotel restaurant where I realised I wanted the wrong things. Before I left South America for the second time, again on the back of failure, I knew that I wanted to be as far away as possible from excessive work, wealth, wants, and consumption. I knew that to keep me at such a distance I had to figure out a very finite thing. I had to work out how much was enough.

The key to prosperity is not more of something, but less, namely, fewer wants. The reduction or removal of wants and desires not only brings prosperity closer to us, but as we are satisfied with what we have, it paves the way to contentment and happiness. A seventh-century Mi'kmaq American First Nation chief had it worked out when he proclaimed, "Miserable as we seem in thy eyes, we consider ourselves . . . much happier than thou, in this that we are very content with the little that we have."[14]

Being content with what you have also has a positive impact on your health because no longer do you have any negative thoughts or stressful feelings about not having enough. Managing your wants and matching your expectations to what you already have takes you that much closer to leading a life well lived. It's as simple as a + b = c.

HAPPINESS IS JUST BIOLOGY (AND ZEN)

Don't you ever wonder why dogs always look so happy? Sure, show poodles seem to force smiles like child beauty pageant queens, and bomb-squad dogs sometimes look a bit gloomy, but these are exceptions to the rule due to their professions. On the flip side, cats don't seem to display much outward or obvious signs of happiness; why is it like this?

It's because happiness is generated internally. I've mentioned it before, but what does it mean? I can't explain it with algebra, as I did with prosperity, but before getting back to the cats and the dogs, I will explain it using biology.

Biologists tell us that happiness is not governed by external stimuli, whether it's money, stuff, rewards, or even relationships. They say that happiness is caused by pleasant sensations in the body. These sensations are a reaction to various biochemical substances (serotonin, dopamine, oxytocin) running around in our blood and the flurry of electrical signals firing in our complex brain biology. So, someone who has just won Bingo does not react to the meat-tray prize but to the biological activity going on within themselves.

Evolution has moderated these pleasant sensations so that while there may be peaks and troughs, they are only momentary; the happy-o-stat will always return from the extremes, and everyone has a different biochemical predisposition to happiness. Some folks are just biologically happier than others. I'll call them resting happiness and range. So, while we can move around within that range, according to biology, no external stimuli can change that range, at least not in 2018.

***

Earlier this morning, Paul and I said goodbye to Daniel and his family. We left quite a mess upstairs at the bungalow after the previous night's feast. It was a kind of gift for Mamma Martin. I know that sounds ridiculous, but on several occasions during our stay, she was visibly upset by our attempts to muscle in on her domain and clean up after ourselves. She is extraordinarily proud of those bungalows and her role in their family business. That's not something with which I was going to argue.

We loaded our bags into Rosie and rounded up and fastened the loose stuff, the plates, pots and pans, knowing there would be a stop after a few minutes as the potholes would expose the remaining noisy fugitives. As we left, I promised my friends that I would return someday, knowing that I might not. Mamma Martin's expression was that of a proud mother with her son heading off into the world for the first time. Unless I was mistaken—and she is in no way house-proud— the look was of relief because she would no longer have to clean up after us.

Three hours later, we are now rolling into Gunungsitoli. It's not quite a city; it's more like a sprawling open-air market. The wet and partially unsealed streets are under constant invasion by a militia of marketers oozing beyond their designated sidewalk stalls towards the rival vendors on the opposing side of the road with both aiming to engage at about the middle. Scooters run the gauntlet between them amid the permanent but individually indistinguishable beeps, rendering them useless as a warning and irritating to no one but me, it seems.

These streets were not designed for a five-and-a-half-metre bus, but the law of the jungle is on my side. My vehicle is bigger than most, and as I am white, I am seen as a threat on the roads. Rosie parts the people ahead of her almost biblically as we crawl past the gawking stall keepers, who no doubt are trying to understand what we are and what we are doing there.

It is here that I notice how oblivious the dogs are to the people, the traffic, and the general chaos. And even though I've seen this phenomenon countless times in Indonesia, it's the first time I think to myself how happy dogs seem regardless of circumstances. Here I see them marauding in squads of threes and fours and more amongst the stalls and crossing streets and half-heartedly snapping at each other. The permanent smiles on their faces defy the wretchedness of their hungry ribs. You know the way dogs seems to smile, panting with their tongues hanging out, almost laughing as if there is some telekinetic canine gag running 24/7? Why are they so damn happy?

I think I know now. Dogs are so active. They are always exercising. Exercise increases dopamine levels in the body. I'm quite sure that dogs don't sit around and have cause and effect discussions about exercise and brain biology; they just know exercise feels good; it makes them feel happy. The supporting evidence is that when you do see dogs inactive on account of injury, age, or confinement, they just look sad don't they? And lazy dogs also don't seem to have that *joie de vivre* in their eyes.

But a starker comparison is cats. Cats seem so moody. Of course, kittens are playful, not having been conditioned by cat society yet, so they do show some outward signs of happiness. This is because they are playful and exercising and dopamine is on a roll. You see adult cats lazily flopped over a sofa arm or sitting pensive somewhere quiet in your yard. They hardly move. Are they unhappy? I often wonder if cats have a relatively high incidence of depression within the domesticated animal world. It's either that, or they are deeply contemplative.

Maybe people are like cats. As we get older and conditioned by society, our natural tendency to play and exercise diminishes, and in so doing steals away our happiness. Biology explains why good health, specifically exercise, needs to be a top priority if we want to be happy.

Biology also explains why prosperity makes you happy. When we realise that we have enough, we feel content, and we get the same chemicals as for pleasure increase in our brains. It's not just the meeting of financial expectations that cause the chemical fiesta. It applies to all expectations. Looking at that in reverse, if in general our expectations are well managed and we've got a handle on our wants and desires, then that feeling of contentment and the brain chemistry party is going to happen more often.

We manage to get the bus through the dense, supposed centre of the village and over to the actual market by the sea on the edge of town. It operates all day, every day, but the fish market section winds up early, so we find a spot on the edge of that. We are careful to ensure when we alight that we don't step in one of the leftover fishy piles strewn about in the mud.

We wander around looking for food for the next few days in the bus. I've run out of cooking gas, and they don't sell the type that I need here, so we need food that we can eat cold. Here also we see the dogs running amok. They are not fussed about their cold food. They seem particularly happy here as the fish sellers abandoning their sites leave piles of ocean-bound plastic bags, foam food containers, and most valuable, the skeletal remains of fish. They forage through the rubbish, yapping as they lunch; their happiness confesses to their expectations' being met. Dopamine strikes again at the fish market.

But this is not for everyone. Halfway along the seaside strip, there is a break in the tarpaulin stalls and some concrete stairs that run down into the water. Partway down the steps I see a scabby, underfed cat, dripping off one step and about to pool on the next as if it were made entirely of some furry, viscous liquid. If I ever needed an animal personification for the word *disinterest*, this is it. We are in the middle of an almost entirely abandoned fish market, a veritable smorgasbord for a cat, and yet I see only apathy. It seems there are no obvious signs of happiness here, and so I know we are in a dopamine-free zone with this cat. Even here in this feline Mecca, it seems that this indifferent animal is unable to meet its expectations and experience contentment and, subsequently, happiness.

The cat and the pack of jolly dogs highlight that the objective circumstance is not as important as the subjective expectation that is applied. Like the dogs, our expectations were quite low here, but we manage to find some fresh avocados, boiled eggs, and cans of sardines, so we walk away a couple of doped up and happy men.

So far, the happiness story has all been based on what the biologists tell us. But I, and I suspect some of them too, leave a bit of wiggle room for sociological and psychological factors. I think they have their place in the formula. Take health, for example. When you are healthy and looking good to yourself, you have a positive self-image. This may initiate a dopamine reaction, but the psychological effect is long lasting, unlike the biological one.

It's a combination of these internal factors that supports happiness. The psychological and sociological ingredients in the happiness formula are contentment, such as in relation to prosperity, connection, and fulfilment.

Social connections have been shown to have as great if not a more profound impact on our happiness than material factors. The cultivation of relationships with friends, families, loved ones, and communities requires external participants, but the psychological participation and reward are internal.

I make no secret of the fact that the main deficiency in my nomadic lifestyle is the connections, in particular to my close family and friends in Australia. I'm reminded of this when I get that happy feeling, forging new relationships with people and communities in my travels.

Daniel, his family, and his community make up an example. In their world, connection is not only more evident than money and things, but also than health. Where they struggle in these areas, family and community seem to fill the gap where they can, and the evidence of this was bulging at the seams when his daughter, Elvira, died. She needn't have died had there been better health services. But the community support after the fact was overwhelming as was their openness to include me in what must be the most personal and private of occasions. The family unit and community there is the highest priority.

I rank my own family as a top priority as well, as I assume do most, but I see fewer similarities between the way our communities function. I question whether the erosion of the Australian community can be explained by the difference in material conditions between the two countries.

Getting back to the dogs and the cats of Gunungsitoli, I wonder how much of the happiness of dogs has to do with their dog communities. I look at cats; they are loners by nature from what I can tell. The last pet I owned, a cat named Tony, was a loner. He had no friends and no community. He had a girlfriend, Fatima, but I question the depth of that relationship. I sometimes wondered if Tony was a happy cat and if his isolation had some bearing on that.

Connections extend beyond people, such as to our connectivity with nature. There is no question that a healthy biosphere is a necessity of life. Forests and waterways provide services essential to survival, such as collecting and cleaning water, moderating climate, and providing food, fuel, raw materials, and habitats for countless creatures including humans. Trees are our partners in breathing, the external part of our lungs. We are interconnected and inseparable from nature at the most fundamental level.

But beyond mere survival, the connection with nature provides one of the keys to happiness. It nourishes the soul. Thomas Moore's inspired book, *The Re-Enchantment of Everyday Life,* refers to this effect as *enchantment.*

> Enchantment is a spell that comes over us, an aura of fantasy and emotion that can settle on the heart and either disturb it or send it into rapture and reverie . . .
>
> An enchanted life has many moments when the heart is overwhelmed by beauty and the imagination is electrified by some haunting quality in the world or by a spirit or voice speaking from deep within a thing, a place, or a person. Enchantment may be a state of rapture and ecstasy in which the soul comes to the foreground, and the literal concerns of survival and daily preoccupation at least momentarily fade into the background.[15]

Think about the trees and the oceans. Besides their irreplaceable functional uses, we see their beauty. There's something magical about them. It explains why nature is such an excellent source of inspiration and creativity in literature and the arts.

Nature presents itself to us, but how much do we take it up on its offer? It is a free source of happiness and enchantment, so why aren't we all over it? The reason is simple. Modernism crowds it out.

The great benefit to be had from connecting with nature is only found with enough time to let ourselves be absorbed within it. It requires a peaceful mind unencumbered by stress and expectation and alight with imagination, inspiration, and playfulness. These concepts are frowned upon as time wasters in the serious culture of work, ambition, and productivity. You could say that modern society is disenchanted in this way.

Another feature of modernism that works against the possibility of feeding happiness through connecting with nature is the need for everything to be explainable. Our modern culture seems hell-bent on explaining the mystery and the magic of nature. It likes to dissolve the wonder of things unknown until all that is left is some logical explanation that allows us to wring from it a practical application.

We don't seem to realise that the unexplained can benefit us too. We like to understand everything in scientific terms, and once we derive an application, the modern economy takes over; this then often leads to exploitation. A beautiful mountain, its potential timeless benefit for all living things is in its pure being, is processed for whatever underground mineral or surface topping can turn the most profit. Because science doesn't neatly explain what it means for something to be enchanted or sacred, it has little value.

It is a mistake that modernism places little value on the natural world and its entwined living things where the only apparent benefit is enchantment. We saw the impact of such a mistake on Easter Island some time back in 2001. We stopped over there for a week on my way to South America. It was the start of my third escape attempt, this time with the company of Lorena, whose friendship had morphed into something altogether different. We had been seeing each other for a few months by that time. The effects of the complete exploitation of anything living on that island were still evident then. The ancient Polynesians may have had a culture rich in tradition and mysticism, but unfortunately, not much of it was connected to or had respect for the living world. To the contrary, it was at its expense.

We had planned to land in the capital, Hanga Roa, stock up on food, and hike the perimeter of the island. We hadn't planned on finding very little food to buy. Due to the soil erosion caused by deforestation, not a great deal was indigenously produced; it had to be flown in.

We managed to rustle up some stale bread and a big bag of avocados, which would be all we would eat for the next few days. As we hiked out of town, a local dog, Steve, joined us. Maybe he was thinking that with us, left the last of the food. I do like avocado sandwiches, but too much of anything can turn a man. Fortunately, dividing the food now into three portions, prevented that from happening. But we were so hungry by the end of the second day, that Steve was starting to look like a fried chicken, stuffed with guacamole. He, like most dogs, seemed happy. His expectations were met and why wouldn't they be. Avocado sandwiches three times a day, I'm sure was better than a stray dog's diet in town.

All three of us could not help noticing the sad emptiness of the land. It was like the wind, now unimpeded by foliage, spread across the island the remorse of the last inhabitants as they toppled the last tree and realised their terminal mistake. This was a land devoid of nature's enchantment. It was only Steve's unwavering happiness that prevented the frowns of the Maoi statues from rubbing off on us.

On the third day, we decided that hitchhiking would increase our survival chances. One picnicking family took pity on us and invited us to join them, on their way back to the capital, to their family barbeque. Up until that point, I'd seen no animals on the island except for stray dogs. So, unless the meat was imported, Steve's eyes, bulging out almost onto the grill itself, cared nought for the fact that this would deem him a cannibal.

We flew to the South American mainland, and after a few stopovers arrived in Bogotá, Colombia. Without a valid passport, Steve remained on Easter Island. We had both agreed on Bogotá as our starting point. I don't recall precisely why, but as both Lorena and I met amongst a shroud of narcotics-laden partying in Sydney, we thought that would be as good a place as any. Cocaine, like highly processed food and indeed buying stuff, increases the rate of dopamine turnover in the brain, and so temporarily boosts feelings of well-being. We could not have cared less for the science, though.

Throughout the country, we boosted our dopamine at every opportunity, which in Colombia, is always. At first, we partied incessantly, but there was something different going on there. Something had changed since I was there four years earlier. On this trip, we were not part of the mainstream on the 'gringo trail'. We saw a new breed of tourist and indeed traveller. We encountered en masse, the eco-tourist. Why were they here? What were they about? Partly because of an otherwise scarcity of like-minded foreigners, but also out of curiosity we infiltrated their ranks and discovered that they were indeed, onto something.

This happy bunch had found a new path—new to us, anyway—to happiness. They were on this continent to experience nature. Our escapades amongst nature, by rivers, in the jungles and the mountain ranges soon began to eclipse those in seedy bars and dimly lit hotel rooms, while not entirely replacing them.

Retracing many of my footprints made in 1997, somehow, I was seeing things for the first time. Had this nature been recently installed? Was Machu Picchu there before? Through Ecuador,

Peru, and on to Bolivia, we were awed. In southern Bolivia, we traversed the Atacama Desert to the Salar de Uyuni, the world's largest salt pan. At an altitude of 12,000 feet and utterly flat, it was mesmerising to look across in every direction and see the horizon reflected as by a giant mirror. For those thinking that by that time we had completely moved away from illicit dopamine sources, we almost had, but come on, the world's biggest mirror?

Perhaps six months into the adventure, we arrived in Argentina and made our way to Iguazu Falls. Here we were entranced. My post-modern brain struggled to comprehend the energy, vastness and complexity of what we saw. Did nature make this all by herself? It was humbling, almost embarrassing. The water was bursting through openings in the jungle in hundreds of cataracts in all sizes and shapes and from a multitude of heights from the bottom to the main river at the top. As water spewed out of the jungle, the jungle spewed out of the water in unreasonably located clumps of green.

The animal life was quite another thing. Excited and noisy birds and monkeys traversed the scene, toucans and macaws appeared as if staged and swallows bomb dived the more significant sections of the falls. For hours, we just stood and stared; I'm sure going through stages of speechlessness and shaking our heads in near disbelief. The spell was such that we then went on to Brazil and immersed ourselves in a different area of the same waterfall complex, and on again to Paraguay for yet another angle. Such is the experience of enchantment.

Beyond the physicality of nature, was the human relationship with it. Many of the peoples we found, particularly in the Andes Mountains of Colombia and Peru and highlands of Bolivia, had enormous respect for Mother Earth, for *Pachamama*. Their connection was celebrated through their spellbinding music, and through what we call myth and superstition. For them, nature doesn't require such classifications and explanations as it is not distinct from ordinary life. When we were in this world, although it wasn't consistent with the way we were used to viewing nature, we had no desire for it to be otherwise. Why on earth would anyone want to explain this away? And besides, do we know what 'real' is anyway? I know from my experiences with Ayahuasca on an earlier trip here, and my reading about Buddhism that reality is not all bricks and mortar. Either way, the entanglement with nature that we adopted here, even though it would only be temporary, felt like it was how things should be, synchronised, content, and happy.

We need to consider that if progress means mastery over nature, it may not necessarily be a good thing. Destroying her in the name of false hallmarks of happiness only drives our separation from her when in evolutionary terms our inherent inclinations and instincts are still very much attached to her. We must as individuals take steps to let the wonder and awe seep back in, so we see the value of not destroying it. Maybe then our communities and eventually societies will see the immense benefit to be had by leaving her alone and reconnecting with her.

When I look back now and try to figure out why that escape failed, I can see that I hadn't quite sorted out the basics of a good life, and that shaky foundation was behind my crumbling resolve that eventually would see my return to Australia. Looking at those basics, in turn, my health, aside from occasional powdered misdemeanours in back-alley bars, was in good shape and well managed. I had a solid handle on prosperity, but I had no strategy for future prosperity This would need some work, and I was somewhat happy. I was with Lorena; we had other groups of friends there and various communities we were involved with. Regarding nature, well, she was at the party with bells on. What I can now see was missing though was another aspect of happiness: fulfilment.

These days in Indonesia I have a lot of time to reflect and theorise. I have come to believe there are several aspects to fulfilment.

Pursuit of meaning. I don't believe that there is any inherent meaning in the world, but whether you think purpose is divine or self-created, pursuing it just feels good. If you have a purpose, it can override a lot of negativity because you feel like you are on a worthwhile path. If you're slaving away on meaningless spreadsheets all day long, as I once did, without any sense of your part in a broader purpose, that's a rudderless ship sailing for stormy seas with a crew just waiting to mutiny.

Creativity. When we're pursuing interests through creativity, we can get into this kind of timeless and spaceless state, sometimes referred to as *flow*. This is caused by elevated dopamine in the system. We get a buzz of satisfaction and contentment during the process and on reflection and completion of our creation.

Growth and education. The experience of learning something new has a similar effect. One of my favourite areas of education is languages. I get a kick out of communicating with people from other lands, especially when it's unexpected. It's not just the smiles and sometimes just outright laughs in my face (I never said I was good at languages) that I get. It's also about the connection created, which often comes from my being bothered to learn other peoples' language, particularly in places where English is widely spoken.

Contribution. This is the least obvious element of fulfilment, but for me it delivers the most surprising returns. Besides feeling good about having done something for someone or something else, we are planting seeds, and we never know if or when they will sprout. I like to plant little seeds of contribution along my way without any expectations. I know just by the law of averages that some of these seeds will sprout in my future, and it's those surprises that give me a buzz.

All of these things can create that dopamine brain effect and have positive psychological impacts on happiness.

In 2001, I hadn't developed my ideas around fulfilment, so I was struggling to be happy. After yet another year and a third failed escape, I found myself back in Australia under fluorescent lights, scratching my head and tilling the furrows of my brow where I would sow the seeds of my next escape.

OK, what has any of this got to do with Zen? The Buddha agreed that happiness is not about external conditions and that something goes on internally, but he took things a step further. He recognised that all feelings, including happiness, are in a constant state of flux. We can be happy one moment and soon after feel pensive or sad.

Either way, no matter what the mind is experiencing, its reaction is typically one of craving. When it encounters something negative, it craves to be rid of it, and when it experiences something positive, it craves for it to remain and even intensify. The Buddha said that it's not negative feelings that are at the root of all suffering but this constant craving and dissatisfaction.

So, what do we do? The Buddha's answer was just to let these experiences and feelings come and go, good or bad as they may be, and accept them as they are. Then there is no suffering. Further, in doing this, because we experience happiness without the craving, the feeling is amplified. Unfortunately, the same thing happens for bad feelings, but who cares? That too will pass. This is all well and good, but we are not all enlightened, so how the heck do we do this?

The Buddha developed a series of meditation techniques that can help us experience reality as it is right now without craving for some other state. In short, when the craving stops and we accept the is-ness and the now-ness of our situation, the mind becomes very relaxed, content, and clear. This state is known as mindfulness which can lead to liberation from suffering and ultimately nirvana, where we become one with everything. This is based on the Buddhist laws of the *dharma*. This path involves recognizing that suffering arises from craving, and liberation from suffering comes from liberation from craving, and liberation from craving can only happen by training the mind to experience reality as it is.

The Buddha's ideas were next-level stuff. Not only is our happiness not determined by external condition, but neither is it determined by internal feelings. It's determined by how we understand and deal with those inner feelings. This is when the penny dropped, and I became enlightened, so to speak, to the quandary of the cats. Cats obviously don't give a shit about external conditions, but like the Buddha, they are not attached to their internal states either. Cats then, on reflection, are not moody, pensive or unhappy. Cats just are.

ENVISAGING A GOOD LIFE

At this stage, I have offered my view of the world in relation to the great lies of success, work, and the economic system as a whole and how it is all concealed within a paradigm. I hope that it is now evident that questioning that paradigm and acting accordingly is the only logical course of action. I hope that folks are ready for an alternative that will give us real improvements in the quality of life without the need for ever-more wasteful consumer products and a disregard for what our world can handle. With that understanding in place, I then described an alternative that centres around having a good life. I have described an alternate way to approach health, prosperity, and happiness. The next step is to visualise what the heck that looks like. The remainder of Part Two is all about the practical preparations for that good life.

The following seemingly logical course of events is not at all how things transpired for me. It is only in retrospect that I can syphon from my escape-related experiments the reactive ingredients that moved me forward from the mostly inert ones that did not. The resultant solution separates into preparation, visualisation tools, and declarations.

Before looking at the preparations, it might be useful to ask yourself the kind of questions that would regularly present themselves to me and drive me towards and along my current trajectory.

- Is life turning out how you imagined it would?
- Are you happy to spend your able years working for most of your waking hours doing something about which you are not passionate?
- Is work-consume-die all you had in mind for life?
- Is life as you live it today getting in the way of your health, prosperity, and happiness?
- Knowing that you are going to die, are you happy to spend the rest of your finite time doing what you are doing now, or would you rather live in a different way where you can have enough without all that stuff and without having to work so much or at all?

Don't answer that last question from a mind-set that is right now telling you it cannot be done. If you do that now, you would be correct. It cannot be done with a mind-set that has been hammered into helplessness and convinced that society and everyone else knows best. The question needs to be answered from a different intellectual and psychological perspective.

First, it requires that you understand the paradigm and what a good life is, an understanding hopefully you have now. Second, to envision your own good life requires a mental blank canvas that is primed for possibilities, rather than probabilities. It is for this that we need preparation.

Preparation is necessary for effective visualisation. Conjuring a good life cannot come from a brain that is full and filling further with conditioning from media, society, and even its human host. Neither can it come from thinking in the way to which it has become accustomed. We need a clean slate, free of mental conditioning and habits, so we can think about possibilities without restriction and judgement. There are some simple ways to set that up.

Limit Media Intake. Media channels include broadcasting, publishing and the internet. Television, radio, newspapers, magazines, books, and the information on the internet accessible via computers, tablets and smartphones all take up time. So much of it is a waste of time, and worse, a lot of it is addictive. It is designed like this. It keeps us plugged into the matrix and sells everything that a good life is not, which eats up the time we could be spending living. We need to discern what types of media fall into this category. And we need to identify the forms and sources of media that are owned by the very corporations whose influence we aim to avoid, and that only perpetuate the paradigm.

There are many media that are beneficial to living a good life; we just need to be particular about which we invite into our lives. One way to do this is to consider media in one of two ways. It can be active, which I describe as voluntary, intentional or purpose-driven. Or it can be passive, which could be thought of as unintentional, unthinking or coercive. Media and information is undoubtedly beneficial to living a good life, we just need to be particular about it.

Mainstream media outlets, be it television, radio, newspapers or their internet equivalents, are often owned by large corporations who naturally will use those channels to further their messages. This is not fearmongering or conspiracy theorising, this is natural behaviour for a profit seeking entity. The aim is to keep you consuming by desensitising and distracting all who absorb it against the realities of consumerism. Further, we increasingly see the news segments in mainstream media suffering from subjective reports and indeed more recently fake news. I consider mainstream media to be mostly passive media and a good one to limit or avoid altogether.

I see very little value in television. It is supremely addictive. The amount of time out of our one amazing life that we spend in front of this contraption can reach obscene levels. If you watch two hours a night of television and you live to be eighty years old, you will have spent a total of seven years comatose in front of the idiot box. And for what? I'm not prepared to surrender perhaps a tenth of my life to watch fake reality shows when I have my own reality, watch sports when I could be doing some myself, watch sitcoms that are so unfunny they require canned laughter, and watch perfect-people dramas that perpetuate your thinking that your life is somehow imperfect. Television is primarily passive media, we just turn it on and it does all the work.

Newspapers, magazines and radio can be passive or active, depending on how they are used by the supplier and the consumer. These channels often consist of mainstream media, so we need to guard ourselves against them in this case. Be intentional when you seek out news, look for independent or publicly owned news sources. Be deliberate in what you read and listen to.

The internet is an incredibly diverse source of news, information, entertainment and communication channels. I get a lot of education from sites like YouTube and Wikipedia and targeted browsing. I find my choice of news on the internet. I'll watch intentional entertainment such as documentaries about subjects I am interested in. And like many, it is my primary infrastructure for communication with family, friends and other groups I am involved with. But being active in this realm is key. Possibly more so than television, the internet can take over our lives, be it social media, random browsing or otherwise it can be a huge time waster and a significant source of unwelcome paradigmatic conditioning. Use the internet, don't let it use you.

A great example of intentional internet usage is as a source of books and music. Regardless of the source, many consider both to be essential to enjoyment, imagination, and growth. Read loads of books. Principally, read books that are aligned with your vision of how you want to live. Well-written, informative, and practical books fill half of my Kindle bookshelf. The other half are creative stories that fuel my imagination and give me ideas about adventures and experiments I'd like to include in this life. As for music, few will argue about the joy and inspiration that one gets from listening to all manner of music?

Ignore Societal Norms. The best way to have an ordinary life is to do what ordinary people do and listen to what ordinary people say. Are they happy, healthy, and prosperous? Probably not. Ignore them. The status quo that I see around me when I am in Australia always has the promise of the good life trinity, but rarely if ever did I see it actualised. It's a lie. The big houses, the three cars, expensive this and that, and all the other 'things' that are part of the promise will not deliver you your good life. From now on, stop comparing yourself to others, as that will create boundaries to your imagination.

Ignore the Naysayers. When you start to visualise and act on your visualisations, ignore the people who want you to conform to your old ways. Inmates of the old system are not only bound by wage slavery and debt but by an inability to accept there is another way. They have so much invested in the path they are on that it will be upsetting to realise this; it will be a knock to their world-view and indeed ego and result in resistance.

There will be claims that you are unproductive and idle. To this I say nonsense. Consider a spectrum with productive at one end and counterproductive or even destructive at the other end. Within the context of damage done to themselves and to the planet, where does the average worker-consumer sit on that spectrum? What about a so-called idle human who spends their days walking amongst nature, studying philosophy, and taking care of their needs responsibly through self-reliance and living simply? Won't they register on that spectrum further from the destructive or counterproductive end of the spectrum than the worker-consumer?

Forget your Reality. For now, this is all about imagining from scratch a way of living that is not related to your existing way of living, so you need to forget about your current reality. Your current reality is something that you can think about later. For now, it's all about unrestricted dreaming. Be reckless in those dreams.

Of course, base your dreams in physical reality. There's no point in envisioning a life on an as yet undiscovered planet with an oxygenated, gelatinous, and sugary atmosphere that can that host human life with all the inhabitants perpetually high, massaging their bodies just by existing in it, and instigating spontaneous and perpetual orgasms just by breathing it. It's just not a possibility. If you find that your dreams are returning

107

aspirations of being a billionaire with fifteen holiday houses dotted around the world's most exclusive destinations, then I think you've missed the point about health, prosperity, and happiness. Dig a little deeper.

In fact, if you're thinking about money at all at this stage, you're missing the mark, and it might serve you well to go back and read about prosperity because money is not an end; it's not a goal. Money is a means. Money is something you figure out later. So, don't think about how much of it you want, and don't let how much of it you have get in the way of visualising what you want.

Meditate. And finally, meditate. I think it matters less what style of meditation you use than that you just do it regularly. It calms and clears the mind. This is precisely what you need to create your blank canvas. I practice Zazen meditation but have used many other styles, and all of them have been beneficial. I will have more to say about this later. After you have cleared the mental paddock of its weeds, you'll need the tools to cultivate your crop of new ideas.

Back in Sydney, after a third but not final year away in South America, Lorena and I moved into an apartment on Bondi Road, a short distance away from the beach. I returned to my office, and she returned to hers. By that stage I had developed a lot of respect for and understanding of Lorena's chosen career, but I could not entirely break free from my chains and follow suit. I donned my business suit instead for what would be another three or four years of wage slavery.

But this time would be different. I had awakened to what I did and didn't want. These ideas, brewed over three escape attempts, were now solidly planted in my mind. I was working for a specific goal now. I'd tasted aspects of the good life, and before I would make another attempt at that summit, I would plan it properly. I would figure out the missing elements, which at that point were precisely how much was enough and what would I use my freedom for to bring me fulfilment.

I was an accountant back in those days so working out how much money I needed to live my proposed good life was a straightforward process of working with cost of living estimates and cash flow forecasts. I talk about that in Chapter 7. I had gone some way to address consumerism, which I talk about in Chapter 5, so I had less money to find. The work that remained revolved around fulfilment. The tools I used to contemplate what that looked like are tools that can be used to envisage all aspects of a good life.

During that time in Sydney, one of the girls from the old Cactus Crew, whom I'll refer to as Ms Cactus, got in touch with me. We had remained good friends and often talked about abstract ideas around the power of mind and the power to fool it, many of which had been spawned back in the Ayahuasca days in Colombia. Ayahuasca is mentally divergent and has a way of wiping the paradigm off your life's viewfinder. It was a theme we would remain interested in to this day. She phoned me about an article she had read about a girl who had been committed to an asylum because of brainwashing by a mysterious cult.

My interest was piqued. Brainwashing? It sounded extreme but nonetheless worth investigating. We did some online research and found opinions were polarised. The reports were either positively life changing, or convincingly life destroying. Most of the latter came from non-participants, family members and friends of those involved. We had a vote, and unanimously decided we should send an envoy, and as I drew the short straw, that envoy was me. I enrolled in the four-day indoctrination process.

In a way, we were disappointed when my report after the first day declared an absence of any cult or brainwashing. My report surmised that this organisation delivered education, an unorthodox and yet practical application of logic, that if followed to the letter, would yield a kind of liberation from one's past and restrictive thinking. As I followed the sometimes uncomfortable and confrontational instructions and practical tasks assigned to the participants, as I was obliged to do based on my agreement with Ms Cactus, and the rules of the organisation, a new world of possibilities opened up to me. This was a course in transformations, not uncommon, but I soon realised, not common enough.

At the risk of infringing copyright, I cannot tell you exactly what happened inside the course, but I can tell you the thinking that changed within me. It wasn't just the thinking, but the doing. The general idea was to take steps to remove from my then-present moment any past personal issues or complaints that were attached to me. To do this, I needed to resolve my past and my hang-ups that were a result of the way I saw things that had happened to me in my past. The organisation provided tools to help me find these incidences and tools to help resolve them. Once I settled the past, I was able to come from nothing and create the future out of pure possibility.

A core belief I already held was reinforced there, namely, that there is no inherent meaning in the universe except that which is added by a subject, by you or me. Nothing matters, and everything is unimportant unless you choose to make it otherwise. To realise this is enormously liberating as it allows you to be the uninhibited creator of your own life and to ignore what society otherwise has in mind for you. It reinforces the idea that life is full of experiments of your choosing or invention. Of course, as I am the sole architect of my life, I am solely responsible for it. There is nobody else to blame if things go tits up.

There were tangible results from this new way of thinking, this 'brainwashing'. Possibilities started to open up. Old dreams became feasible and would be fulfilled in the years that followed.

For as long as I can remember I've dabbled in environmental activism. But I was always frustrated with just protesting. I felt I should be doing more. I remember being borderline angry, partly at the injustice perpetrated on the environment but equally at my inability to do something more significant. I was mentally disorganised, paralysed by indecision, and could not visualise a future and future experiments from the space of nothingness.

However, once I had resolved my past, disintegrated my hang-ups, and understood the emptiness and subjectivity of the universe, I became empowered to make stuff happen. Overcoming my confidence issues, I corralled a posse of lieutenants and between us, dreamt up what for me at the time was an experiment in not only the environmental action I sought but in building a community. We gathered one hundred city folks and teamed up with drought-stricken farmers in what would be the first of several tree-planting raves.

Yes, you heard it right. We combined our desire to contribute to the environment and the drought effort with the desire to party and dance to electronic music by blending farmers with ravers over the course of a weekend. We planted over 10,000 trees during the days and danced and partied throughout the nights. By some standards, this might seem a meagre effort, but for me at the time, it was a revolution in possibility.

This and other projects like it were just the seedlings in the test bed that proved the theory of creating possibilities from nothing. It was the foundation for things bigger and more elaborate to come, including my current existence, dreamt up from an uninhibited position of emptiness. Creating this mind-set is just the preparation of our mental fields, tilling the synaptic rows of our brains before we go to work with the tools that we can use to plant the seeds of our future.

One such tool or approach is acknowledgement of death. I am dying. I don't have some terminal disease, neither do I know when and how I will die, but I am acutely aware that someday I will. I see death not just as birth's partner in bookending the story of this life, but also as something inspirational and invigorating. I use it to envisage how I want my good life to look.

I'll mentally travel through time to some point in the future to look back at my current self and see if I am happy with my life's trajectory. I'll fast-forward all the way to my deathbed. For the macabre and sadistic amongst you, you can even lie in bed, breathe shallowly, and for further effect cough and splutter to set the scene. I don't do this, but it's just a thought.

The more you can visualise it the better because death instils a sense of urgency and priority. When people are dying they have been known to be very lucid and often voice their regrets and what they wish they had done in their life, so why not leverage that? From my faux deathbed, I'll make lists of the things I wish I had done or done more or less of.

Some friends and I, including Ms Cactus, took this idea a step further during those years in Sydney. We came up with the Death List Game, which resembled what would become a popular notion in the years to come known as the Bucket List. The game was accompanied by inspirational death-related quotations to help us come up with Death List items and an agreed-upon set of rules that governed the getting of those things done, complete with punishments for not.

Looking back, I see this may have been quite a militant approach to avoiding regret, but it was an excellent source of inspiration and guidance in running my life. The lists were more about specific tasks and achievements than general ways of living or being, but having to do these tasks, in some ways,

112

directed general life. For example, a specific item on my list was to learn a musical instrument. This triggered the purchase of a ukulele. I practice simple songs from time to time, and the act of practising and enjoying that instrument has taught me to slow down and just enjoy something for the sake of it without any specific goal in mind. It has helped me to awaken the creative spirit even though my spirit appears to have no musical ability whatsoever.

Another specific item on the list was to write a book. The experiment behind the book I chose to write, *The Consumption Cleanse*, instigated an enormous lifestyle change, and it had an unbelievably positive impact on my diet and other consumer habits. So, it's OK to dream up specific things if they come from the right place. They will be microcosmic representatives of a more general way of being.

The game did not endure, even though one of the rules was that you could only leave the game by dying. However, the principle is still active for me, and I still have those lists. I occasionally review my list and even add to it. Under the rules of the game, deleting items is prohibited. In fact, I write this from my current experiment in Indonesia in the planning phases of a future grand experiment that I can best describe as Death List Tourism.

Another tool that I sometimes use is to steer the present from the past. As we move through life, we cannot help but collect the expectations both of ourselves and others, social conditioning, and other conformist ideas. A child has little of this. Children are full of ideas of adventure, wonder, and possibility about the world. They are still enchanted. As they have a relatively short past, there is less for them to be attached to.

Adults are comparatively predictable, even boring. As we grow up, we use logic and practical explanations to banish all those things that excited us as children. By mentally returning to childhood, we can recover some of this imagination and free-thinking and forget about the ways of the paradigm where we think what we are supposed to think. The process may even regurgitate ideas that we had when we were children, which now from the position of nothingness might seem like a good idea again.

I suspect this is how I generated another item on my Death List: to build an ecologically sustainable home with my own hands. As a child, perhaps like many kids, I used to excel at building cubby houses. My young siblings would use building materials such as household furniture, pillows and blankets to construct their poorly engineered hideaways. Elsewhere on our family's property, I would be found using brick, scavenged timber, and sheet iron. I'd kidnap my father's power tools to fortify my new dwelling, only confessing to the minor crime when I needed help with the inevitable injuries that followed. This Death List item is that childhood dream resurfacing on steroids. It may be that some ideas will be straight-up impossible based on the laws of physics, but it remains a good way to generate ideas about what it is you want.

When folks look to what they want for their lives, they often think about what they want to have first. For example, they might say they want a million dollars. Next, they will imagine what they want to do with that million dollars, such as buying a luxury beachfront property and concentrating on fishing. Finally, if at all, they might consider what or who they want to be, such as a happy and fulfilled fisherman.

The transformation course that both Ms Cactus and I signed up for taught us something that wasn't so obvious and turned the Have -> Do -> Be thinking on its head. By thinking first about who or what we wanted to be, rather than do or have, and then believing in that, our internal thought processes aligned with that state of being. Then any actions that we took, any doings,

114

were consistent with that new way of being, even if it was not the way we usually thought about ourselves. Second, old limiting beliefs even those we may not have been consciously aware of just seemed to dissolve. Third, by focussing on what or who you want to be, we found that we often didn't need to go through many of the haves and dos at all.

To be happy and fulfilled, if that is what you want, might drive different actions, and by not focussing on the haves, in all likelihood you will get there a lot faster. For example, if being a retired-from-work fisherman is who you dream of being, I assure you there are ways to go about that other than working your ass off until you have a million dollars and then blowing that million dollars on property.

In my case, for example, in applying the Be->Do->Have logic, I start by telling myself, and of course, it requires that I believe myself, that I am a writer. This drives what I will do. I pick up a pen, and I write. That's what writers do. Soon there will be words on a page. There you go; I have a pen; I wrote something; I am a writer. I wanted to be a more active environmentalist, so I just said it; I declared that is what I was. Next thing you know I was doing things in accordance with who I believed I was.

A few months later as I drove away from our tree-planting rave, I saw the beginning of a forest that we created. I doubt this could have happened without the belief in who I wanted to be and if I had just focussed on getting trees in the ground. It would not have happened as seamlessly, in any case. As Gandhi said, "Be the change that you wish to see in the world."

It was during my Sydney time and after I had learned from previous escape attempts that I found myself using these tools and general contemplation to envisage a good life for myself, particularly around the idea of fulfilment. The ideas that I dreamt up could still be categorised into what I didn't want (freedom from) and what I did want (freedom for).

My freedom from concepts were very general.

Freedom from Work-Consume-Die. Even though I was in the thick of it and participating as much as anyone in the work-consume-die cycle, when I stepped outside the paradigm and observed its impact on myself, the environment, other people, and the future, none of this behaviour struck me as OK. Around that time, I resolved to get away from all three hyphenated aspects. The focus on work, money, and material belongings was something I wanted freedom from.

Freedom from Separation from Reality. I also knew that such a life was shielded from the reality of what it does to the planet and our communities. The fact that it was an intentional separation to keep us consuming was not clear at that time, but I decided that I wanted to be free from the paradigm and propaganda that made those impacts invisible. I wanted to live in communities that were closer to nature so I could be closer to the impact of my choices. I wanted to neutralise my negative impact as a proof to myself that sustainable living was possible.

Freedom from Bad Government. I am one who believes in the administrative function of government. It seems to be a good way to manage infrastructure and public services. I am also a backer of representation - a government by the people, for the people – a function I see less and less of, as time goes by. In fact, in Australia, the United States and I'm sure many other countries the government looks more like the political branch of the corporate ecology. With their political class elitism, corruption, cronyism, short-term politicking, disregard for facts, unaccountability, and misguided representation of corporations and lobby groups instead of individuals, the government is now out of control and has lost the sense of its purpose. Consequently, I aim to minimise my relationship with government.

My Freedom for Ideas. In 2005, these were a combination of rough ideas around ways of being and specific tasks such as those from my Death List. Since then, I've found that by focussing on ways of being, the doings just surface as expressions of that way of being.

My list of the ways of being and the resultant doings and havings is long. So, I'll only include a few examples here. I wanted to be fit and healthy as a direct result of my lifestyle. So, I did a great deal of research, wrote a book about food, completely changed my diet, and studied Pilates, yoga, Qi Gong, and meditation. As a result, I have an additional education, a healthy lifestyle, and a fit and flexible body.

I wanted to be in control of my finances and satisfied with enough. So, I practised minimalism and became frugal and more self-reliant. As a result, I have sufficient money to not be concerned with it, few material desires, and a lifestyle that is full of experiences and adventure.

I wanted to be a writer, photographer, and salsa dancer. So, I began practising those vocations and activities, taking classes, and self-educating. As a result, I have some books and a photography portfolio, and I'm still waiting for the salsa dancing skills to take hold.

This process of envisaging my good life took place in 2005, and it came from nothing even back then. When I re-envisage these days, which I do from time to time, ideas still come from the same space of nothing, so the list is hardly different. Even when I look at the new projects and experiments I am planning today, I see they are consistent with those from the past.

By putting myself in a space that was outside of the pervasive paradigm in which we live, restricting the inbound information and societal conditioning, and then forgetting my reality of the day, I was able to picture a good life. Creating a mental space of nothingness and possibility and using visualisation tools and games, I came up with more detail about how I wanted to be in this life, and with my Death List I drove the things I would do to produce the things I have: Be->Do->Have.

I was not concerned about how or when I would do all these things and instead focussed on making declarations about who and what I wanted to be, which then spawned what experiments I would do. I found writing it down a valuable exercise. In a retroactive way, as this document did not formally exist back then, it appears to have been something of a blueprint to guide my decisions from then onwards.

By having it written down now, I'm also able to be grateful when I look at it and see that my life is turning out how my future, past, and present self, wanted, want, and will want it to. These declarations of being pull me through life and maybe, when I am on my death bed, breathing shallowly, and coughing and spluttering, I'll also be chuckling as I look down at my utterly ruined, abused, and spent body and think that was a life well lived.

4. Ritualise Health

WHY WE STRUGGLE WITH HEALTH

My idea of a good life rests on a core belief that nothing is more important than being healthy. There would be no point in escaping and gaining time and freedom now if my lifestyle were so unhealthy that it erodes my time and freedom from the other end, the death end.

I also believe in having a lifestyle that is intrinsically healthy such that my physical well-being does not require any explicit buying or doing. My nomadic lifestyle would fluctuate in and out of a healthful state if I did not work out every day, which many would say is explicitly doing something. So, my mission became to integrate that workout into my lifestyle so that I was not consciously doing anything, so that I did it as unconsciously as going to sleep every night.

Throughout my adult life, I have sought out health education. Perhaps if I were honest with myself, I'd say that was because I was hoping to stumble across the "do nothing, be healthy" system. I have come to realise that the most significant impediment to building and maintaining the best physical version of myself is not in the knowing but in the doing. Of course, lately this has become more about the being, but I'll get to that later. If health is the most important thing there is, then why did I and why do so many of us lack motivation to do what is necessary?

It comes down to excuses. Armed to the teeth with fitness information counted for nothing if I weren't getting out there and working out. I had developed a whole raft of excuses. These included:

1. I'm busy reading about working out.
2. I'm busy having internal conversation about which workout to do.
3. It's too early, too late, or I just don't have enough time right now.
4. It's the wrong time of my energy or food cycle.
5. I have work to do.
6. I have play to do.
7. I can always do it tomorrow.

My healthiest version of myself wanted to work out every day, but my actual version of myself thought about the effort and then found an excuse to match every occasion.

To resolve this, I figured I would rely on willpower to override the excuses. How could I best use willpower? I did a bit of research. It turns out that willpower is like a mental muscle, and it helps to think of it as such. It doesn't have endless stamina. The tank empties, and the more you use within an eating and sleeping refuelling cycle, the less remains. So, I surmised that at the start of the day, after your longest sleep and recovery, and perhaps after a light snack or a coffee, you're likely to have the most willpower at your disposal. It wouldn't have been used for around eight hours so it should be raring to go. Consistent with thinking that one's health is the most important thing there is, it made sense to use that fresh tank of willpower to begin my daily workout before I needed it for anything else.

So, this is what I began doing. It wouldn't be my final solution, but it is one of the reasons why my workouts are always the first thing I do each day. Later I would discover something far easier to work with than willpower, so easy in fact, that no effort at all was required.

THE MINIMALIST WORKOUT

I wanted to devise a workout framework that would endure the passage of time, so I was methodical in the design phase. To come up with my solution I first set out to identify what I wanted from a workout. A viable solution for me would:

1. Include aspects of both mind and body. I wanted a daily process that was beneficial to my mind, energy, breath, flexibility, core and general strength, and overall fitness. (Yes, I'm asking a lot, aren't I?)
2. Require no equipment, gym memberships, or classes (I am a nomadic, frugal minimalist after all.)
3. Be able to be done anytime and anywhere, in hotel rooms or in nature. (Why not get a nature fix while I'm at it?)
4. Be comprehensive and challenging but no longer than it has to be (one-hour maximum).

5. Be integrated into my daily lifestyle with no buying and no conscious doing (as automatic as brushing my teeth).
6. Bypass my excuse-making mechanism.
7. Be adaptable to changing personal physical needs, goals and the advancement of knowledge. (I have minor back issues, so I want to focus on my core.)

My daily workout design using this list needed to include elements from quite a lot of disciplines. Over the years I have enjoyed the benefits of meditation, Qi Gong, yoga, Pilates, and resistance and interval training, so I had those in my toolbox. I'd taken courses and self-educated in all of these fields. Instructor-led classes are useful for starting out, and I recommend them for getting educated. Even do refresher and advancement courses from time to time, but given my minimalist, mobile, and frugal nature, classes are the exception rather than the rule. Looking at what I needed my body to do for me, I came up with the following sequence:

1. Meditation (Mind and Breathing)
2. Qi Gong (Energy and Warm Up)
3. Yoga (Flexibility) & Pilates (Core Strength)
4. Resistance (General Strength) and Interval Training (Fitness)

There are other applications and benefits of the disciplines that I am leveraging, but this is what I draw from them and how I glue them together.

To allay boredom, I designed each phase to last no more than fifteen minutes with one hour in total. I find this removes a lot of the pre-workout excuses and procrastination. By keeping it short and interesting, I find each morning I look forward to getting started, getting it done, and feeling great about it.

The phases are fixed. The contents of each phase can vary, and mine tend to vary slowly with my education because I aim to squeeze more benefit out of each phase without taking more time. I use no equipment, which means I need to use body weight which helps me know my own body and work on other things like balance. Most exercises involve many muscles working in coordination, resulting in great overall fitness and strength. For folks who are just starting with strength training, bodyweight is often more than enough anyway.

The progression of the workout has a symbiotic flow with the progressive waking up of the body, starting very passively and becoming more active with each phase warming and waking me up for the next. This awakening is not something I want to be doing at the end of the day when I'm trying to wind down. More detail about the ritual phases and the specific exercises can be found on my website.[16]

One hour after waking up, which for me lands me at about 6 a.m., I am done and dusted. I have been great to my body, covered all health and fitness must-dos for the day. (Diet is another story I talk about later.) I am fitter and healthier than I was yesterday, and hardly anyone is even awake yet. I've been to the beach or the park, and instead of looking at my reflection in a gym mirror, I have enjoyed a sunrise and even a dip in the ocean.

THE RITUAL HABITUAL

My morning ritual still required willpower, particularly when I gave myself an opportunity to use one of my excuses. Making excuses was a bad habit I had not quite kicked. I seemed to have an affinity for habits whether nail-biting, beer and coffee drinking, or otherwise. Habit is a powerful force, but it needn't be all about things that are bad for you. I brush my teeth each night before I go to bed; I kick my flip-flops off whenever I enter a building almost without realising it. I certainly make no effort or use any mental energy for such things. Such is the nature of habits. If I could think of a single thing I wanted to do for myself, it would be to do this workout every day. I don't want to be disciplined or use willpower because that's too hard. So why not turn it into a habit?

According to research, it takes an average of sixty-six days to form a habit.[17] So, after sixty-six days, I had a 50 percent chance the morning ritual would become a habit and require no willpower. As an experiment, I committed to doing my wake-up ritual every day for 66 sixty-six days. I can confess that by the end of that period it had indeed become habitual.

***

I woke up a few moments ago and thought to myself that no matter how much I like living in my bus, I never sleep as well as I did last night, in an actual bed, in an actual room. I creep past my brother who is apparently experiencing the same thing, out for the count on a mattress on the floor.

I pry open the wooden door and slip out on to the balcony. The creaking doesn't wake him as he can't hear it over the white noise of the fast-flowing Bohorok River over which this cabin is perched. I sit down and look across the river into the pre-dawn blackness where I know the wall of the jungle to be. The only light is the sinking moon's reflection on the rapids below me. I guess it must be about 5 a.m.

We left Nias two days ago after some of the most remote surfing either of us had ever done, or rather, not done. We found a deserted beach, accessible by dirt road at the far north-western tip of the island. We had no real directional plan, but when the road ended, and the jungle opened up to an expansive beach with what looked to be a neat little left-hander out beyond the western point of the bay, we figured we'd set up camp—that is, park the bus. After paddling for a bit less than a kilometre, our hopes sank as we watched the wave break directly onto rock. I wasn't game; neither was he. We bobbed around for a while, both agreeing as we looked back to the distant and deserted coconut palm-lined bay, that we might well be bobbing in the remotest waters we had ever bobbed in. It was a good feeling; it was good to be out there in that isolation with my brother, but we couldn't surf there.

Now, after packing up that camp, making another visit to Gunungsitoli, taking a turbulent ferry crossing back to the Sumatran mainland, and enduring a long, hard slog on the Sumatran roads, we are back in what is fast becoming my second home here, the jungle by the Bohorok River and my room at the Mboy Guesthouse.

It's a very different air from that which one gets along the south-western coastline, but I enjoy it just as much. Rosie enjoys the rest too. I come here for the intense green, the vivid and dense envelope of the wild, hiking the ever-changing trails, and as much as anything to visit my friends Masa and Nor, who own the Mboy Guesthouse.

Masa is an ex-ranger in the national park. He left the role many years ago because he loves the jungle. I know that doesn't at first

125

make sense, but most of his ranger colleagues were on the take from the logging companies. Instead of protecting the jungle, the endangered Sumatran wildlife, orangutans, Asian rhinoceros, Sumatran tigers, and much more, they were facilitating their demise. The foreign and indigenous logging and palm oil companies bribe the rangers with an amount that they can at least live on, unlike their salaries.

Now Masa is a cook. He lives for the jungle treks, carting his kitchen around on his back and helping to spread awareness to the tourists whom he sees provide a better chance of saving the wild there. Last time I was here, we hiked for five days in this jaw-dropping wilderness. I'm sure when we are in amongst it, we feel the same way about it, awed but saddened.

Masa also covets Rosie the bus. Such a vehicle is unknown in these parts. He often volunteers to come with me on my errands just to get to ride in the passenger seat. I think he gets a buzz out of being seen in her as well; I'm not entirely sure why.

Nor is his wife, boss, and financial controller. She manages his jungle activity schedule and the Mboy Guesthouse. She reminds Masa that he has obligations in the village as well as in the jungle. She does her reminding, regardless of the hour, in a high-pitched and coarse scream. This is why I know they are also awake now. This I can hear over the sounds of the river. If they are up and about now, it means Masa must be taking a group into the jungle today, and they'll be preparing meals and equipment.

Most folks don't realise how generous and caring Nor is as she is so often behind the scenes making things work with only her scream as evidence of her existence. But in the time that I have known her, I've met her kind and quiet side, and I understand that for all her fussing, she is just seeking the best for their children and Masa. Admittedly, I think Masa needs to be yelled at. Keeping him on task often seems like trying to manage a wild orangutan.

They keep this small room for me when I let them know when I'm coming. Nor calls me *Bung Toyib*, which means something like 'Uncle Who Never Goes Home'. She yells at me sometimes too. They know I love the space because from my balcony perch on the solitary chair or the hammock, I can just sit and gaze across the river to the jungle wall. I can spend hours like this. Almost as if it's like one of those magic eye puzzles, the more you look at it, the more pops out of it, from gibbons to orangutans and birds and all manner of monkeys. At around sunrise and sunset, on most days, I spot wild orangutans make their way down the jungle wall, not so much like a magic eye puzzle but more like a sixty-metre-high *Where's Willy?* jungle book. First, I see the lighter branches and the bamboo rustling. I know the path they take from around the top of the canopy down to the water's edge opposite me about thirty metres away, where they become easier to spot.

Right now, it's too dark to see the branches moving, and it's too early to walk down to the spot by the river where I would normally do my morning wake-up ritual. It's too early because Paul, who wanted to join me, is still asleep. This throws a spanner in the works.

I decide to do the first phase of the ritual on the balcony alone, and I meditate for fifteen minutes while belly breathing and listening to the sound of the river and the noises of the jungle day-shift animals waking up.

I'm not sure how much time has passed, but I come out of my trance, and it is now quite light. Paul has woken up. I go inside and make a cold coffee for us both. We return and watch the jungle wall together.

Then I see it. One of the sugar palm fronds is bouncing up and down. It's just light enough to discern colour. The primate's ginger arm is reaching out from his cover amongst the fronds to the bunches of sugar dates as he scores his breakfast. No matter

127

how many times I see these human-like creatures in their orange hair-suits, I am always amazed by them and their simple living. I sometimes think we could take a leaf out of their books. We watch him while the coffee lasts, and then I break the spell.

"OK, let's do it."

Outside of the phases and the contents of the morning wake-up ritual, the environmental factors are always different, depending on where I am, but nowhere is as perfect as here. We grab water bottles, yoga mats/towels, my iPhone, and notepad and hit the path. I got all this stuff ready the night before. It's not a great deal of preparation, but just putting these items in a pile by the door helps me operate in zombie-mode autopilot in the morning. I take the iPhone as I usually have a downloaded guided meditation on it and to listen to music or podcasts during the remaining phases. I also use Microsoft OneNote to track improvements in the workout, which I continually evolve. Each morning I'll add a repetition here, correct a posture there, or add something I've just researched on YouTube to one of the phases.

We walk along the river past the village football field to a flat grassy patch which is set back five metres from the river. It's wet from last night's rain, but despite the mosquitos I like the connection with the muddy earth. I usually locate my workout zone at least by the night before, so there is one less thing to think about in the morning. I want to avoid thinking and let habit run the show.

Since I did the first phase at home, we start on the second phase, mostly a Qi Gong warm up, as I narrate the steps for my brother. I have a shoulder complaint that just won't seem to go away. My self-diagnosis tells me it bursitis. It's been with me since I arrived in Sumatra so I'm careful to thoroughly warm the area up.

A group of spectating long-tail macaques, the rats of the monkey world, and Thomas leaf monkeys cling to the surrounding bamboo branches and climb higher along the shoots, making them bend towards us and giving us the impression they are closing in—no doubt to scan our belongings for anything of value to them. I love the jungle activity during the workout. It's eventful, so the ritual passes more quickly. On the other side of the river, a different militia of macaques is walking the narrow sand path between the turbulent river and the jungle wall. The youngsters are pushing and shoving each other. I'm quite sure if the intention of their tomfoolery transpires, a young macaque will meet a watery end.

We move through the third phase, yoga and Pilates. As we start the fourth phase, my least favourite and most strenuous, the circuit training, I hear a hornbill screech from above. The sun is showing above the canopy now as we finish the one and only thing we have to do that day, and indeed, most days.

Ordinarily, I'd be by myself here with my notepad and iPhone. I find this environment with my blood running at exercise velocity through my veins and my brain and the backdrop of the thing most inspirational to me, nature, highly conducive to creative ideas. As the workout itself is on autopilot and not taking up brain capacity, fresh ideas come at me at a pace I don't experience anywhere else. That's why I take a notebook with me. Other times, when no light bulbs are going on, I'll listen to a saved Podcast on my iPhone, and that may trigger ideas about this or that. I write them down. Perhaps they are useful ideas, perhaps not. Lately, I've been listening to language podcasts as well. My Spanish has been slipping somewhat, so I listen to the morning news broadcast in Spanish, not for the content of course, but for the words.

It's such an immensely beneficial part of the day for me in so many ways. But for today we chit chat and admire the spectacle of the jungle at sunrise. We finish up dripping with sweat, wrap up our belongings to be safe from the monkeys, and place them by the water's edge. We wade into about a foot of cold, clear, but very fast-flowing water. This is the most exhilarating part of the ritual. We each find a spot and, holding our breath, submerge and grab a rock on the river bottom to slow our downstream slide. The rapids bounce over our backs in a river massage to finish the workout. After a few minutes, we flop closer to the shore, roll on our backs, and watch the jungle wall now alive with the day crew.

As I've tailored this habitual fitness ritual to myself and my needs and made it a daily habit, which anyone can do, I no longer see health and fitness as a chore. I can think of no better way to start the day. With this exercise ritual and my diet, which I follow mostly per my findings in *The Consumption Cleanse*, I have never felt in a better physical and mental condition.

The last piece of the puzzle needed to satisfy the shopping list was to ensure the ritual was adaptable. The contents of the phases in my ritual are continually changing except for starting the workout and the phases themselves. I like to think it is always improving with my changing requirements, the advancement of knowledge, and the advancement of my age. I used to be all about buff and muscle, but these days at forty-four I'm all about keeping my life vehicle alive, supple, and healthy so it lasts. Variation also keeps it interesting and keeps me challenged.

So how do I evolve the ritual? Slow change is the best; it helps me remember the sequence of exercises. I tend to make changes in only one of the four phases on any given day, and I make a change every single day. Sometimes it might just be to add a repetition or focus on improving form on one particular exercise.

My sources of ritual evolution I find in instructor-led classes and YouTube internet classes as I've mentioned above. I also subscribe to a handful of online newsletters that I scan each morning for anything interesting or applicable to me. I'll save and read them whenever I'm looking for some enhancements to my routine.

5. Prosper as a Frugal Minimalist

THE MYTH OF BEING FRUGAL

Terms and labels incite reactions, often alarmist ones. When I utter the words consumerism and materialism, the immediate reaction of many, other than tuning out and scanning for the nearest exit, is surprisingly not a negative one. However, if I mention the words frugal and minimalism, the instant reaction is often negative as those terms imply that a sacrifice is required.

These reactions are not visceral; they are mental. They originate from a structure in the brain called the amygdala. Its responsibility is to react quickly and instinctively, and it is most useful and often critical in flight-or-fight situations. It is the quick responder, whereas the intellect meticulously processes all situational information. It then ruminates and prepares a well-informed response including a bullet-point action plan, explanatory notes, references, and glossary, and then faxes it to you in carbon copy triplicate for appropriate action. The amygdala is often correct but not always. It reacts based not on a full assessment of the situation at hand, but instead takes a quick glance, and then as per its job description it draws on historical and sometimes genetic behavioural responses for guidance.

So why does your amygdala advise you to disengage upon hearing the terms consumerism and materialism? And why does it tell you to put up a blockage or freak out when someone talks about being frugal or living with minimalism? It's because the amygdala can be programmed intentionally as much as genetics and history programme it.

Beware, your amygdala is a double agent. That's right, that sneaky little gang of nuclei in the centre of your brain has been turned by the repetitive message of the paradigm and pro-consumerism forces. They train it through constant amygdala-washing to think that indulgence is good for you and any reduction, minimalism, or frugal behaviour is self-oppression.

The amygdala, after so long working as a turncoat, thinks that if we stop focussing on stuff, we will need to make sacrifices. It worries about the demise of consumerism and the growth-driven economy because of all the conveniences and nice stuff we will have to do without. In this case, the amygdala is incorrect, and we need to turn for guidance from elements and agents that are on our side, such as the intellect. The intellect will tell us that not only is there no self-deprivation associated with frugality and minimalism, but that sacrifice is actually associated with consumerism and materialism. That's how twisted our amygdalae have become.

In the absence of the amygdala, which has now slinked away into the shadows out of embarrassment, I can explain the two conclusions I have drawn from my briefings and cross-examinations of the intellect.

First, frugal minimalists favour experiences over things. As such, they tend to need less money and consequently less work. Such people have more time and energy to devote to the things that make them happy like the quality of their relationships, time with their children, time spent in nature and in pursuit of health and creativity, or perhaps just loafing about in a hammock and watching the rain. This is not self-deprivation.

The second is that more of something is not always better. Take leprosy, flatulence, and cellulite for example. Even more of supposedly good things, like money and stuff, is not always better either as it doesn't make us happy. It has us spending most of our lives at work to pay for and maintain stuff. We sacrifice the time we would have had for the things that do in fact make us happy. This is self-deprivation.

I defined consumerism and materialism in Chapter 1. My focus when I refer to consumerism is on the extraction, production, buying, consumption, and disposal of stuff. It's about the movement of stuff, which in accounting terms would most likely have a financial representation on a profit-and-loss statement. When I talk about materialism, I'm referring to the ownership and maintenance of stuff, something that is more likely to be represented on a balance sheet. This chapter is about two intertwined transitions. On the profit-and-loss side, I talk about going from consumerism to frugality, which is the practice of being "frugal, sparing, thrifty, prudent or economical in the consumption of consumable resources such as food, time or money, and avoiding waste, lavishness or extravagance."[18] And then on the balance sheet side, I talk about going from materialism to minimalism. Minimalism has a much wider variety of definitions, but the extent to which you employ it is related to the magnitude of the side effects. My interpretation is to only own those things that are useful or bring me joy.

Adjustments in this direction for both the balance sheet and profit and loss will have the same benefits in terms of needing less money and therefore needing to work less. Both adjustments produce many additional benefits as well, which I will get to shortly.

My first step before taking any action in this direction was to get a thorough intellectual understanding of the benefits of such a lifestyle change, without my amygdalae yapping away in the background, and to acknowledge that there was no sacrifice in living as a frugal minimalist. The sacrifice was in my old way of life. As I shifted focus from the quantity of my stuff to the quality of my experiences, my spending reduced dramatically; thus, I needed to work less.

I didn't stop consuming; I would have died faster than had I had leprosy. Consumption was not my target; consumerism and overconsumption were. I started buying carefully and consciously, eyes open to the costs and benefits, both immediate and long-term, obvious and hidden. And once I accepted that the best things in life are not things, I found that I was living with fewer of them, but I was living with a lot more of everything else. Moving away from consumerism and materialism and becoming more frugal and practising minimalism are not self-deprivation.

THE SACRIFICE IN CONSUMERISM

Once upon a time, sacrificing our time by going to work to make some money to orient ourselves more towards the enjoyment of life was the intent of both our reactionary amygdala and our patient and thoughtful intellect. These days, though, the amygdala, hijacked by the persuasive forces of the paradigm, continues to drive us to work to fund endless and pointless consumerism, but it has lost sight of what that sacrifice was initially intended for. The amygdala has sold you out. We must awaken the intellect and encourage it not only to stand up to the amygdala's deception but in so doing repatriate, re-educate and realign the amygdala's intentions and ideas with those of its own.

When we take our time and think about consumerism and materialism at the intellect's speed, we start to see things differently, even ourselves. We used to identify, express, and measure ourselves by who we are, by our nature, and by our civility. We had connections, responsibilities, and obligations to our fellow citizens and our communities. But these days we have become and are now referred to as consumers; we are even called that by our representatives in the gilded halls of government. We identify, express, and measure ourselves through the owning of stuff, the consumer goods we display, the size of our wardrobe, the job we have, the car we drive, and the place in which we live. It is derogatory because being known and referred to as a consumer plays down the importance of the human character.

So long as we use stuff to identify and express ourselves, we are convincing ourselves that this contributes to our self-confidence, and we end up relying on it for such. So, it is a leaky boat, despite the shiny façade, because all things, all stuff depreciates, falls apart, or wears out. So, our purported self-confidence is on shaky ground because it is attached to shaky stuff. It's not genuine self-confidence.

Instead of deriving self-confidence and filling our needs with real and lasting stuff like internal qualities and connections to those around us. Using material stuff just creates an endless appetite for more of these temporary solutions. And it goes on because as it is endless, it never fully satisfies, and this cycle is what spawned the 'keeping up with the Joneses' mentality. As we can't be keeping up with everything, we end up feeling less satisfied and experience negative emotions. If we continue on the path of materialism and comparison, we won't find the satisfaction we seek. We will only have this constant desire to have what is new and better.

This dissatisfaction can then go on to affect other areas of our lives. The constant comparison can instil an inferiority complex in us. Anxiety and depression can develop from that, both being based in deep-seated dissatisfaction.

It's tiring to keep on buying things. The velocity of purchasing is always going up, and it seems the utility of the stuff we buy is always going down. Being materialistic is mayhem. It's impossible to keep up with the endless desires and cravings. It takes up so much headspace that there's barely any room left to sit back and enjoy the finer things in life.

This never-ending pursuit of more is also time consuming as it takes time to earn money, go shopping, and spend money. Not only are we taking away valuable present time, but we are also striving for some theoretical future time, a future time that will never come and the same future we are destroying with consumerism.

By always buying your solution instead of figuring stuff out for yourself, you lose a lot of skills and know-how. Automatically purchasing stuff and services is making us less mentally and physically equipped to make and do stuff ourselves. All these things that do everything for us now, can make us feel a bit useless.

We participate in consumerism and materialism, even though it leads to the sacrifice of those things that satisfy us because the amygdala reacts faster than the intellect does. The intellect will tell you that being more frugal and practising minimalism is not self-deprivation. Doing so is likely to provide the time, the urge, and the energy to seek out genuine sources of happiness.

FRUGAL MINIMALISM IS GOOD FOR YOU

Consumerism and materialism are indeed sacrifices we make unconsciously and daily and for no particular reason as we have lost sight of the reward. The freedom that we once sought by working falls in our laps without any sacrifice when we pursue frugality and minimalism.

The definition of frugal living is well understood, but what about minimalism? Minimalism is concerned with our relationship with stuff, tangible or intangible. It is a philosophy that encourages the removal of the non-essential things from our lives, removing obsessions with material things and allowing us to work less so we can focus on the things that bring utility and joy to our lives.

It covers physical stuff where buying and maintaining are replaced with alternatives like making, sharing, and borrowing. The focus is on utility and enjoyment rather than ownership. My own application of minimalism is mostly about physical stuff. Besides my bus and the things that make it run, I own very few things. It is about simplifying life, carrying little, and living lightly. In a way, I am materialistic because I like the few things I do have. I use almost all of them every day, barring clothes. Most of my things have multiple uses and are durable, high-quality things. It covers non-durable physical items as well such as food, household consumables, and health and hygiene products.

Minimalism covers more than just physical stuff. Minimalism is also about reducing the clutter of your busy schedule, simplifying your work life, minimising bureaucracy, clearing out negative relationships, and all the unnecessary running around you might normally do. It's about simplifying not just what you have, but what you do.

Minimalism is not a distinct state or an end in itself. It is a journey that unravels differently for everyone. It is not a definable goal. It's more like an idea or an understanding, and for those who grasp it and appreciate its benefits, it provides a way to have more freedom, more time, and more room in life for what is important. It is a path to less worry and more pleasure.

My journey into minimalism began a few years after the time of the tree-planting raves in the late 2000s. My relationship with Lorena had fallen apart a few years earlier. At the time, I felt like a hooked fish, gutted of its organs but still gulping for air, rejected on a lonely jetty someplace. Fortunately, self-preservation kicked in before I became fish jerky in the sun as I scooped up my vitals and flopped back into the sea where I had heard there were still plenty of fish. I've come to realise that sometimes things just happen at the wrong time, and I'm grateful today that I can still call Lorena one of my best friends.

Her moving out of the apartment was in a way what started it. With her gone, I wanted to get rid of many of the things that reminded me of her. I began disposing of them, but once I got going, I found it was hard to stop. It wasn't just that removing reminders of her removed the related noise from my head but getting rid of other stuff also seemed to create more mental space as well as physical space.

Living with new flatmates, I also felt the need to withdraw into my personal living space, which required further shedding. I hosted a few garage sales from the Bondi Road apartment. It was nice to see a bit of extra cash coming in as a result.

Finding myself back in a share-housing arrangement, I was grateful that Lorena and I had never thought to buy a place together. Dealing with a jointly owned property would have been difficult. I had always rented my home up until then and indeed until today, excluding my bus, and I do not see that changing.

Eventually, I wanted to move closer to the beach for easier access to the surf and the sand. It was as easy as terminating one lease and starting another. I had no concern for property prices. I was not concerned whether I had made enough money to cover all the interest, repairs, and rates I had paid had I owned the house. Neither was there any of the usual stress that comes with buying and selling a property. I just picked up my then much-reduced belongings and moved.

Where I live these days, I have the complete utility of Sumatra. I have such unfettered access that I sometimes like to say that I own Sumatra, which I effectively do, albeit in co-ownership with about fifty million other people. I need to add one more since my brother arrived a little while ago. He too has become part owner.

I haven't always been so devout about non-ownership. In my travels in my late twenties and thirties, I would often stumble across a beautiful place and feel an urge to buy a small, inexpensive plot of land there. I felt that I needed to own it to assure the enjoyment of it. When I acted on those urges, the result was usually more headaches and financial cost in the long run than had I simply enjoyed those places. Fortunately, I am cured of that reactionary urge these days. In any case, I doubt I would have enough money to buy Sumatra.

I would much prefer not to have to own everything I use for another reason: expertise. It's highly likely that the folks who look after the shared facilities that I enjoy and use such as national parks, libraries, guesthouses, and mobile-home car parks do a better job than I would if I owned such things and had to care for them myself. In a way, not only can I say I own Sumatra, but I also have a staff of around fifty million people who look after it for me.

After leaving Bondi Road, I moved in with some good friends. It was a house full of women they called the Shakti Abode, and with that came all the utility of living right by the beach in the heart of the Bondi party zone within which I was still at that time very much enmeshed. I had utility without ownership in the Shakti Abode housed with an eccentric collection of inmates. There were the permanent girls, known as The Timekeeper and Evil Kate, and a revolving door of itinerants, sometimes a few at a time, who could be found bedding down in every nook and cranny. I would end up moving in and out of that house repeatedly over the following few years in line with my growing travel agenda.

Throughout the second half of the 2000s, I found myself taking long annual holidays, usually for three months. The nature of my work was not full-time; it was based on project length, and without a mortgage or any other significant assets that needed funding and maintenance, I had plenty of disposable income. I certainly did not need to work for more than nine months a year.

At the end of one such trip, I found myself by the Adriatic Sea in Croatia. By that time, I was well into my minimalism journey, but I was not immune to temptation. I was also still working to make money, so when I came across the opportunity to buy an old stone house that had been half-destroyed during the recent Balkan War (the price was just a few thousand dollars), I leapt at the prospect. I was thinking not so much about owning an asset, but about restoring and selling it to bring my last work day closer. It seemed straightforward.

As I was coming and going on these trips, I enjoyed the benefit of not having a lot of things. I could abandon whatever room of the Shakti Abode I was in at the time at a moment's notice so it could be rented out to someone else while I was away. While I was away, I incurred no rent at home but still had a vague claim

141

to a roof over my head when I needed it. My allotted space in the house was not fixed as the itinerants tended to seep into vacated spaces as soon as they appeared. Getting rid of things, and just as important, not accumulating them were becoming a way of life for me.

I was soon at the point where I could tell you by item name every one of the things I owned, perhaps excluding clothing. That was not something I had control over. Evil Kate would plant new clothes on my clothes rack, maybe out of pity, probably out of embarrassment for me, so I was never sure what I owned in that department. Much of her offerings would find their way to the garage sales that we would periodically host on the pavement.

I was so hooked on minimalism, I started disposing of my flatmates' stuff as my need to simplify spread like a virus throughout the house. I'd see unused stuff and inquire as to whether we could include it in the garage sale. The girls kept constant vigil over their belongings, wary of my light fingers, often not realising I had relieved them of items until they saw them in the basket on the pavement labelled *All Items $3*.

With the disposal of each extra thing came the freedom from having to own, maintain, and worry about that thing. A few dollars may also have been earned if the disposal were via the garage sale route. Although, I must confess that all garage sale proceeds were liquified into beer almost immediately upon receipt. Pursuing less had become more than a lifestyle. It had become an addiction.

Another notable buzz I got from the realisation that I was moving towards the skinny end of the minimalist spectrum was knowing that minimalism was good for the environment. As a tree-hugger from way back, I knew that a life of less stuff meant that less stuff has to be produced, needing less natural resources, polluting less and creating less greenhouse gas emissions. If we all adopted the minimalist lifestyle, there would be a lot less demand for non-essential consumer goods, and the corresponding impact would be anything but minimal.

In 2007, I returned to Croatia for the second time to check up on the restoration work on the ruined house. The remote renovation was turning into a nightmare given the language differences, communication difficulties in general, and my mistrust of the builders who were cutting corners in my absence. Already I was regretting doing the deal. Costs were rising, the real estate market wasn't moving an inch, and every month I had to pay $200 in accounting fees as I purchased it through a local shelf company.

The experiment was not a total waste, though. It would cost me yet one more visit, but each time I bundled it with a visit to see friends in the region, and this was priceless. (Note the comparison, own a house = bad time, enjoy friends = good time.)

The monthly $200 went unnoticed while I was working, but a few years after my final visit after the turn of the decade, with work halted on account of ongoing disagreements and my no longer working, it became a thorn in my frugal side that needed removal. And removal it would be, with a drastic and yet thoroughly satisfying solution.

Less stuff means less worry, and in particular it means less worry about money. Stuff doesn't just cost money to buy; that is just the opening ceremony of the wallet drainage party. There can be financial costs for maintenance, repairs, insurance, damage, theft, and even disposal. With less stuff, you have less to do with money. I found that the further down the frugal minimalist path I went, the faster money was accumulating. As I needed it less and less, I stopped giving it so much importance. When money is not so important, work becomes less necessary. Minimalism is one of the most important consideration if you want to work less.

That is what I did; I worked less. I worked for nine months of the year for most of that decade. After that, it would further dwindle to no months of the year. As a side note, a couple of those three-month vacations were in conjunction with another land purchase experiment in Burma. Mother nature helped me exit that venture when her 2004 tsunami turned that land into ocean faster than our garage sale proceeds dissolved into beer. Another couple of trips were to Guatemala, where we purchased several coffee farms. This experiment I do not regret . . . yet. It is a joint venture with Ms Cactus and two others; it cost next to nothing to purchase and costs nothing to maintain. For now, we just let the jungle grow and retake its ancestral lands. Where that experiment goes next is anyone's guess.

More time and freedom to undertake these projects were less on account of what I was earning as I was earning the same as my peers and more because of what I was not spending (a few minor international property forays notwithstanding). That is what made the difference and bought me time. I would ask myself before spending money, "Is this thing, this gadget, car, or appliance worth my freedom?" Even down to the smallest thing: is this coffee worth my freedom? At some point back then, I even used to think about the cost of everything in minutes of slavery. A $3 coffee was four minutes of wage slavery.

My freedom and my time had a tangible price tag. The time that I gained in my life was not just by spending less, and therefore working less; having fewer things just uses less time. I wouldn't need to look for things, organise things, or clean and maintain them. And then, of course, there is shopping. Aside from my basics, shopping ceased to exist. Shopping became this weird thing to me where people made a hobby, something to actually do, to go and throw away money they worked hard for on stuff they didn't need that would then steal more time and money from them in the owning of that thing. I began to find it quite bizarre. Minimalism eradicates this idea of shopping as a thing.

So far, the benefits have all been about freedom from worry about money, work, and debt. Minimalism provided me with a path to one of the keys to a good life, to prosperity. But what else did it afford me? Surprisingly, it also paved the way to more happiness and better health.

Happiness oozed from the walls of the Shakti Abode. The girls and I would spend long hours on the front porch entertaining ourselves by solving the world's problems during our regular wine from a box (the frugal alternative to bottles) appreciation sessions. We'd discuss problems closer to home as well, such as how to keep that very old and crumbling home, perhaps the last of its kind in a gentrifying Bondi, from crumbling to the very ground. We could put our fingers between the old sandstone brick courses and flick out the powdery mortar, which now that I think about it, may have enabled the happiness to flow from them so liberally. It was in constant need of repairs, and friends would find it curious that we wouldn't contact the landlord for such but do them ourselves.

The Timekeeper would often have multiple enjoyable and creative projects in train. She specialised in having no particular employment but many occupations, paid and unpaid. Each day I would come home from work, and she would have been making something out of some garbage she had found or making artistic and beautiful decorations out of magazine paper waste and peddling them to local craft shops. With each paid project, she would proclaim that this time she had hit the jackpot. While we never saw a pot of gold anywhere, maybe the gold was in the pottering itself.

I spent many hours renovating the kitchen just for the joy of it. I used only discarded materials that I found in the streets from

145

leftover renovation projects. There was no pay for this. It was a rental property. It was about the joy of creating.

Evil Kate was the resident handyman before my arrival. I'd come home from work, and she'd be busy working on some weird and wonderful home improvement. She'd be looking for the source of a new leak in the roof, botching the installation of a clothes rack, or making a meal of installing a magnetically activated cat flap. We often wondered whether Tony, the house cat, suffered at all from having the powerful magnet, required to deactivate the cat flap lock mechanism, permanently tied around his neck. But it was always fun; after all, we didn't own the house, so projects half-finished and others that went completely wrong were not unusual and not a concern. As an aside, the cat flap project paid for itself. Tony would return from his nightly neighbourhood prowls, often with coins amongst the metal objects stuck to his collar.

All of the residents of the Shakti Abode were excellent scavengers. Bondi Beach in those days was like a suburb-sized high-end building site, so the most remarkable things could be found lying idle bound for the landfill on the streets. The entire house was furnished from what by definition was garbage. Like a flock of humanoid-sized bowerbirds, we'd come home to the nest of an evening and display our proud finds: an old ornate lamp for the lounge room, half a bicycle to decorate the front yard, a broken terracotta plant pot, an ironing board, an old spoon. All of it was either useful or brought joy to the house with zero money down.

The junk also could have walked out the door without much resident sadness. In fact, a lot of it did leave through the garage sale channel. It was like some kind of alchemy, turning rubbish into cash and then into beer. And while the Shakti Junkyard was often cluttered, it was more of a way station for random objects of curiosity to pass through on their way to some other place.

146

Amongst all of this, I remained on my minimalist mission. My personal belongings were few and functional. Most of what I used, my room furniture and household contributions, I had no attachment to. I would leave them with the house not knowing or caring if it would be there when I came back. Invariably when I did return, the house was reconfigured to suit a different population of drifters, and a new space was assigned to me. I did sense that I was losing status with each successive trip, though. My last designated sleeping area was in fact, the laundry, sharing the room with Tony.

For me, the simplicity of non-ownership was one of the secrets to happiness. I learned to enjoy less, and many of the things I did enjoy, in that house, for instance, I did not own. We had no idea who owned half the stuff in that house. Hippies would come and go; ownership became difficult to track. The real happiness came from the friends, the laughter, the creative projects, and the ridiculous notion that we were secretly renovating the owner's house without his knowledge or consent.

In between the boxed-wine conferences and renovation projects, having relocated to the beach, good health became difficult to avoid. I had the time and location such that beach running and beach volleyball formed something of a backbone to a health regime that would feature to this very day. That regime was based on the frugal minimalist guidelines. That is, it involved no spending and no owning; I leveraged only that which was publicly available.

And we ate very well. The kitchen was not a zone to heat up leftover macaroni and cheese in the microwave; it was a laboratory for culinary experimentation and a hub of social vivacity that all too frequently would erupt into full-blown parties. The girls were inventive and excellent cooks.

Even though the neighbourhood was inundated with and some would say famous for its restaurants, the frugal and creative

147

nature of the house-holders drove us into the kitchen each night for home-cooked and cheaper meals.

Practicing minimalism is also a great way to improve self-reliance. With society's general inclination towards specialisation, we humans have forgotten how to do and make many things ourselves. As a frugal minimalist, this trend is reversed. This became evident when the Shakti Abode renovations took on a whole new level. A photograph of a Mediterranean Pizza Oven was circulated at one evening's boxed wine conference, and we decided we needed to have one. To have it built would cost $1,500. The house democracy voted that I would learn about and build a replica, with a maximum budget of $100. We estimated the project would take four weekends of work, allowing for the drying time of cement and render.

My father came to Sydney for the breaking of the earth and to instruct me on the correct brick laying technique, as he watched idly by, doing his crossword and listening to the cricket on his wireless. He took being, not doing or having to the extreme, almost sage-like, although on that weekend I would have preferred some doing. But he preferred to observe, occasionally lobbing a corrective instruction my way, often well after it was possible to implement.

Restricted by the budget and the frugal minimalist's dogma, we had to find or pilfer most of the building materials. My father was more excited than I when we found a large construction site nearby and stole a length of iron rebar, and another demolition site that was happy for us to take a hundred bricks, bound for the landfill, off their hands. He was proud as punch, walking down the glamorous main café strip of Bondi Beach parading his gnarled, rusty eight-metre length of fleeced rebar and like me, as an ex-accountant, doubtlessly calculating the money saved as we walked.

The oven was built to withstand category five hurricanes and in my opinion to a professional standard, but it took a bit longer than four weeks. Our rate of materials scavenging slowed, and the general lackadaisical approach to completing projects in that house took hold. The oven construction site in the corner of the yard served in chronological order as a wood store, dancing podium, plant nursery, fire platform, and cat kennel. It wouldn't produce a pizza until one Sunday afternoon, when we finally laid the decorative tiles that The Timekeeper had hustled from a nearby bathroom renovation, some two and a half years later. All of the enjoyment that we had along the way and eventually with the finished product was one thing. Quite another were the skills I picked up through my internet research and education and the trial-and-error building process and just not taking the easy way and buying a solution.

Some years later when the house would sadly be demolished to make way for some generic townhouses, the pizza oven would be the only survivor. Rather than excavate its stubborn reinforced foundations, the new owners evidently worked out a way they could live with it.

Minimalism forces us to be resourceful, it uncovers those hidden talents and helps us to develop new ones. It helps us to become generalists instead of specialists. Self-reliance is an important part of human autonomy and mobility, and so I'll devote an entire section to it later in the book.

Beyond all of the functional reasons to become a frugal minimalist, it can also be a lot of fun. No part of my days now involves switching off and working for someone else in some mind-numbing exercise that serves to keep me in the work-consume-die cycle. Sure, I do without all of the money and things I once had, but in their place, I have experiments, adventures and genuine challenges that keep me mentally active. And because I have to come up with my solutions, of course, I'm going to make them as fun and ridiculous as possible. Most of my joyful memories, in these last few years especially, of being frugal were born out of the figuring, the planning, and plotting as much as out of the bumbling journey itself.

BECOMING A FRUGAL MINIMALIST

As I sit here in the dense and sticky heat of the Medan wet season waiting for my regular breakfast of boiled eggs, I place a mental bet with myself that those eggs won't be to my specification. The Angel Guesthouse is my mainstay when I'm in Medan, and my breakfast request here never changes. Hard-boiled eggs are not a complicated recipe, and yet I am regularly surprised by the variations of this basic dish that these and other Indonesian folks manage to concoct.

I'm here waiting for my ride to the airport. An unscheduled trip to Australia has come up after the exciting events of the last few days. My two road companions are gone. My brother's stay came to an end, so I took him to Medan airport a few days ago and on the same day left Rosie with Dedi, the head of my pit crew at the Medan Isuzu workshop, to deal with a recurring clutch issue. I'm quite confident Dedi will instruct his team to go 'Jungle' on her because original parts for Rosie are hard if not impossible to come by. I am not concerned, though; mechanics in Sumatra are as creative as egg chefs.

Earlier this morning I returned to the workshop to find they were still debating a solution. As it happens, my plans have changed drastically anyway, on account of the unexpected happenings that kicked off two days ago here at the Angel. I asked Dedi if he could take his time, two weeks or so. With his acquiescence, I snagged two weeks of free parking and security for the bus.

As I left the workshop, I packed a small bag and thought back to the South American backpack size competitions. I thought, *what amateurs we were.* Sitting here now waiting for my eggs, looking at my bag and my stuff, I think about my journey since the Shakti Abode days. I really have become a frugal minimalist

Frugal minimalism lies somewhere between an art form and a discipline. But wherever it lies on that spectrum, it is a journey, an adventure, and a challenge.

Frugal minimalism's most obvious adversary is physical stuff. It is about not buying or owning stuff that is not essential, stuff that is not regularly used, or does not bring you joy. It is also about being vigilant and defending yourself against useless stuff trying to creep back into your life. It requires a rethink of what consumables and durables are necessary. Everything that is not necessary, goes. The result is that you find that the things you do have are appreciated and used a lot more.

A couple of days ago, on the afternoon after I said goodbye to my brother at the Medan airport, I met a Malaysian chap and a girl he claimed to be his girlfriend in the bar of the Angel. I say he 'claimed" because she did not confirm it. She did not speak at all. Even when I directed the conversation to her in Malay (Malay is about 90 percent the same as Indonesian), she would look to him, and he would answer for her. He had been at the Angel for two days, but he was a bit out of place in this haunt of cheap-end backpackers and predatory local businessmen looking to bed naïve western women.

This chap, who also claimed he was in the export business, was riddled with bling. The bar table between us was littered with electronics and wires and shiny stuff so much so that I refrained from putting my own phone down for fear it would be abducted by the commotion. He had gold and silver chains around his neck and wrists, a ring on possibly every finger, and every brand of clothing I've ever heard of stencilled on far too many items of apparel. He clearly was looking to be identified through his stuff because there was so damn much of it that he was hardly to be seen.

This guy was a marketer's dream and spoke every bit as slick as his outfit in almost perfect English while intentionally leaving his seemingly mute girlfriend isolated. But there was something about this chap I didn't like, didn't trust. I didn't know if it were the way he treated the girl or that anyone with such an absurd amount of not-him-ness was hiding behind it for a reason. I rejected his invitation to go out later and party with him alone, took my leave, and went upstairs to my damp room and pushed in my earplugs to block out the midnight and 5 a.m. call to prayer that would come from the adjacent central mosque.

It was a restless night. I again forgot to put cardboard I'd found outside by the bins up against my window to block out the spotlights from the mosque. At some point during the night, there was an awful racket out on the street from the clanging of bins. Maybe a pack of street dogs was crashing through them, looking for leftovers from the Angel's kitchen.

In the morning, I went downstairs for an early breakfast and some desperately needed coffee. Susi the owner was already downstairs and rushed at me all hullabaloo, grabbing both my arms and in a panic, pushing me out onto the street in front of the guesthouse. There, she explained what had transpired during the night. It turns out that I was right not to trust the Malaysian fellow. He was in the people-smuggling business. The racket of the night before was one his unfortunate prisoners, one of three held captive at the Angel, jumping from a second story window and crashing into the pile of debris below. At some point during Susi's frantic explanation, I figured it might be time to find a new guesthouse.

The Malaysian chap, aside from his distasteful profession, is a useful example of how not to be a frugal minimalist. To be a frugal minimalist, there are a few general tactics that you can deploy to smooth your transition away from consumerism and materialism.

Turn your back on consumer society. The first and perhaps obvious step is to look out for opportunities to enjoy the simple things in life, which are usually not physical things. It's not easy to do because you will be relatively alone in your battle. But remember that consumerism is not an inviolable fact of life. It is a manufactured policy with resultant behaviour. It was made, so it can be unmade, most easily at the individual level.

Stop watching television. The first thing you must do, as I've earlier mentioned, is stop watching television. The constant barrage of advertisements, and often the programming itself is not going to help you go cold turkey. It's like quitting junk and leaving your drug paraphernalia lying around all over the house. Advertising executives know exactly how to get to you and how to make you think you need a product, this is all they do all day, they should be good at it. So, don't let them into your living room. Besides, it is a living room; do you feel like you are living when you are watching television?

Reconsider shopping as recreation or a hobby. You might think of shopping as entertainment, recreation, or a hobby but consider that it is also a mechanism to keep you shackled in wage slavery. Find other ways to entertain yourself. Shopping for pleasure is nonsense if you consider all of the effects of buying wasteful things, on you, others, and the planet.

Stay away from malls. Shopping malls are like television advertising in 3D. You have made an effort to drive there with the intention of buying something; you are not going to leave empty-handed. And these places are set up to feed you the object of your addiction: useless crap. They are a vortex of impulse buying and are acutely aware that you will arrive having been primed to spend money from years of exposure to advertising and consumer society.

Think about your environment. There is one final, general thing you can do put a brake on spending and lubricate your slide into frugal minimalism. If you are not already, become environmentally conscious. Get educated about the things you buy, where they come from, what damage can be caused to our planetary home every time you buy a new gadget, trinket, or unnecessary extravagance.

Every single thing that you buy, the entire spectrum of consumption of things, at some point, must come from the earth. Even if it is sustainably produced (a loose term), it requires natural resources at some point. If you make this connection then like me you might feel a little selfish that perhaps an orangutan has to die for you to use the latest skin-tightening cream that has been proven not to work. Where you must consume something, know the total cost, other than dollars, of doing that, and for heaven's sake, buy stuff that is produced locally to avoid the damaging environmental and often social cost of international trade and transport.

Once you have kicked the habit of shopping and you have a handle on what is non-essential, there will still be some things that you need and want to obtain. But often those things are still impulsive or unnecessary so applying delaying tactics can be useful. I use a wish list system. When I think I need something, I write it down. I leave it on my list for a while, it might be a month, but it might be a week or a year. The most common things that happen is the item falls off the list with the passage of time, or I just lose the list. If something stays on the list for a while and the need for it arises repeatedly, I will deem it useful and proceed to the many ways of obtaining something that I list below, the last of which is spending money.

Additionally, when something sits on my list for a while, it can be joined by other items. I've been opening wine bottles lately by putting the base of a bottle inside a shoe and smacking the shoe and bottle combination against a wall. This works, but it is not so elegant, and sometimes I lose a bit of wine if the cork is too eager to escape. So, I added a bottle opener to my list. It sat there for weeks, maybe a month, and the need was reinforced with every bottle that I drank. But during that time, I ruptured my toenail clippers on my hoof-like toenails and snapped my knife on an arrogant coconut. Both were old, but more important, beyond repair. So, I was now in need of these three items, and realising I could not find, swap, borrow, share, make or rent them, decided to take my time and find a high-quality, durable multitool that could do all of those things. When I found such a tool, I happily spent money on it.

If you've overcome the consumer mind-set and a specific item survives your delaying tactics, perhaps you should go ahead and obtain it. Needing to obtain something and needing to spend money are two different things. There are many ways to obtain something. I use money, as a last resort.

So how do I get stuff for free? I don't have a problem with stealing, if in my judgement, the heist is of such immateriality, that the victim would not notice or hardly care if he did. However, I do prefer to call it redistribution or confiscation in the name of the overall benefit to humanity. Like stealing, most of the approaches to obtaining free stuff are well known. Unlike stealing however, they are underused. They usually rely on social interaction either in person or more commonly and efficiently via the internet. Because the very nature of getting something for free tends to be social and involve something second-hand, there are benefits in terms of greater community interaction and less environmental damage. Obtaining used stuff reduces landfill and the need to produce new stuff.

Find it. My favourite option to obtain something is to find it. I prefer not to focus on the distinction between finding and stealing something, subject to my theft guidelines above of course, and instead focus on the adventure. Like the building materials for the Shakti pizza oven, finding stuff often involves an element of adventure.

Swap it. You can swap things for things or things for services and for your time. I've swapped books for books, cigarettes for mechanical assistance, and accommodation in my bus and English lessons for food and beer. If you have a skill, it is swappable. If you have stuff you don't want, it is swappable. You can even give stuff away in exchange for Karma, although I am not sure who keeps those accounts.

Borrow it. Especially for big-ticket and infrequently used items, borrowing might be the best solution. Living mostly by the beach or in the jungle I occasionally find it necessary to vacuum the inside of my bus. Am I going to own a vacuum cleaner or even a small dust buster for this? What a waste of space it would be. Instead, I just wait until I see one in a guesthouse and then borrow it. One of my rules for borrowing though is to return the favour, so I might vacuum their foyer or perpetrate some other uninvited cleaning crime.

Create it (Stuff). If none of these options is possible, I'll see if I can make the item. With the considerable amount of how-to information on the internet, you might be surprised by the number of things that you can make yourself. And I'm not talking about consumables; I'm talking about durables. I make things out of rubbish and things that occur naturally in the environment. I made the kitchen in my bus from waste plywood I collected over a short period and borrowed tools. I stitched my tattooing kit together from leather I seized from the waste bins of a tannery and information about leather from the internet. Making stuff is fun. I see lots of folks now using discarded wooden pallets to make furniture. The options are endless, and everything you figure out and create yourself makes you more self-reliant.

In-house it (Services). Aside from making things instead of buying them, you can also learn to do things instead of hiring someone's services. We've been conned into thinking that we need specialists to do everything for us, but many of these things we once did ourselves and can be brought in-house. It just takes a bit of learning. Again, the internet is a fantastic resource. It saved me from electrocution when I wired up my bus for lighting. I do more and more of the mechanical work on my bus as I learn more from both mechanics and the internet. I'm currently learning more about solar power so I can size and install a bigger solar system for Rosie. I don't do this because I have to, but because it's interesting and enjoyable and I have the time. Many of the things we outsource are not just because we don't think we can do them ourselves, but because work puts such constraints on our time. It's crazy that we have to outsource simple things like laundry, clothes mending, hair and nail cutting, and grooming.

Rent it. Sometimes there is no way around spending money on something, but that still does not mean buying it. You might need a garden tool that is only in use once a year such as a chainsaw. Instead of paying retail to own one, maintain one, and watch it slowly depreciate as it rusts away in your garage, team up with neighbours and rent one for the weekend and have a street-wide chainsaw festival.

Share it. Or if you cannot find, swap, borrow, make or rent it, and it is an expensive item that many could benefit from, share the purchase price and the use of it. Do we all really need a lawnmower that sits in the garage for 167 of the 168 hours of the week? Why don't we have one per street and share it? We'd all have saved that money we spent to buy it, the thing gets more utility, and we'd probably have a better street social life as we wheeled the thing around from place to place on the weekends.

Spend as a last resort. Finally, when all other avenues are exhausted, and it is clear that I must buy something, I will happily exchange money for it. Once a fortnight I like to rent a room with a shower and bathroom so I can have a proper wash, do my laundry, sleep inside a room instead of my car, and just mix it up a little bit. I happily part with $6 or so for a night's accommodation in a basic room because I get a lot of utility out of it. I don't need a terrace with a fantastic view because for the other thirteen days I have unbeatable vistas from my bus. When I have friends with me, old and new, I don't quibble about spending $2 on a bottle of beer—probably a lot more than one. I get a lot of joy out of it, until the morning, that is. I know that I am not going to brew my own beer, not yet, and I can't find, swap, borrow, or rent beer. Beer is a personal item that for me must be bought, so I buy it, and I buy it happily.

Once you've got your approach to obtaining additional things down pat, it's time to do a comprehensive audit of your existing spending habits to get a handle on where your money goes. Spending is such an automatic process that it's often hard to know what all your money gets applied to, and there are leakages out of your bank account for usually small amounts, like subscriptions, that you don't even realise you have. This is a seek-and-destroy mission; it must be done with military precision as you remember the reason you are doing this, which is essentially your freedom from slavery; freedom from the paradigm.

To do this, I prepared a simple spreadsheet budget, with individual days going down the page and spending categories

158

going across the page, but how you do this is up to you. For three months, I tracked every cent I spent in cash. I carried a notebook and transferred the information to my computer. At the end of each month, I checked my credit card statements to capture all the amounts spent directly from cards.

Even by the end of the first month, I was amazed by what I was spending my money on. I found several small items that were coming out as direct debits for subscriptions to magazines that were going to a previous address and some online subscriptions to rubbish I didn't even know I had signed on for. My ATM withdrawal fees were astronomical, as I cared nought for finding free ATMs for my cards. I wasn't surprised but a bit depressed by the amount of money I spent on booze, cigarettes and other party goods. My coffee bill was also quite large when I could easily have been making coffee at home. On the other side of the coin, I was pleased to see I had spent no money on clothes and a satisfyingly minor amount on rent and utilities.

By the end of the three months, I prepared a summary. I then ordered each item, not by the amount spent, but by their priority in terms of being essential. And then, gradually, from the end of the list that contained the least essential item, I started looking for ways to remove or replace that item such that I did not spend money on it. I did this over the period of a few months, but it was incredible to see the growing amount of my monthly wage that was left in my bank account each month after subtracting my dwindling expenses. And it was enjoyable and satisfying to know that I was not sacrificing real lifestyle and setting up reduced spending habits that would eventually facilitate not having to work.

This should now start to have an impact on the frugal aspect of being a frugal minimalist. But there is a lot more that can be done to bolster the minimalist side of the equation. I'm referring less now to reducing spending and more to reducing ownership.

I am not suggesting owning nothing. Just like spending, ownership is OK if that thing brings you joy or utility. For example, a passport brings you utility, and that brings me back to the Malaysian people smuggler story. I did leave the Angel that day and found an alternate hotel, a few sweaty and dusty blocks away. I crashed out early that evening, exhausted from the night before and the unrelenting heat. Without a fan in the room, I left my window open. It was secured with galvanised iron bars. The only thing likely to come in through them would be mosquitos and the aroma from the designated bin area, which was directly outside my window.

The following morning, I woke and went about repacking my bag, as I had planned to collect Rosie and leave that day. I'd strewn my stuff around the floor near the window the night before, too knackered for order. It was then that my stress level, usually non-existent, went through the roof.

My passport. I didn't have a lot of stuff, just a side satchel, so it didn't take me long to figure out that it was no longer with me or in the room. I had used it to check in to the hotel so it must have somehow been taken out of my room. My door was locked, so the barred window was the only way to access it. I went outside and saw that the area outside my room was indeed just a bin area, so someone either got into the bin area from inside the hotel or from the neighbouring property. I kicked into sleuth mode.

Now, while there was an element of stress going on, I did also recognise that my passport was just an object and it was replaceable, and I was very quickly getting right into this as an adventure in itself.

It wasn't long before the nervous staff, possibly suspecting I might be some kind of agent of an unknown foreign agency, submitted to my demands to inspect the CCTV cameras from the night before to rule in or out the inside job scenario. Sure

160

enough, after reviewing the tapes for the seven-hour window of possibility, I saw nothing suspicious.

It must have been an outside job. What would MacGyver do? What would he do if the options were to catch the thief and recover the passport or go through the bureaucratic and costly process of obtaining a new one? He'd set a trap, wouldn't he? That night I cleared all the stuff I wanted to keep away from arm's reach of the window. I placed a packet of Marlboros, prized cigarettes in Indonesia, on the low table by the window. On top of that, I put a shiny can of beard oil, thinking the glossy surface might attract the offender. I turned the lights out and went to bed at about the same time as the previous night, only this time I sat on the bed in the corner, vigilant, poised like a funnel web spider patiently awaiting its prey.

I didn't immediately consider the significance of it, but I awoke to the call to prayer and saw that it was light enough to make out the features of my room. Dawn had arrived. I had fallen asleep. Dammit! Not only that, I soon realised that some crafty Indonesian was now walking around with not only my passport but a very shiny beard.

In retrospect, I look back to those events and wonder what the heck I would have done anyway if I had have caught him. Would I have grabbed the arm protruding through the bars? Then what? It's not as if he would have reached through the bars with my passport in his hand. Who knows? But the fact that I would not replace my beard oil probably means that it was non-essential anyway.

As a frugal minimalist, I am all about utility, appreciation, and enjoyment without the need for ownership. I am interested in doing, not buying and experiences, not stuff. There is so much to appreciate in the world around us if we can just slow down long enough to see it. I much prefer, instead of paying a king's ransom to watch a predictable Hollywood movie, spending those ninety minutes watching unpredictable life or taking a walk in the jungle or even the city.

Occasionally, usually when I had guests, we would seek the utility of expensive and lush resorts. Before you get excited, I'm not saying we paid for it. On more than one occasion, we have skipped our morning cup of coffee in the bus and wandered into a nearby resort, which are few in Sumatra. We'd buy our coffee there instead. Granted, we'd have to shell out $2 instead of having it for nearly free in the bus. But we would then spend the best part of the day, at least all morning, using the resort facilities, the infinity pool, fluffy towels, warm showers, and sometimes a sauna. We would still sleep in the bus, but when I'm asleep I don't know where the hell I am, so it doesn't matter. We effectively had the utility of a five-star resort, without having to buy it. On at least one of those occasions we encountered the proprietor. He was wise to our escapade, but nonetheless seemed happy to have sold at least those coffees, and even happier to spend a bit of time practicing his English with us.

The focus on experience applies everywhere. Instead of buying expensively prepared food from an overpriced restaurant, I'd rather spend an afternoon experiencing the life and madness in a local market, handpicking each item of food carefully and then making the food preparation a festival of fun, rather than just a function. We have to eat, so why not appreciate the entire process and potentially learn or improve our cooking skills? Instead of driving and taking taxis or buses to get around, I prefer to walk. Or you could cycle. Besides the health benefits, getting from one place to the next can be an enjoyable thing, an experience in itself. Why make it drab and lifeless just by getting it done. Learning to find pleasure and enjoyment in even the most seemingly mundane tasks is a skill; this is mindfulness. This is what the Buddha was getting at with his meditations aimed at helping us to experience reality as it is right now. And by doing this, one is less likely to need to seek enjoyment and pleasure by buying it.

Earlier this morning, after I finished grieving the loss of my beard oil, I moved my things back over to the Angel, where I now sit awaiting my ride to the airport. I must go to Jakarta to begin the passport recovery process. It's been about an hour now since I ordered the eggs. They finally turn up at the precise moment my ride does.

The eggs are fried.

After understanding that you don't need to own to enjoy, appreciate, and use something, the next step to becoming a frugal minimalist is to start shedding stuff. But first, you need to identify it. This is about doing an audit for utility and joy, and everything is fair game. Every single object that you own is up for assessment. Starting with your material objects and then later moving on to the non-tangibles, the simple question to ask is whether a thing is truly useful or brings you joy. If it does not, then its days are numbered. This task can be done gradually or in large doses, but either way, you'll find it becomes quite addictive as the benefits materialise. It is a constant effort as well because some stuff might be useful today but become useless tomorrow, so while frugal minimalism is still new, a conscious, repeated assessment of your things is needed.

I arrived in Brisbane with an embassy-issued emergency travel document and started the passport recovery process from my parents' place a few days ago. My mother and father had a good laugh at my misfortune while we ate breakfast, Dad looking at me over his glasses in disbelief initially, Mum just smiling and shaking her head. Even though I only just saw them recently, I'm happy to be back because every day with them is a precious gift.

Today, though, I have set myself a mission in minimalism. When I first left for Indonesia, I went through a process of disposing of the vast majority of my things, but I did leave a few sneaky chests and milk crates full of objects that I wasn't ready to let go of yet. With each trip to Brisbane since then, as my minimalistic mind-set became more embedded, I went through those chests and boxes and found items to dispose of. This trip would be no different.

I rummage through my stuff in my parents' garage. I find a bunch of old diaries I was keeping for god knows why. In one of them, I find a schedule that my 25-year old self had written about wealth accumulation: by 30, \$x, by 35 \$y dollars. The numbers are astounding. I'm glad I didn't wait around to achieve that!

With each item, which is now down to just memorabilia, I admire it one more time and then let it go, for the most part assigning it to the rubbish bin. The interesting thing is that there is no sadness involved. I feel relieved. It is like letting go of the past. And with each thing that I thought was me, discarded, it is like the space it occupied is relieved of its duty and assigned to the present.

I'd carried some of this stuff for most of my life. I had hung on to it just in case. Just in case of what, I still don't know. I assign sports trophies and pendants from when I was five years old to the rubbish bin. Do I ever plan to study Tae Kwon Do and Kung Fu again? And do I think I'd fit those uniforms anyway? Of course not, out they go. Curios from my travels when I was eighteen, a wooden poison-dart blowpipe, quite a treasure and useful as a kid. As for me now, I'm not so sure. I bin that too. Oriental pillow covers I was keeping for? No idea, in the bin. There was a roll of about a dozen screen prints and canvasses I had collected during my years of travel. Throwing them out seemed like a waste, but

164

here they just gathered dust. I give the roll to my mum and dad with a "Merry Christmas; these are yours." At least now some of them will be hung on a wall and enjoyed as good artwork should be.

By the time I finish, I am left with one chest, which now only contains photographs, a few of my favourite books, a couple of high school assignments I was particularly proud of, some handwritten letters, the earliest of which was addressed to my grandmother and dated 1977, and some music. Aside from that I still have my collection of stamps, coins, and Phantom comics. In the next few days, most of that would be gone as well.

The thing about the 'just in case' reason for holding onto something, is that just in case will probably never come. So, excluding memorabilia and photographs and the like, if that just in case ever eventuates, well, you can probably just find, borrow, or buy that item when it happens. We hang on to so much stuff just in case when it's unnecessary.

**

A few days have passed now since that last purge, and I've been thinking about what to do with my last chest of personal items, mostly an assortment of my history and my collections. Until a few days ago, I had three or four times that amount hidden away in the dark and under the dust. That stuff was banished under the law of the sparse jungle of minimalism. If it doesn't bring joy or utility, get rid of it.

I am drawn to the idea of only owning that which I have on me, being ultimately mobile, and being as much me and not my things as possible. I get no utility from the remaining memorabilia. If anything, it is the opposite, as it needs to be stored, which is not a big effort but one nonetheless, and my parents would be responsible for it should they move, which they would do in the near future. What about joy? The truth is that on the rare occasion that I look through my chests of goodies, it does generate a lot of emotion, good and bad. So, in that way it has utility. But I didn't need all that stuff to get this utility out of it. In fact, the less of it there was, the more likely I was to use it for this purpose as I could potentially take it with me on the road.

I take another crack at the remainder. I look for things that would make suitable presents for my five nieces and nephews, like my old collections of coins, stamps, and Phantom comics! I have had these items since I was a child, but what value do they bring me now? Nothing. But kids love collections and collecting stuff. Well, I did. So, I leave those inside the house to be cared for by my parents with instructions to disperse them next year on birthdays or at Christmas. I look now at the last lonely chest. *You are next*, I think to myself.

One of my rules to live by, and do excuse the language, is, "It's got to be fun, not shit." I apply it at every possible opportunity. And it applies to the act—or should I say, the art—of disposing of your stuff. I learnt a lot of my disposal skills at the Shakti Abode through the garage sales and dealing with the constant traffic of inbound and outbound stuff. I have an order of preference of disposal as well, but this is personal; yours might differ.

Sell stuff. Keeping in mind the bigger picture, which is to become a frugal minimalist in part to have more cash, selling stuff where it makes sense is my number one option. I sold many big-ticket items, like my car, and then did not touch a cent of the proceeds. I put it straight either on my highest interest debt or into my savings account. It is true that the girls and I at the Shakti Abode were in the habit of drinking our garage sale proceeds, but this was on account of the conflicting "It's got to be fun and not shit" doctrine. Something had to give. Any sales, where possible should go to improving your balance sheet. Other than preparing for your escape, this approach also allows you to see the benefit of becoming a minimalist each time you look at your improving balance. If proceeds are turned it into beer, the benefits do not have a lasting effect.

The nature of the item determines the best place to sell it. Cars are often best sold on online car sales sites. Other substantial items like furniture, appliances, electronics, tools and popular expensive accessories might be best sold on eBay, Craigslist, or with a flyer on a community notice board. Books might be best sold to second-hand bookstores. Other items, like clothing, trinkets, and other bric-a-brac can be sold at a market stall or as in the case of the Shakti Abode, a garage or yard sale. At the Shakti garage sales, we would fire up the barbeque and sell hot-dogs and cold beer as well. This encouraged more attendance, livelier negotiations, and more frequent police visitations. Garage sales are good for bundling things together. I kept for many years hundreds of donated tubes of sunscreen from the Tree Planting days. Even though they were many years past their use by date, we gave away a free tube of expired sunscreen with every purchase.

Wear it out. Often when you just have too much of something, such as clothing, just use it up and don't replace it. I did this with my clothing recently. I was carting around in the bus too many items of clothing, so I just wore my least favourite items every day until they were ruined.

Up cycle, down cycle. Once I decided that underwear was non-essential, as each pair of boxer shorts became more holes than fabric, rather than throw them out immediately, they first were repurposed as dishcloths, car cleaning cloths and rags I'd use for mechanical work. Google "Upcycle" for a list of blogs and other sites that have loads of ideas about re-purposes decaying and dead belongings.

Give it away. Giving stuff away in a meaningful way has so many benefits that I feel like it's a selfish act. Consider my stamp, coin, and Phantom comic collections. First, I get to be relieved of the item. Second, it goes to someone who I have thought would appreciate getting their hands on it. Third, if it is for a birthday, for example, you don't need to spend any money. And finally, it saves you from buying useless junk that more than likely will just add to the landfill.

Donate it. There are so many places to donate stuff that almost everything you have to dispose of has a receiver somewhere. There are goodwill stores in every neighbourhood. Donating also earns you Karma points to be cashed in at some time in the future.

Trash it. Last and least is trashing something. Ideally, there will be very few things that end up in this bucket, particularly if you have time to dispose of your stuff methodically. If something is bound for the trash, then don't hesitate, get rid of it, so it is no longer taking up space in your house and your life.

You will see how liberating this process can be. Don't be like me though. Once your stuff is gone, don't start eying other people's stuff to dispose of, that is their problem.

6.   The Frugal Minimalist Hit List

FRUGAL MINIMALISM AND CONSUMABLES

Alongside the general strategies of a frugal minimalist are tactics for specific consumables, including food, personal care products, household products, utilities, entertainment, and gift giving. As always, the primary consideration is still joy and utility, but I also consider their impact on me and the environment.

Food. Many moons ago, the foraging lifestyle of our ancestors provided sufficient, some might say ideal, nutrition. They were foragers for a long time, so it stands to reason that their bodies adapted and thrived with that lifestyle and diet. They ate a wide variety of natural, local, and seasonal foods and certainly had no concept of processed food. They were opportunists. They'd gorge themselves when food was abundant, and when it was scarce, they would have to fast. Genetics evolves very slowly, and our current DNA is still suited to the hunter and gatherer diet.

169

With the arrival of the agricultural revolution, we had a more reliable food source, so we ate more, but we ate less variety. We ate a lot more of what we farmed and a lot less of what was wild. We started eating lots of grains, and we started eating domesticated animals that also had a less varied diet. We began to consume dairy.

From the industrial revolution and urbanisation through to the advent of consumerism came the availability of almost any food one could imagine. Processed food shuffled onto centre stage. We continued to gorge ourselves because we could, and we did it all the time. But the problem was and still is that our genes have remained virtually unchanged. This reduction in variety, particularly in wild and natural foods, and the gorging contribute to one of the biggest health crisis to afflict humanity: obesity. Our genes want us to run around chasing down a variety of whatever unprocessed food is about, gorging sometimes, and fasting others. But our reality sees us hunting highly processed and unnatural food in a supermarket and feasting every day. Minimalism suggests we return to the lifestyle our genes are set up for.

So, what is that precisely? Eat less food prepared with fewer but more natural ingredients and use fewer preparation steps. We should also eat more sustainably, which often ends up being the result anyway, and enjoy the ceremony around food.

Many people would agree that in developed countries we overeat. The minimalist solution, as crazy as it may sound, is to eat less. Forget about diets and cleanses and all that fancy stuff, which often can turn out to be an expensive waste of time and effort, and just eat less. There are many ways you can go about eating less without feeling like you are making any sacrifice, and I discuss them at greater length on my website.[19]

Minimalism extends beyond what and how much you eat to how you prepare your food. I try always to eat fresh food and

170

avoid anything processed. My favourite type of meal preparation is my one-pot wonders. For me it works because I spend a minimal amount of preparation time and use a minimum of cooking tools like pots and plates, so there is a minimum of washing up. These days my favourites are simple daals or bean recipes. I just soak the beans or pulses so I need less boiling, and then end with a quick boil, adding fresh vegetables and some basic spices. I then eat it out of the pot. This process works well for one, maybe two; an entire family scooping gruel out of a single pot might risk being called uncivilised.

That's not to say I don't love a good dinner party. When I am cooking for more than myself, I tend to get a bit more elaborate. We don't all sit around and eat out of a big pot like a pack of hungry dogs. I'll even use plates in such cases, but the meals themselves are still quite basic, cheap, easy, and tasty. Food is something to celebrate, and yet in our busy lives we tend to dispense with meals as conveniently as possible. With more time to do the stuff you enjoy by being a minimalist, why not learn more about food and cooking it? It's part of culture and society. Make the procurement, preparation, and eating of food an occasion even though on your plate it is a bit smaller and simpler.

And then there is eating sustainably. The argument around meat-eating is a hotly debated one, particularly as it relates to human health. But beyond that, I don't believe there is any evidence that can dispute that eating a plant-based diet is better for the planet and definitely for the animals both those we eat and those that die from habitat loss as a result of animal agriculture. Animal agriculture is responsible for 18 percent of global greenhouse gas emissions. This is more than the combined exhaust from all transportation.[20] Whether you choose to stop eating meat and dairy, or at least take small steps to reduce it, it is a step in the direction of sustainability and in my own opinion, better health.

Eating locally sourced food also takes out a lot of the environmental cost of transportation. Of course, eating natural food, as opposed to the processed junk that lines supermarket shelves, with less processing requires fewer resources from the earth.

Over 2016, I researched and conducted an experiment on myself. At the time, I was six months an escapee and living in Ubud, Bali, where every imaginable cleanse is available. One can just select one or two random nouns and add "cleanse" to the end, and someone will be selling it. The fruit and soil cleanse, breath and ear bud cleanse, and the tea and toadstool cleanse— you name it. In this environment, surrounded by the clean and conscientious auras of the folk of Ubud, who seemed to have a contradictory high level of consumption, I came up with *The Consumption Cleanse*. For fifty-two weeks each Saturday, I selected a category of consumables, researched it to verify the item was either bad for me, bad for the planet, or both, and then quit consuming that item for the rest of the year. The first thirteen weeks were all about food and the topic of the book. I then quit thirteen other health-related things like gyms, supplements, smoking, and classes. On Saturdays for the next thirteen weeks I stopped consuming certain household items; toilet paper was one! I ended up making many of the things I needed. Finally, I stopped buying products from thirteen of the most destructive multinational corporations that I researched.

The format was first researching to prove to myself a reason to quit, then looking for suitable alternatives where necessary, and then purging. I then wrote about the experiment. The experiment was educational, and most of the items I still won't consume because of what I learned. It was an awareness shift on a massive scale.

In order, I quit consuming sugar and artificial sweeteners, beer, confectionery, soda and bottled drinks, coffee, land-based animals, wheat, deep-fried food, anything with genetically modified ingredients, dairy, seafood except for small fast-reproducing fish, and food additives. In the final food week, I focussed on those habits and tactics that help people to eat less. By the close of week thirteen, I had lost a lot of weight and was feeling the best I had ever felt.

These days, when I'm not on a self-imposed ban, I'll consume beer. I'll drink a coffee or two in the mornings, and sparingly something with wheat in it, but other than those exceptions, I adhere to my conclusions from that experiment. You can replicate this experiment by just eating organic fruits, vegetables, nuts, seeds, some seafood, and eggs without going the long way around. It makes life in relation to food simple, healthy, and cheap. Now, I have no use for a fridge, except for beer, but some sacrifices are made.

Personal care products. Pharmaceutical multinationals have hijacked our innate ability to heal ourselves. I do not blame them; it is in their interests to do so. They are human creations but do not work for humanity; neither should they. They work for profit by design.

Before you default to buying pharmaceutical products, search the internet. There are usually many options you can try out that do not cost any money and are from things found in nature. Medicinal marijuana seems to be growing in popularity to treat many ailments; conventional hydrogen peroxide can be used as a disinfectant, and the allicin in garlic has been found to deal with some viruses better than commercial antibiotics. It's all there; you just need to look. I am not saying that all medical advice on the internet is valid. I am also not suggesting you stay away from doctors. But you have nothing to lose by investigating the alternatives and where they seem viable, giving them a go.

173

Vitamins and supplements can also be found in nature in the food we eat. If they're not, then you probably don't need them. Do some research if you think you need more magnesium; instead of buying tablets, eat more broccoli and kale. If you think you need calcium, eat more almonds and bony, canned fish. There's almost always a way to get the vitamins that your body needs just from your food.

As for personal hygiene and beauty products, as you might expect, there are simple solutions. In my bus, I carry a bottle of apple cider vinegar and another of cold pressed coconut oil. They are incredibly versatile. Google them along with any other personal hygiene products and you'll see that most can be made, found or are just unnecessary. I have not yet found a replacement for dental floss though. Maybe seaweed?

Household products. Being obsessed with cleaning and cleaning products steals your time and money. Besides, so many store-bought products contain irritants both airborne and on surfaces and loads of chemicals that harm the environment in the making. They cost money and will harm the environment again when disposed. My house is my car, so I don't have space for many cleaning products, but neither have I found the need. Again, vinegar is my main ingredient here, and it suffices for almost everything. Add baking soda and lemon juice, and you have everything covered. Forget about your fancy and expensive plastic bottles of every imaginable cleaner for every imaginable cleaning concern.

For dishes I just use water. I don't understand the obsession with dishwashing liquid; my dishes are clean with just water and a scouring pad. If I'm parked by the beach, I take the dishes into the ocean for a swim with me and rinse them with fresh water when I get out. Sand is great for scouring.

I wash my clothes when I swim in fresh water in rivers and waterfalls; waterfalls are nature's washing machines. If this is not readily accessible for you, use home-made mixture that can be found on the internet for your washing machine.

Utilities. My bus's electrics run off the battery and some solar cells, so I'm conscious to only use light when I need it. As it happens I tend to do stuff during daylight hours. For all your electrical products, turn them on and off at the wall. Electricity leaks when things are on standby. Use manual appliances whenever you can. An electric can opener? Come on. Not only is it wasting electricity but doing it yourself uses energy and skill. Do we want a world where no one can open a can without the help of a machine? Use gas water heaters as they heat on demand, and you won't have hot water getting cold in the tank. Ideally, use solar power; it's cheaper and environmentally second to none. As for town water, if it is potable, drink it! Tap water is fine and is often what is in bottled water anyway. If you have concerns about fluoridation of municipal water, add a water filter to your tap that addresses this.

Entertainment. Entertainment used to be one of my biggest expenses. Hanging out with my friends in Sydney usually meant going to pubs, restaurants, and concerts, all enjoyable and all expensive. But lately, I've been drifting away from this partly because I drifted all the way to Indonesia, but also out of choice. Even when I am in Australia, I much prefer to hang out in more personal environments, house barbeques, and dinner parties. Where I live, I almost always cook at home in my bus or occasionally eat in cheap, local restaurants. Drinking and eating out in the developed world can disintegrate your budget.

Another thing I've become interested in is creating my own entertainment. I've been learning the ukulele and having fun in language exchange environments; I find it more personal and as entertaining. Each new town I arrive in, I also check out what "meetups" are around (meetup.com) to see if there is anything that piques my interest. I usually find volleyball crews this way.

Gift giving. This is an emotional and reactionary topic. I need your amygdala to be out of the room for this one. This item requires clinical and intellectual honesty. I am talking about gifts, but specifically I want to focus on the events of the twenty-fifth of December or the evening before, and for those still practising the pre-Reformation period custom, such as in some European countries, the sixth of December. I'm referring to the traditional ceremony whereby families will gather at the assigned distribution point and apply in assembly-line fashion the unpack-stack-repeat procedure to a small mountain of wastefully wrapped and often useless gifts.

This procedure encourages materialism and consumerism in children and perpetuates the throwaway mentality. It re-enforces that Christmas is about material things not about thoughtfulness and the sharing of time and experiences with family. In my own family, I've seen some obscene situations on Christmas morning. Children were shredding through wrapping paper, disregarding cards (about the only nice aspect of a present), and often unknowing of the giver, hurling the junk over the shoulder and moving on to the next piece of rubbish. It is a brutal and disheartening exercise when one considers the children are the future. All that wrapping and all those presents took many resources to make only to come down your chimney for a quick stopover at Christmas on their way to the landfill. If not, they create clutter, the nemesis of minimalism. The vast majority of the junk will not be appreciated anyway because as we know material things do not satisfy.

Do we need to ask ourselves if this way of giving is really giving? If you find yourself giving something with one hand and then taking away with the other, albeit unbeknownst to you, then is it in fact giving? This is my angle on the modern-day gift giving spectacle that is Christmas.

Here, I must raise the concept of net giving. You buy and give a junk present to a child. On the face of it that is giving. Behind the scenes, though, perhaps in Bangladesh, there is an exploited child producing it, using up resources, and creating toxins in the process. Then a shipping company burns oil and fuel to get it to you in the developed world. Then there is consumerism and dissatisfaction encouraged in the child receiving the present, and finally you've got clutter, landfill, and pollution at the end of it all. This does not mention all the lost opportunities to use Christmas for something more wholesome. So, with all of that in mind, is it still giving? I propose that regarding the net effect, you are taking away from your child's world and future when it doesn't have to be this way.

Frugal minimalism provides a solution. It does not economise on pleasure or quality. Without buying junk, there are other things with which you can be generous. The key is to avoid buying material gifts and instead make, do, share, or experience something. This teaches kids the value of time and creativity and to favour quality over quantity. Think of something that will constitute net giving. Think of adding value. Isn't that giving? Some might say I'm a cheapskate, that I'm ruining the spirit of Christmas, or that I am a killjoy. But let's be real. Consumerism doesn't bring joy; experiences and connection do, so in fact giving thoughtless material gifts is what kills the joy. I am talking about being a "create joy."

If you're stumped for gift ideas that will facilitate your net giving of something that will not take from the planet, other folks, and the future of your children, take a look at the list on my website.[21] I guarantee each item will have a longer lasting memory than all the thoughtless, impersonal, plastic crap often bought just to fill a stocking.

FRUGAL MINIMALISM AND DURABLES

And then we have durables, such as clothing, entertainment, technology, cars, transportation, and even your house. Then there is memorabilia. I will deal with this last, since this was the last category with which I myself dealt.

The trick to becoming a minimalist with durable items is to take your time and enjoy the shedding process. Have fun. Get the most you can from the disposal, cash or otherwise. Of course, you are a habitual creature, so for many things on your first pass, you will think that you need them. When you go around again after experiencing the mental and physical spatial benefits, you might find your answer has changed.

Clothing. First, a minimalist considers clothing to be durable goods. For clothing, be especially careful with the just-in-case reason for keeping something. Look at each item and ask yourself, "Have I worn this in the past year?" If not, it can go. If it's a tuxedo you keep for rare special occasions, get rid of it and rent one next time. There's no need to carry that excess when there's a chance you may never use it again.

Then look at where you have duplication. Do you need eight t-shirts? I need two and one button-up shirt. But I didn't discard my excess clothing immediately. I wore them out and didn't replace them. And try to hang on to and preserve your well-made clothes. I'll mend them or have them mended rather than discard and replace them. I'd rather give a local seamstress a few coins and support her in maintaining my quality clothes than pay a big box store for cheaper, poorer quality clothing.

When you acquire additional clothes, why not make second-hand stores your mainstay? Not only will you most likely buy better quality items, as older clothes tend to have been made better, but you'll get unique pieces, save money, and support charity and the environment. I have not bought new clothes for several years now, except for footwear. Footwear tends to mould to its wearer's feet and finding a good fit can be a challenge.

Technology and appliances. The proliferation of time-saving technology and appliances hasn't always resulted in saved time. It has resulted in more stuff being done. I wash items of clothing after I have worn them for about a week. Folks tend to wash their clothes after just one wear even if they are not dirty. Why? The washing machine makes it possible. But if you add up all the time spent in a week doing washing, drying, ironing, folding and so on, perhaps you'd spend the same amount of time as I do, maybe more. The washing machine does not save time; it just has you washing more. If you look at other time-saving technology and appliances, you'll see a similar pattern. Folks used to live close to their workplace because they either had to walk or ride a horse. Did the automobile save time there? No, it just means people move further away from their place of work and do more driving.

Many other activities that people used to do themselves have also been turned into products. So instead of being self-reliant and even enjoying a task, you spend that time working so you can buy a product that can do that task for you. Your life skills are downgraded as you come to depend on appliances, and you need to work more to pay for it. In general, I opt for the manual way, not only because of the time-saving myth and I enjoy it, but to burn more calories. To do something manually typically requires more energy, strength, and sometimes endurance. Do the work of your appliances. Open all your cans of food manually for exercise, and trade in your gym membership.

Appliances by and large are just unnecessary gimmicks. I was amazed when I saw the first garlic press and annoyed when I had to clean one. Imagine my reaction when I saw an electrified version. What the heck is wrong with a knife? It is unnecessary. I love using a mortar and pestle, taking in the aroma as the ingredients pulverise and blend into the perfect curry paste. Where's the fun in blending that with an appliance?

Some other technology, such as televisions, computers and smartphones are particularly dangerous because they tends to upgrade faster than appliances, so if you are a sucker for the latest and greatest, you've got an exhausting and endless battle ahead of you. There are always going to be enhancements, upgrades, and new and improved versions. You didn't need it before it was conceived, and you don't need it now.

The slow approach is the best when it comes to minimising appliances and other technology. I am not suggesting you cut everything out immediately. Start by removing those things that are stealing your life away. Can you do with fewer television sets? Can you manage with none? For kitchen appliances, ask yourself if you need them and then sell them or just don't replace them when they die. There's not much that one high-quality kitchen knife and a mortar and pestle can't achieve. Why not teach the kids knife craft?

Cars and transport. The freedom that cars provide comes at a cost. They cost enormous amounts of money to buy, run, maintain, and garage. Yet they typically spend 95 percent of their time in your garage.[22] Car sharing makes a lot more sense, and even renting vehicles for those weekends away is more cost effective than owning one, let alone two or three. If you live in a city and have public transport options, ditching your car will return so much freedom both in time, money, and worry that you will never look back. If you must own a car, perhaps because of your family, or on account of your location and unavailability of public transport or car sharing options, at least make it as frugally minimal as possible. Don't buy new cars because they immediately become second-hand, and you lose a bundle. Buy it with what you can afford in cash and look for fuel efficiency.

Housing. When thinking about minimalism, housing can be a touchy topic. The paradigm heavily influences home ownership. What is needed is thoughtful consideration as to whether your current housing situation is serving you, or you are serving it. Is it conducive to the life of freedom that is available through frugal minimalism? A house is a building; a home is something that comes from your input and your subjective appreciation. So just remember the building alone is not a home.

Just as with all material things, deriving status from your home is illogical because that asset is prone to depreciate. Your house will always be bettered by the Jones's house, so trying to derive status from it is futile. It's important on this mission not to be attached to your housing situation but to be mindful of the usual minimalist tenets of joy and utility. Here are some useful considerations when it comes to housing:

Size. Bigger is not better when it comes to housing. A bigger house usually comes with a bigger mountain of worry. It requires more organising, more cleaning, more space to furnish, and usually more debt. None of these are good. Europeans, in general, tend to have smaller houses than folks from the United States or Australia. They'll not have a movie room and three entertaining areas because they have cinemas and coffee shops for this. Small is sexy for them. Small homes are easier to manage and free up time for the activities they like to engage in outside of the house. They are more interested in qualities like location and function.

Location. Location is important, not because of the real estate speculators mantra of location, location, location but because it makes sense to sleep close to where you do most of your living and working. This also means it's less likely that you will need a car. There is much benefit in being able to walk to work or your social venues. And wouldn't it be handy if your kids could ride their bikes to school? Why live an hour away by car from them?

Function. Function is as important as location. If you live close to where you work and don't need a car, then you don't need a garage. If you eat out for most meals, you mightn't even need a kitchen; a kitchenette might suffice or perhaps just a kettle. If you are eating mostly nutritious and fresh foods, you don't need the giant refrigerator. When you don't need these extras, you have so many more options available to you.

Storage. When I say you don't need a garage, some might cry, "What about storage?" Sorry, there is no storage needed as a frugal minimalist. As Francine Jay, a popular minimalist blogger, says, "Your home is a living space, not a storage space." Storage areas are fertile grounds for finding stuff to shed. Maybe that's why they're sometimes called storage 'sheds'. Why is the stuff in storage? It is probably because you hardly ever use it, so get rid of it. Do this for all of your storage areas, and then once they have been vacated, close them down as a storage space. If you leave it available, you will just find something to fill it. You might find that you can liberate entire rooms that you thought were necessary.

With these considerations, how does one go about creating a frugal minimalist housing solution? After decluttering, shedding your stuff, reducing storage spaces, and closing down entire rooms, you'll be ready to rework your housing solution that emphasises location and function instead of size and storage. The process of shedding is an ongoing one, but you don't want to take stuff that you plan to shed to your new housing solution. You'll only have to deal with it there. So, pack stuff that is yet to be disposed of in one set of boxes marked *Storage*. Find a storage space separate from your living space. In my case, this was a disused garage at my parents' house. Paying for a storage unit can be advantageous as the monthly rent might encourage a faster shedding process. Don't let the storage boxes make it into your new house or apartment; you can take your time whittling away and disposing of these boxes as you adjust happily to your new living space. Then, considering the space and size that you need with your living things, find a well-located and functional rental property. Don't consider storage spaces, and ideally don't seek car parking if a car is unnecessary in this new location.

Renting in such a way helps you adjust to living with less but better, and it's a useful interim step regardless of whether your next step is to buy a frugal, minimalist housing solution, rent one, move offshore, or become a nomad.

Owning and renting are not the only options in the quest for less. There are other options that the pending escapee might find particularly palatable. With these approaches, it is possible to save even more money and live even more like a frugal minimalist. These ideas might become attractive as you get closer to your escape date and as you get ready to take the leap.

You can rent a single room in a house, like I was doing at the Shakti Abode. You still have all the other rooms like a kitchen, lounge, and bathroom, but those rooms you share. And why not? I'd spend maybe ten minutes in a bathroom each day, so why would I pay for twenty-four hours? And then if you get it right regarding housemates, sharing housing adds a lot of joy to your life.

There are other options that are just free. See Chapter 11 for more on that.

Back in Brisbane, I am sitting on the porch with my mum and dad. I've been thinking about my last chest in the garage. Memorabilia is proving to be the hardest things for me to get rid of. But I begin to realise that I am not, in fact, getting rid of the memories. I'm getting rid of objects. My memories are not my things. My memories are inside my head.

We've just finished breakfast, and the newspaper sections are being pecked and squawked at like seagulls fighting over fish and chips at the beach. I withdraw from the battle, and both of them look up at me, curious.

"I'm going in again. I'm going to find more stuff to get rid of."

Dad's eyeballs do a lap of his eye sockets before landing hungrily back on the pile of newspapers. Mum, who I think has an idea why I am doing this, puts up no protest. I go back to the garage and open the door. The sun beams in through the dust and rests on my one remaining chest, sitting there in the centre of the otherwise empty garage. It reminds me of a scene from *Raiders of the Lost Ark*.

I rummage around in the chest. I decide that I am not going to reread those books, so I flick through each, ask my parents if either would like them, and otherwise hurl them in the bin. I feel guilty knowing I should have found a better solution to a landfill. But I was on a roll; forgive me. I decide to rationalise my music and photographs. I get rid of repetitive teenage drunken photographs and hundreds of scenery photographs that mean nothing to me. I contemplate digitising them but then they would only clutter up my computer. I keep just a handful of nice pictures with each of my friends and family through the years. What remains, perhaps a hundred photographs, I put into a waterproof protective sleeve that I will take back with me to

184

Sumatra and the bus. I make a mental note to at some point digitise those pictures, so I don't have to carry them at all. My music suffers the same fate. I fill my parents' council bin with hundreds of CDs. I regret not having planned a garage sale, but I am in a frenzy. I need immediate disposal as I will be returning to Indonesia in a few days. I haven't listened to that music in over ten years; what makes me think I ever will? I keep about twenty CDs, which I plan to digitise and add to my iTunes library, and then I'll throw those out as well.

Then I go through my letters, which suffer the same fate as my photographs. Some letters were to and from people I don't even know anymore, so they make their way to the recycling bin. To my remaining photographs I add about a dozen letters, including that one from 1977 to be digitised later, I think.

I add a few more items to the rubbish bin, and the chest is now empty. As I clean up the scattered debris lying about the garage floor from the purge, a rush comes over me, a physical rush as I realise that I now own nothing, nothing at all, that does not bring me joy or utility. I have my bus in Sumatra and my small travel bag with around forty things in it on my person, and it feels good! I feel light, unencumbered, and free.

I close the garage door for the last time. I would never need to go in there again. I would spend no more time looking at my past. As I close the garage door, I realise that perhaps for a decade now, the only reason I had looked at that stuff was to decide whether or not to throw it away.

I also realise that throughout this visit to Brisbane I have spent perhaps four hours in there sorting through my stuff. I could have spent four of those hours with my mum and dad. These objects of the past were getting in the way of my experience of the present. As the garage door clicks locked it sounds like the click at the end of a film when the last frame leaves the spool; perhaps it is a documentary about a historical journey, a journey

185

that can now be left in the past, as the current film about the present rolls on.

FRUGAL MINIMALISM AND INTANGIBLES

The last category of stuff that minimalism applies to is the non-stuff stuff. The stuff of spaces: your relationship spaces, your workspaces, mental spaces, and internet spaces, all of which can to some degree be a waste of space.

Applying minimalism to the intangible areas of life is governed by the same principles and follows the same process as for objects. It still has the same fundamental goal of less but better, by removing all those things in your life that suck up your time, money, and energy. It's about eliminating bad habits, time-wasting activities, relationships that bring you no joy, and unnecessary paperwork and digitising only the essential stuff. By doing this, you can free yourself up to spend time and resources on the things you do want in your life.

Relationships. Be it family, friends, partners, work colleagues, or anyone else, relationships occupy our time. Many relationships are formed out of geographical, professional, or educational convenience rather than because of shared values, beliefs, interests, or just the plain old fun factor. Minimalism suggests making and keeping relationships more deliberately. You can do this by identifying those that are energy draining, unsupportive, and lacking in value, and then you either change those relationships into something better or just cull them.

There is a species of friends that can be the biggest time wasters of all. I'm referring to your social media friends on Facebook, Instagram, Twitter, and the like. Posts and updates flood your feeds and not only waste your time because you actively have to ignore them but often drown out updates and information from those whom you do want to hear about. Go on an unfriending binge and scale back to only those who are your real friends or post information that interests you. If you use social media as an avenue for promotion and influence, then remain friends and just un-follow their posts.

Commitments. What is the obsession with being busy all the time? Why is busy a good thing? Is it so that you can be productive? Productive doing what? Producing more stuff? More stuff and more waste and more consumerism? Or busy making the world a better place? I'm pretty sure the world was a better place before we started trying to improve on it. One could argue that busyness and productivity made a difference when we were venturing out of the cave and establishing more reliable food sources, better shelter, and better health systems. But I think now we have gone well beyond that, and many who spend their lives plugged into work-consume-die are making the world a less tolerable place. I refer you to all my previous reasoning on why consumerism and even modern life is not productive. Inversely, it is destructive, and as such, I think busyness is a ruse.

We need to rediscover what it's like to be idle, to do nothing, to sit still, and to enjoy silence. We need to put more space in between things instead of cramming them together all the time. Let's stop being busy and start being happy. Busyness is just gunk that gets in the way and takes away our ability to relax, kick back, and enjoy the world for what it is or what's left of it.

Busyness and commitments are like the intangible partners in crime, of stuff. They will just creep into your life if you don't make a conscious effort to block them out because the inflow is as endless as the pursuit of more stuff. So, the first step is in relation to the paradigm to accept that busyness, like work, is nonsense. A good life and the good things in life come to those who are idle.

An excellent approach to repel busyness is to set your default response to requests for your time to "No," and make exceptions only for the bare essentials when you say "Yes." Commitments take up time, headspace, worry, and effort, and often you're getting no reward.

Next, chip away at your recurring commitments. These are the worst kind. Whether it's work, social, or otherwise, exit from those commitments that are not beneficial to you. Even write a list of everything you do in a week that consumes your time, including unproductive work and social meetings, household obligations to family and flatmates, social stuff, school stuff, everything. Do it on a spreadsheet; then you can have fun ranking them in importance, say 1–10, and then sorting the spreadsheet so you can clearly see the items from which you want to start extracting yourself. Just like with stuff, enjoy the process of whittling away at it.

And finally, you need to install protective barriers, especially at work. Insert blocks of time in your schedule for the things you do want to do. In my last paid project, I found that my days quickly filled up with people booking thirty-minute or one-hour meeting in my online calendar, often for things I could sort out in a two-minute conversation or an email. If you have the space, it will fill up, so block out entire chunks. I would block out each day from 8 a.m. until 10 a.m. and from 1 p.m. to 3 p.m. I would book a meeting in my calendar for myself so that no one else could take that time, and in that time, I did my thinking work undisrupted. When people requested meetings, I'd respond with a tentative no and ask if it were something I could just walk over to their desk to resolve or send a resolution email.

Bureaucracy. Undoubtedly the most significant time waster of all is bureaucracy. We want as little bureaucracy in our lives as possible. It exists mainly to take up your time, measure measurements, monitor monitors, and create unnecessary work just to keep people busy.

So, one way to ditch bureaucracy is just to leg it and let it try to catch up with you. For me, I wasn't initially conformable with this approach, so I used the catch-and-release method. For about a year, after I knew I would be making my final escape until my final escape, I tracked every piece of official mail, email, or other paperwork that demanded my attention, and dealt with it in a terminal fashion. For stuff like electoral notifications, I found out how to get off the electoral roll and did that. I do not vote in Australia's corporatocracy because by participating in that system I send the message that I condone it, which I don't. It is neither a genuine democracy nor representative. Letters that required my feedback from my local council, as I was leaving it soon anyway, I responded with a "No Longer at this address." I'd sold my car, but I still got notices about insurance and roadside support membership. I contacted them and asked them to remove me from their databases. Owning a phone and a plan comes with bureaucracy, so I stopped my phone plan and got a prepaid phone without a plan.

Credit card offers coming my way were met with a complaint and in persistent cases a threat of contacting the ombudsmen if they continued to harass me. I closed all credit card accounts except for one. Paper bank statements I discontinued in favour of online statements.

I terminated all of my remaining insurance. Health insurance premiums are worked out by really smart people so that on average the health insurance company makes money out of your policy. So, instead of trying to "beat the casino," I do what I can to reduce the need for insurance, meaning I just have to live healthier than the average person that fits my profile. This will likely be the case because I treat my health as my number one priority. Of course, I am taking a risk here, albeit calculated. Even if I am living healthier than my others in my health profile, random accidents happen. In life insurance, I have never participated. As a man without dependents, it's an investment that I would pay for all of my life only to get the benefit by dying. As a dead person, I can't see how this would be beneficial to me. I don't need employment insurance because I don't work in the system, and I don't need house or contents insurance because I have no house or contents. Having a house or a normal job may impact on these decisions, but all insurances are designed to be profitable for the insurance companies. Insuring my bus is not only impossible for a foreigner in Indonesia, but it is highly complicated and impractical to make a claim.

In a physical sense, I had become effectively vanished, an e-person, a ghost safe from the harassment of bureaucracy.

Before arriving back in Medan, a short while ago, after yet another breakfast of eggs Benedict with my mum and dad, I packed my photographs, letters, and CDs that I'd designated to the digitise-and-dispose of pile. And mindful of my recent passport experience, I digitised a copy of that and some other travel documents and emailed these to myself for safe keeping. I did the same for my driver's licence and all of my other cards.

I go straight from Medan airport to Dedi's workshop. I am keen to avoid the Angel; who knows what dramas are unfolding there? Dedi is milling about in the car parking lot. I can see Rosie parked there, clean as new after their free cleaning service. Dedi sees me coming down the driveway, and his face erupts into a toothy smile that threatens to burst through his cheeks. This is a sign that he has resolved the clutch issue.

"Did you bring me my souvenir, Mr Mike?"

Only now I remember that he asked me to bring him a kangaroo, which I initially thought was a joke, but when I see the scale of his disappointment, I realise that he possibly didn't understand the practicalities of bringing a kangaroo to Indonesia, especially as carry-on, the only way to fly.

He takes me through the list of repairs I left with them, and then I see the cause of his uncontainable happiness a few moments earlier. They did indeed go 'jungle' on the clutch. With a part from a different make of vehicle, some extra scraps of metal, a welder, and some Indonesian bush mechanic's determination, Rosie is rigged to change gears. This is a handy thing because, in a few days from now, one of the Norwegian girls, Ane, and her family would be joining us for some adventures. They would be Rosie's last adventures before she would be boarded up and left in the jungle in Masa's eager hands.

7. Financial Mumbo Jumbo

There are two ways to be rich: one is by acquiring much, and the other is by desiring little.

—Jackie French Koller

A REALITY CHECK

2013 was the year of my fourth and final failed escape. Throughout that year in voluntary exile, I kept good health thanks to my morning wake-up ritual. I was happier than I had been in a long time with various projects in fulfilment underway. But what about prosperity? Even for an accountant, when it comes to finances, if you fail to plan, you plan to fail.

I thought I had my financial situation under control; I thought I had a good grasp of enough. But while I did have an excellent theoretical grasp, I had not made a practical plan that I could follow to ensure enough was in fact enough. Perhaps it was my arrogance and my belief that I had an intuitive grasp of what I was doing on the money side of things. It may also have been that I always had a safety net in being able to return to work, so being disciplined with my finances was optional. But I would soon discover that I had been unrealistic about my financial position and about how much I spent and earned each month on the road. Unplanned expenses both abroad and at home were eroding my balance sheet and shrinking the available monthly cash it produced. As that year approached its end, my ears began to droop again with the realisation that failure number four was nigh.

I had to sort this financial mumbo-jumbo out once and for all, make a plan, write it down, and stick to it. That is what I would have recommended for a client in the days of yore; why the heck wouldn't I recommend it for myself? Before returning to Australia, I activated the old accountant's brain. I documented my financial situation, as it was then, not as I wanted it to be. I listed all my assets and liabilities which at that time included two mortgaged investment properties in Australia and two speculative or dreamer properties abroad: one in Croatia and one in Guatemala. I had a handful of credit cards. I had no house that I lived in, no car, furniture, or household effects.

Next, I did a monthly cashflow budget. I had a net income from one Australian property and a net loss from the other. I did not have any salary income. In that year away, one of my projects was to develop other passive income streams, doing only things I loved, things I wouldn't call work. I had started to earn small amounts of money with stock photography and travel writing. I added those to the budget. I then listed my monthly expenses. What I ended up with was my realistic financial position at that time.

MINIMALIST FINANCES

My version of escape involved living abroad and living light, with as few assets returning as much cash flow as possible. From my recently created budget that I knew that I needed about $1,000 each month to live the life that I wanted, and I was not clearing that amount during my fourth escape attempt. I also decided that to allow for unexpected things such as health issues I would add a $500 contingency and aim for $1,500 per month, or $18,000 per year. In Australia in 2013, this was considered below the poverty line for single person ($503.71/week or $25,689/year),[23] but in the countries I choose, it provides a comfortable life.

It was time to devise a plan. I returned to Australia one year after I left it, and it may come as no surprise that I planned a return to work. My goal was to work on my balance sheet with the objective of having it generate a net cash flow of $1,500 per month.

Having salary cash coming in was an essential part of knocking my balance sheet into the desired shape. I returned to work without accumulating any stuff aside from my everyday clothes. I did not rent a property or buy a car as for most of the project I would be on the road. When I wasn't on the road, I stayed with friends. In this way, I was able to stay lean, stuff-wise. Together with my cash flow target of $1,500 per month and my estimated savings rate, I was able to set an escape date. My last escape, surely.

That date would be one year from then. If I came up short in terms of cash flow, I decided that instead of continuing to work I would come up with shortfall projects to make up the $1,500. I'll talk about those later. I needed a fixed date to save me from slipping back into endless slavery and to motivate me to achieve the target. I applied all of my disposable income to my balance

194

sheets, paying off my credit cards first and then closing the account for all but one credit card account, leaving it open with a balance of nil for travel convenience.

As for assets, I listed and sold the Australian house that was costing me money. I put the stone house in Croatia up for sale. The story of what transpired there is still coming. I did not sell the coffee farms in Guatemala. These had a zero cost of ownership and are likely to come into play in the short-term, but that's another story. Besides, they were not only mine to sell. All that remained was one rental property whose total cash return was higher than the total cost, including the interest. It was putting money in my bank every month. My plan was to have no liabilities and keep only those assets (and associated finance) that put money in my hand every month. The resultant cashflow, if all things went to plan would make up the biggest part of my escapee income.

AN ESCAPEE'S BUDGET

It is the middle of January 2017. I'm sitting on a decaying leather couch on a second-story rickety veranda overlooking a courtyard busy with plants and cats. I am at a guesthouse called Nokky's Place in the Old Town of Chiang Mai, Thailand. Nokky is the Thai owner of the establishment. She wears a permanent smile and smokes a permanent cigarette. I suspect those two activities are linked based on the relaxing wafts that drift from her exhalations through the courtyard and up to the veranda when the breeze is favourable. She likes to saunter around in various spectacular kimonos, either watering plants or serving elaborate meals to her many cats.

195

I arrived here a week ago from Malaysia, and since then I have worked out that the pecking order of the beings that command her attention here is: cats, plants, and only then, guests. I am still not sure she knows or cares who of the eccentric bunch who call this place home pay their way or not. Sporadically, when I pay her for my $4 room, she pockets the money without looking at it, smiles, and then dreamily scans the courtyard, no doubt trying to figure out whether it was the plants or cats to which she was tending. With her feet hidden by her kimono, she then glides off as if on a cushion of air to tend to whichever of those she determines it was.

This last month, since I left Brisbane, has been a rollercoaster of action. Ane and her family joined me in Sumatera for Rosie's last adventure. Having three adults and two rather wild children crammed into Rosie's belly was a challenge. It was three weeks of madness, laughing, crying, singing, screaming, waterfalls, rivers, beaches and jungles, and above all, enjoying four of my favourite people in close quarters and sharing with them my life with Rosie. It was incredible to see the transformation in the children in such a short time as they adapted to a life of less, but more. Less toys but more adventure, less sugary sweets but more of my infamous daily sardines and eggs, and less television but endless wildlife.

By the time we had spent the first days in the jungle, they had realised that the treats of home were just not available and there was no amount of whining that would make them so. The realisation turned these children into amazingly independent and explorative assistant jungle guides under Masa's close tutelage and sometimes over Masa's already weighed-down shoulders as he carried them aloft with his pots and pans. I think all of the grown-ups were quite proud to see the children not only adjust but, in the end, thrive, so much so that they did not

196

want to leave Sumatra and—perhaps only in my imagination—me.

Neither did I want them to leave. But my time too was up. I had decided that I needed a change of scenery. I loved my life there, but at times, given the cultural differences, it could be a bit isolated, and I needed a fix of something different. Masa was almost too happy to babysit Rosie, perhaps because I gave him the green light to unfettered usage of her. Maybe because that's just the kind of generous man he is.

I packed her up. I went through her insides and discarded or gave away anything that might perish. I contemplated sprinkling some mothballs I had purchased about the place. But as "mothball" was an Indonesian word I was yet to learn, I could not be sure they were not those soaps you find in men's urinals, so I thought better of it. I had known this was coming for a few weeks. I conjured a plan to do one of the things I had dreamt of doing for more than a decade, which was to ride a motorbike around Southeast Asia. I estimated it would take me about a year. I would be back for Rosie.

I packed a bag, not unlike the one I had recently taken with me to Brisbane. I found I did not have enough stuff to fill it. I counted the items, and I found that I still only needed forty things to live. Since this number of things had popped up previously, at that point, I decided that I would live with only forty things from now on. Thankfully, airport security would assume ownership of my toenail clipping multi tool, creating a place on that list for a motorbike. You can check out my list of forty things on my website.[24]

We said goodbye to Masa and Rosie, and the five of us left for the Medan Airport. From Medan, my jungle friends flew home, and I flew to Chiang Mai, which would be my starting point. I had done my research on the cost of living in the countries that I wanted to ride through and figured that I would focus on

Thailand, Laos, Vietnam, and Cambodia, hopefully making it back to Sumatera towards the end of 2017. With my research and my escapee budget done and with confidence that I could live on no more than $1,000 each month in the chosen countries, I set my plan in motion.

How did I know I could live on my $1,000 escapee budget, my personal enough? How did I know what my costs would be in this latest version of escape? By 2014, I had spent four years in an escapee situation, so I could estimate my needs and, with a bit of time on the internet, associate dollars with those needs. Additionally, I was always moving further along the spectrum of frugal minimalism, and my monetary needs were ever becoming less, so these days I save money even out of the $1,000 each month. My escapee budget is actually $1,500, but $500 is just a buffer I save for unanticipated costs.

An escapee budget is personal and geographically dependant.

For many, the escapee lifestyle may be new, and their escapee locations may as yet be unknown. The task of deriving an escapee budget is not easy because it will depend not just on your lifestyle requirements but also on the geographic location of your escape. As I enjoy living in places like Indonesia, other Southeast Asian countries, and Latin America, most of which have a comparatively low cost of living, I don't need as much as someone who is committed to living in Vancouver, Sydney, or Tokyo.

Finding a country to live in doesn't need to be a laborious process. In fact, it should be downright enjoyable. There is no hurry as you are most likely working away each day to get yourself into a financial position to escape, so the process may even be a relief of sorts, living the dream life only in your imagination and on the internet for now.

I want to live in the places where I like to travel. I also see a lot more opportunity in the developing world, so choosing

Southeast Asia and Latin America was easy. I eliminated Africa because it seems too volatile for my tastes. North America, Europe, and Australia I marginalised because they are too expensive. Perhaps you can start with a list of every country and use a process of elimination. Perhaps language is important to you. Perhaps safety is important. Ideally, you would be able to eliminate enough countries so that you are left with no more than a dozen that you might research in more depth. You might even like to take fact-finding trips or short holidays to candidate countries. Of course, they would be frugal holidays.

Some countries offer foreigners incentives to move there, such as an easy passport or investment incentives. When I was there in 2014, Nicaragua was offering foreigners residency if they were willing to spend $10,000 to set up a business. Other counties might have an abundance of shortfall project opportunities. Hanoi in Vietnam is currently starved of English teachers, full- and part-time. This might be a good way to make up any shortfall in your required monthly income. Ecuador has a thriving retirement scene and encourages foreign retirees. Other countries might focus on sports or hobbies that you like. Columbia is a big draw for me as, according to my Death List, I need to become a salsa dancing expert. I like Indonesia because of the jungle and the waves. You might like a country as it has good international schools for your children. The selection process is very personal, and each selection criteria should always be assessed alongside its cost.

Once you have your shortlist, get to work on the internet.[25] Sign up for Expat blogs and Facebook housing and community groups for the countries and cities you're interested in. Automate your feed of information to both continue your short-listing process and start feeling like you are already there. And you don't need to get it right on your first go. If you move somewhere and don't like it, you can always move again.

You may not want to relocate at all. That is fine; at least you will already know the cost of living. But do consider that the lower the cost of living in your escapee country, the sooner you will be able to escape.

Updating my budget for the countries on my motorbike trip was no different from the process you would follow for your first escapee budget. Once I'd chosen the locations, there were three types of modifications I made to my previous Indonesian budget. The first was to remove expenses in my old location and situation that I would no longer incur. I removed much of the vehicle-related expenses, for instance. First-time escapees might remove household expenses, subscriptions, memberships, services, and utilities. You might also remove some insurances. My second alteration was to add the new location's expense data. I'd researched food and accommodation costs and fuel costs for a motorbike. I also knew that I would be socialising more and moving more and faster than previously, so I had to modify my entertainment and travel budget. And the third type of modification was new expenses. I would have visas to consider and contributions to local law enforcement as I would be riding illegally without the correct registration and drivers licence paperwork. Some new expenses I would not anticipate, but this is the purpose of the $500 contingency amount each month.

All the while you are preparing your budget for your first escape destination, there are a few other general considerations to keep in mind.

This is not a holiday. When you consider yourself on vacation, you tend to spend more as you try to do a lot in a limited time. But when you take your time, you need less money. There is no hurry. You'll spend money thoughtfully, taking the slow and inexpensive option when possible. Slow travel is usually cheaper than efficient travel. So, don't factor in expensive and regular flights to far-flung destinations, daily jet-ski or motor boat hires, golfing extravaganzas, and regular polo tournament attendance. Budgeting for such expenses not only goes against frugal minimalism but also will see you working under lights for a very long time.

Be conservative. It is more likely that you will spend more rather than less than your budget, so it's important to be both realistic and conservative. Round up, not down, and factor in buffers on every budget expense line. Even apply a 10 percent markup on every item to be safe.

Consider inflation. Depending on how far away your escape date is, factor in inflation. In Australia, the government aims for between 2.5–3 percent inflation each year, so if your exit date is three years away, scale up every budget line item up by 3 percent compounded each year (i.e., 1.03 x 1.03 x 1.03).

Consider taxation. Your escapee budget might call for an income that will be subject to taxation. This you must include in your expenses. Another reason why I like $1,500 per month is that it equates to $18,000 per year, which is below the Australian tax-free threshold. Aside from the massive amount of wasteful and counterproductive government spending that I don't want to contribute to, I do not live in the country, so I don't carry any guilt about paying no tax in it.

Have an emergency fund. I include $500 a month in my budget to be allocated to an emergency fund. This is there should I need an unplanned flight or have a health issue. As I don't want health insurance, I need a security net for it. The amount of this is entirely up to you and will be influenced by your current health and other personal factors.

With your escapee budget, you now have the amount that you need to live free. Now you can draw a line in the sand. This is what you need to come up with. It's your money or your life we are talking about. Remember that even on a minimal income, $18,000 in my case, it is possible to live very well and be prosperous. Down the track, if you decide you need more money, either because your estimates were off or because your cost of living rises, you always have your shortfall projects you can beef up.

EARNING "ENOUGH"

Up here at Nokky's veranda, I am joined by Denzo, a beanie-and-dark-sunglasses-wearing South African ex-diamond trader. He has been here for a few months. As he sits down on a neighbouring leather chair, also doomed for the reupholsters or landfill, he flips open his laptop and starts tapping away. From time to time he lifts the ageing computer up and puts it against the stand-up fan that we have scanning our faces.

"Laptop's fan is busted, ma bru; doing some heavy processing," he explains.

Denzo is also an escapee. He is one of the many colourful characters that have made Nokky's their home for now. He's working on his shortfall projects without realising it. For him, he is trying to get some cash to live. He relies 100 percent on shortfall projects, which in his case is part-time work harvesting email addresses from open databases and selling them to shifty characters online. I'm not suggesting this as a way to go, but I can tell you that Denzo works for about an hour a day, maybe two, makes enough to fund his good life, and then has much the same day as I do.

Denzo hasn't necessarily planned things this way but has the same idea about financial freedom, which is about creating a comfortable gap between your outgoings and your revenue that lets you avoid undesirable work. I'd say one hour a day is pretty comfortable. I prefer a different mix of investment income and shortfall projects, but the principle is the same. As long as my time is my own to live how I choose, I feel I am winning.

The name of the game in achieving this state and in funding the escapee budget is to increase income or decrease expenditure such that you are living within your means happily and healthfully. Now that you have become or are becoming a frugal minimalist, your outgoings should be diminished or diminishing. And since you are addressing your balance sheet, it also should be contributing less to your expenses and more to your income each month. Your net income should be approaching your escapee budget. The forecast date at which it meets your escapee budget will represent your escape date.

So, aside from reducing your escapee budget by cutting out more expenses and pushing your balance sheet productivity without delaying your escape date, how do you expedite your escape? The answer is shortfall projects. I deliberately don't refer to these projects as work to distinguish them from the type of work I earlier referred to as nonsense. The idea with shortfall projects is that they be enjoyable, something you love doing or might even do in absence of remuneration and certainly don't feel anything like work.

On my last escape to South America, in 2013, I started building an online portfolio of stock photography images. I was taking photographs anyway, and the whole exercise itself improved my photography skills. By the time I had returned to Australia, I was earning about $60 a month from stock photography. Once the photographs were uploaded and accepted, no additional work was required; it was all royalty income tied to purchase downloads. This $60 might not sound like much in a pre-escape scenario, but as an escapee, it meant that two days of every month would now be covered by the passive income from this shortfall project. Besides, I don't think of it as just $60 a month. I think more along the lines of $720/year, every year. It all adds up. It was 6 percent of my living expenses covered just by taking a few hundred amateur photographs.

During my last year of work, regardless of how determined I was to improve my balance sheet, I could see a few months before my escape date that I was not going to reach my target of $1,500 net per month from all sources. I was going to be short about $200 a month. Admittedly, this would only dig into my contingency $500, but I didn't want to start out on such a note, so I spent some time looking into other shortfall projects that I might enjoy or that were easy money and fun.

To bridge my deficit rather than look for a cheaper country to live in or push out my escape date, I came up with a list of shortfall project possibilities. Some were one-off gigs, and others were projects I would continue to this day. Some I have tried already, some I have not yet undertaken, and others I had not yet conceived by my escape date. Stock photography turned out to be a great way to explore places on my travels, looking for interesting shots and doing city tours and the like. There are many sites for stock images, and I have tried a few, namely istockphoto.com, shutterstock.com, and esp.gettyimages.com, the latter seems to be give me the best returns for my amateurish pictures.

I also tried export-import during my final failed escape attempt. The idea was to find products that had a significant price differential between Guatemala and Australia. I shipped a load of hammocks, ponchos, and other textiles and made a useful profit from their sale. It was quite an enjoyable and educational process. I then mentally noted that I should pack an extra 20–40kg of luggage with every trip home and transport profitable goods, provided they are ethically and environmentally sound, for resale. A few thousand dollars on each trip, well, that pays for the journey.

Other projects that I noted down at that time were copywriting, blogging, translation services and English teaching, all of which I would eventually try my hand at and learn a lot. But it would be with the writing of articles and essays of a similar content to that which you are reading now that I would enjoy the most, and perhaps partly on that account, make the most pocket money, usually around three to five days' worth of living each month.

And then I thought about a few ways that I could spend less money, which I view as the same as making money. I still call these shortfall projects. Interesting accommodation solutions showed the most promise. Before I had finished my last employment project, I noted some options in each of my locations like renting a house instead of a room and subletting rooms to my advantage. I also figured that if I were staying for more extended periods of time in places, I would be able to negotiate cheaper accommodation deals. A monthly rate is always going to be cheaper than a daily rate. There are many options where you can trade your skills and labour for free room and board. I discuss these in Chapter 11.

There's also the possibility of skill swapping. I figured that most places I stay could have some use of my decaying accounting and computing skills. I might offer to automate some of their accounting systems or develop a simple website in exchange for free accommodation. As I drift in and out of Medan these days, I'll work on the website for the Angel Guesthouse. Unfortunately, it has never been developed to a stage where it can protect itself against the staff's best efforts to run it into the ground. Either way, I do an hour here or there for a free meal or room.

And then there is volunteer work. There are many options in developing and developed nations for volunteer work. I have done such work in Indonesia, and it is highly rewarding. I am finding more and more, however, that one has to pay to be a volunteer, which turns the tables to some degree, but there are still good options out there. If you volunteer for a month, you can get housed and fed and save your entire month's escapee budget, which you apply to your balance sheet.

Between this list and other shortfall projects that would surface after my escape, I would easily make or save an additional $200 per month.

Now as I sit here at Nokky's veranda with Denzo snoring on his couch next to mine, probably caused by Nokky's floating a little too close, I flip open my laptop to work on a shortfall project. This one I did not expect to have some eighteen months after my last day of work. You see, when my final project wound up in July 2015, it did so on a high note and with the prospect of further work with the client. At that time, I had a great relationship with my employer and said that if he needed me to do anything for him after my escape, I would be open to it, provided it was small and discrete pieces of work that I could do remotely. It turned out to be a handy shortfall project with small clumps of work, a few hours here, a few there, and now a two-day piece on which he has asked me to work.

Why the hell not? That kind of money in this sort of life is often a godsend, although never a necessity. As time goes by and I get more out of touch with that industry, I am quite confident my utility will fade, so I'll take the work while it comes my way. I like doing this kind of work when it is not exactly a job and I'm not in a traditional workplace.

A handy shortfall project can always come from your existing job. It's always a good idea to leave your job on a positive note, not because you want to leave the door open to return, but so that you may negotiate the occasional remote part-time work to make up your shortfall while you grow other projects. You might even find, as I do, that in small doses and from certain very mellow atmospheres, working on an old job is enjoyable.

A few hours have passed, and the Nokky effect has become too potent for me to concentrate. Some of the other residents are shuffling in from their daily doings and creating a distraction anyway, so I shut down work for the day. I see Carlos and Socrates chatting in the courtyard downstairs. Both men are around seventy years old and hail from possibly Greece and definitely Slovakia, respectively. Both men have been at Nokky's for years. Carlos is here by choice. Socrates is stranded. He never suspected he had marital problems until he discovered his wife had drained their bank account in his absence and left him without the means to buy a return ticket.

Carlos is the stereotypical ageing hippie with his long beard, dreadlocks, and colourful clothing, but he is also a legendary soccer player. He has been teaching young teams here in Chiang Mai for decades and has mastered the art of living on next to nothing. Tonight, we will all go with him to the local stadium where he coaches and I usually do my wake-up ritual. We'll join him afterwards at the adjacent Hindu Temple. There we will participate in a prayer session for about two hours and, as remuneration for our efforts, be invited to a smorgasbord. Carlos tells us that he does this once a week, every week. He must be praying a great deal as not only does he fill his belly in exchange for his prayers, he also fills an assortment of take away containers to feed him through the next few days. I'm not sure I will follow suit with the Tupperware on my maiden prayer night.

Socrates is a different story. Staying here at Nokky's suits him because Nokky doesn't seem to care about timely rent payments. He has established a new room on her premises, which is just a mattress on another veranda with a piece of string holding up a sheet to act as the wall of his room. Nobody here knows or can remember his real name. We call him Socrates because he spends all day collecting blank pieces of paper and flyers from the streets and then writing out philosophical quotes on them in his room, or rather, his area. He seems to like his name, and that encourages him both to write and recite his writings throughout the day, not necessarily to welcoming ears. At Denzo and my office, he knows to keep it brief.

He has no money at all and struggles with his shortfall projects. Writing out second-hand philosophy on pizza pamphlets might be a bit too niche to turn a buck. He comes to our veranda from time to time to declare that he has a solution to his money problems. Almost always it involves a new business of buying and selling some peculiar object he has found at the markets, and his business model usually puts him in direct competition with the Thais. We try not to be negative, but the flaws in his plans would pile up higher than his stack of pamphlets. From time to time we throw ideas at him, but more often than not they involve access to a computer and the internet, so they are not that useful for him.

Over this last eighteen months, since I have been drifting around Sumatera and now in Thailand, I have come across many other previously unconceived shortfall projects, some undertaken and others pending.

Recently on my way through Malaysia, as I was moving faster and more extravagantly than usual, I spent too much money, so my current spending game is to stay here at Nokky's in a $4 room and make a game of eating as cheaply as I can. Fortunately, just around the corner, I can get sardines and eggs for just $1, so it's not turning out to be too challenging. I am not opposed to staying in a dormitory as a savings experiment. Sure, it might at first seem a bit creepy with a forty-four-year-old man staying in a backpacker dormitory, but I have done this before at my advanced age, and it has always been a heck of a lot of fun.

208

I would happily exchange work, in other than my area of knowledge, for accommodation or cash, though perhaps not here at Nokky's as I would only be saving $4 a night, and I'm not entirely sure she realises I am staying here. But perhaps where my rent was more significant, I would gladly work the bar or restaurant or do some cleaning to save cash. Bar work is fun when it is not absolutely necessary and working in any place will give you a deeper appreciation of it.

There are many options out there to bridge your shortfall, should there be one. You may not have any shortfall, or you may have only shortfall. It comes down to the urgency of your need to escape and your escape date. I know of many more projects that I won't mention here because they go against the grain of what I believe in. I don't want a shortfall project that involves creating and consuming an unethically produced physical product or that results in degradation of the environment. Why would I preach anti-consumerism only to dump it on someone else? So, I tend to lean towards services and intangible products rather than physical ones.

So, once you have some ideas, shortlist them, research them, and instead of waiting start working on them right now. Set up your stock portfolio account; even start taking photographs now in your hometown. Do an English teaching course; why wait? Having these projects in place, and ideally already generating income before your escape will take the pressure off having to do it later, and it may well see you achieving your escape budget well before you even get on a plane.

Part 3: THE ACT OF ESCAPE

8. The Fear Factor

THE PSYCHOLOGY OF FEAR

With my designated escape date fast approaching, and the lessons from four failed escape attempts now assimilated, you might be thinking that there was nothing left to figure. I had grasped the logic that demanded an escape and processed the psychology required make it successful. This I shared in Part 1. With each of those attempts, I unwittingly uncovered the essential aspects of escape preparation, which I discussed in Part 2. Poised to make a run for it, I had one last mental morsel to digest.

I was poised to hit the big red button labelled *The Act of Escape* just before August 2015. But there was one last thing: fear. I had not experienced a fear of escape in any of my previous four escape attempts. I know now that was because with each of them I embarked with an inkling of pending failure that would eventually see me back in the safety of the paradigm. The paradigm is indeed a safe place. So much is assured in the paradigm. It is why so many are stuck there. You have your home, your transport, a job, income, a government that, according to it, will take on many responsibilities for you, and a system to ensure you don't need to think about what to do with your time. But safety is not freedom. You can be safe in a cage.

But this escape would be different. A bit more than one month out from my planned escape date, it was the confidence that this escape would be successful that gave rise to the fear. Because the perceived safety of the paradigm was at risk, there was a fear of freedom, which meant I had to be responsible for myself and my time.

But my confidence in success also eroded that same fear. I had done the work. I could do no more mental groundwork or escape preparations. I did not need the safety of the paradigm. That aspect of my fear was unfounded.

In addition, this escape included fear of the unknown. But that too was only perceived. I had been through this four times before, for heaven's sake. My fears there were also not real. One of my possible future selves reminded my current self of Mark Twain's words, "I am an old man and have known a great many troubles, but most of them never happened."

One of the spin-offs of this fear of freedom was that I found myself debating whether to delay my escape. This was an instinctual reaction to fear, which is to postpone the object of the fear, the escape. I found myself inventing excuses so that I could delay the decision and therefore delay dealing with the fear. I found myself saying to myself things like, "Just wait until you have $x more," and, "Do just one more project." I even started looking at seasonal aspects of my destination and saying, "If I wait a few more months, the weather will be better."

But these were all just excuses originating from my pesky amygdala, and none of them were significant. I knew that had I waited a few months or amassed a bit more cash I would then have found a new set of excuses. It was around this time that something from the transformation course of many years before popped into my head and stayed there. It was a little line, "If not now, then when?" With that in my head and understanding that I was already living my worst-case scenario, the escape date remained unchanged. I knew I could always return to that worst-case scenario. I'd proven that enough times.

9.   No Turning Back

THE POINT OF NO RETURN

Mental alignment?
Check.
Escape preparation?
Check.
Fear factor?
Check.
It was time to take specific actions that would set me irreversibly upon my new trajectory, the Act of Escape button would take me past the point of no return and cried out for my attention.

Throughout the last few months of my employment, I was flying regularly between Perth and Toronto with my work kit, an assemblage of old-fashioned, restrictive, and downright uncomfortable items of the compulsory uniform in my industry. These you would know as suits, business shirts, and ties. Ties are the most bizarre of all and fittingly as redundant as the need for work. Their distant ancestors back in the 1700s were made of leather and served partly to protect the neck against bayonet and sabre strikes. Now, I do understand the need for workplace health and safety, but in the accounting game these days such attacks are quite rare.

While I was on each of the Perth legs, I would sneak off to Bali where my then-girlfriend, Amber, lived. These were not only reconnaissance missions to what was to be my first escape destination, but strategic sorties. We were hatching a plan to build a home inside her bus and travel eastwards across the Indonesian Archipelago. My escape destination would not so much be a fixed location as it would be a mobile adventure.

I handed in my notice several months in advance of the escape date to afford an easier transition process for my employer. This approach mightn't be possible in everyone's case. I suggest handing in your notice at work with at least the minimum notice period and, if possible, more than that, so you are committed and can start getting excited sooner rather than later.

I also had the conversation about what work I would be happy to continue to do once I had escaped. This would turn out to be a fruitful move as I'd see small amounts of work trickling in over the following year and a half and petering out at about the same rate as my shortfall projects petered in. I didn't need to have a specific arrangement with my last boss, but this might be useful in some cases. You might even specify five hours a week or something along those lines. If this is rejected, great; you've got other stuff to do.

If your work is actually a business or you are self-employed, then you would have started an extraction plan long before now. It might be time to remind one and all that there are just four weeks left until your disappearance.

On the day I pushed the button I was like a sleepwalker coming awake; my dream became very real. Escape #5 was underway. From here on in, it was a race to the finish line—or should I say, the starting line.

Handing in my resignation solidified my escape from something. Making plans and reservations confirmed my escape to something. Sleuth-like, I had been keeping an eye on flights and working out the patterns in pricing. As Bali is a popular, even overrun, weekend destination for Perth's population, Sunday evening return flights to Perth were always full. Monday morning outbound flights were the cheapest. I booked my flights. Sites like Skyscanner.com make it easy to make price comparisons. They'll even show you all routes, airlines, and times for a given month ordered according to price. Pretty handy.

Accommodation was the next factor. Amber had her own compound in Bali where I could stay, so that was done. Had I not had that option, I would still have prearranged my accommodation. It's a personal thing, but when I fly, I like to pre-book at least the first night in a new location. If you don't have contacts that will house you in the new location, before you automatically book a hotel look into some more fringe options, about which I'll speak more in Chapter 11. Most of these options will save you money and provide immediate and useful contacts in your new location.

If you do go for paid accommodation, book somewhere just for a couple of days, as the situation on the ground will always be different and often cheaper than what you find on the internet. Long-term apartments and accommodation options are always best arranged in situ once you have the lay of the land.

BEYOND THE POINT OF NO RETURN

A crucial symbolic and functional next step was to identify or obtain my "Go" bag. As a frugal minimalist, one wants to travel as light as possible but with the right things. I still had my work kit, but I knew that would be discarded ceremonially after my last day of employment. A couple of plastic shopping bags would be more frugal, but even for me that was going too far. In those last months of travel between Toronto and Perth, I chose a fifteen-litre bag that endures to this day and set it out for packing in my living room. It was like a shrine to Saint Christopher, the patron saint of travellers. And he was hiding inside it like an immobile, miniature Pied Piper calling hither the things I would need for the road. With my last day of work scheduled and flights and accommodation sorted, anything that did not heed the call of Saint Chris or that I did not need for the remainder of my work days, were drawn to the beat of a different drum, coming from somewhere inside the street-side, municipal rubbish bin.

This is the stage where you will want to sell your car if you still have one or at least plan its disposal if you still need it, along with all other household effects and furnishings. Use storage options if you need. I did at this point still have those chests in storage at my parents' place in Brisbane.

It's worthwhile getting such stuff out of your way, one way or the other, and to begin getting used to living like you're on the road. Have a final garage sale to make a few more dollars or throw a giveaway party where guests can help themselves to your stuff in exchange for your helping yourself to their alcohol. Ideally, you'll have as little to deal with as possible on your last days before your escape.

I was travelling and working right up until my escape date, and my accommodation was part of my remuneration. It was not my responsibility. But this might not be the same for you. A week or two out from escape, once you are down to just your work kit and your Go bag, you must also close out your accommodation. Either take up one of the housing solutions described in Chapter 11 or move in with friends or family. Besides the fact that it might be nice to hang out with such people before your imminent departure, it is like a practice run of living out of the Go bag. In this way, you can make adjustments, get rid of more stuff, recoup, and obtain something that you find you need. You'll also save a bit of cash.

A week out from my confirmed departure date, I dispensed with the remaining minor but vital financial matters. I phoned my banks and informed them that I would be travelling indefinitely. Many a time I have had a credit card frozen on account of transactions that did not suit whatever algorithm banks use to detect fraud. If they see transactions popping up in unusual countries, it triggers an alert that may leave you stranded. When you call to advise them of your new situation, they may ask to which countries you plan to go. You can tell them if you know, or if you don't, you can do what I did and list all 195 countries just to teach them a lesson for being nosey.

Because those same banks together with their foreign accomplices will tax funds faster than a Sumatran ATM can eat your card, I set up an online account with transferwise.com. This fantastic service allows us to transfer money from our home bank to a local bank in most other countries with a fraction of the charges and at the spot foreign exchange rate, saving loads of cash. Jump on the site to see if they will transfer from and to your required source and target countries. Soon after my arrival in Indonesia, I set up a local bank account to avoid ATM withdrawal fees. It is a straightforward process.

The moment finally arrived. It was a warm Toronto afternoon and my last day of this kind of work, ever. From that day forward, I would only ever do things that I enjoyed; I would only earn money doing things I loved doing. It was not a sad day for me; it was a debauched night.

Evidently, the celebrations were commensurate with someone who knew that it would be their last opportunity to avail themselves of employment-sponsored drinking and dining. I woke up the following morning and could see that I had indeed made a ceremonial disposal of my work kit. My shirt and tie of the previous day were now a glob of melted imitation cotton in the kitchen sink. Some kind of ritualistic fire had taken place. My suit and other work accessories were nowhere to be found, as was my small work suitcase. *Never mind*, I thought. *I no longer need them.*

My flight back to Perth was in a few hours, so I packed what belongings I could locate in a small satchel and, with my suitcase missing, reverted to using a plastic shopping bag. I ordered a taxi to the airport.

As I locked the hotel room door and turned for the elevator bank, the suitcase mystery solved itself. I could see the debris of the inebriated efforts of a man celebrating metamorphosis. The door to the hotel garbage chute room was held ajar with one of my work shoes. Opening the door, I saw what looked like the garbage chute giving birth to my suitcase with two-thirds of it still wedged in the birth canal. The square case had been jammed into the smaller oval shaped chute, such that it would neither go any further nor be extracted, even had I had forceps. I smiled to myself and thought it was fitting that my last memory of my relationship to work was a square peg in a round hole.

As I checked out, I let the concierge know there might be a problem in the 10th-floor garbage chute. Hoping that he had some experience in caesarean sections, I took my last free taxi and flight. In Perth, I had just a day to say goodbye to my friends, collect my thoughts and the Go bag, and escape.

Part 4: ESCAPEE

10. Escapee At Large

> *"Twenty years from now you will be more*
> *disappointed by the things you didn't do than by*
> *the ones you did do. So, throw off the bowlines,*
> *sail away from the safe harbour. Catch the*
> *trade winds in your sails. Explore. Dream.*
> *Discover."*
>
> —*Mark Twain*

HITTING THE ROAD

Around October, 2015 and after three months of life on the road, trundling through the islands to the east of Bali, my relatively new girlfriend, Amber, and her daughter, found ourselves just outside the tumbledown town of Moni, Ende Regency on the island of Flores. Specifically, we were parked on a flat gravel shoulder at the base of the Kelimutu Volcano complex, opposite an immense expanse of rice paddies, tended to by the folks of a small satellite village of Moni. Somewhere within those flooded rice fields was the secret Kolorongo Hot Springs, the motivation behind that day's camp location.

Three months before the arrival at Moni, I landed in the active-wear mecca of Ubud, Bali. There I joined Amber and at that point her completely unknown-to-me ten-year-old daughter, Rocket. We spent a few weeks there applying the finishing touches to her big, blue Isuzu bus, Bessie, and preparing it for the rough road ahead. We less successfully applied the same treatment to Rocket, who didn't share our enthusiasm for the journey. For the foreseeable future, Bessie was to be our snug little home, although, in retrospect, a fly on the freshly painted upholstery would have called her more of a laboratory, and Rocket, a gulag.

When the day finally came, we hauled Rocket out of school, kicking and screaming, confident that this would be the worst time of her life. The girls packed up their lives, and we started driving east. As if vindicating the Rocket's insight, within twenty-four hours we were stranded roadside with not only a flat tyre but also a rusted-through rim. But the roadside was also ocean side, so the only suffering was my own, as the designated first mate and responsible in that case to have the issue rectified.

For the next few weeks, as I was adjusting to escapee life in general, all three of us were adjusting to each other and our shared, five cubic metres of living space. Rocket eventually accepted that there would be no retreat, there would be no surrender, and this was her lot.

We lived an ostensibly simple existence, just the kind for which I had hoped. Each day we'd take turns in making the driving plans. Some days it was a random target, some days just a direction, and other days no movement at all. Every third day, at least for the first few weeks, we would have to use various bribery techniques to persuade the smallest inmate that our general direction was eastward, not as per her repeated request, a westward return to home base.

Other than a general pull towards the east, we had scant ideas about where we were going; we stayed in places until we no longer wanted to stay and figured out where we were going only once we got going. It was a lot more about living the life than driving to a destination. With no plan, no two days were the same, although there were some doings, some patterns, that started to emerge.

On driving days, we tended to drive no more than a couple of hours, and we'd aim to park near running water, of which in Indonesia there is no shortage. Our favourites were waterfalls, rapids, and rice paddy aqueducts. Like nature's multi-appliances, they served as clothes and dishwashers, showers, and water massage units. A quality waterfall would hold us up for a few days and, without any driving, those days saw a higher density of the less externally adventurous goings on.

I don't recall another time in my life when I read as much as I did then, and writing was becoming a thing. Then there was the least enjoyable part of most days for everyone, home-schooling. Rocket knew it would happen every day, but the same amount of fuss, distraction, and semi-violence came with each school's-in bell.

It was through her resistance to the home-schooling sessions that I discovered her penchant for aggression and eventually her love of home-made weaponry. It was one of the few things over which we bonded. That is to say, she would develop a new weapon made from nature's gifts and then test it out on me to ascertain its pain rating. Warcraft and weaponry activities usually trumped school, and I agreed that it was a heck of a lot more fun.

Considering her age, my jungle and weaponry craft were superior to hers, so many a time I had to fall on my bamboo sword, so to speak, to even up the battles. But I did not always submit. I recall one day she had developed some bamboo-and-vine nunchakus and came careering around from her workshop behind the bus to test its sting on me. Little did she know that I had developed a mace and ball with bamboo, a length of vine, a coconut, and cactus spikes. She came skidding to a stop, as I reeled on her with my deadliest medieval grimace, letting the

226

coconut ball drop to the full extent of its vine chain. She was sent packing back to her workshop, scratching her scraggly blonde head and no doubt working out how to replicate my new invention. The energy and aggression expenditure took a lot of potential friction out of bus life.

With no imminent driving, we'd often wander off into the jungle both because of a love of it and to keep an eye out for food. In the bus, we had a lasting store of dried beans, peas, lentils, rice and spices, and this we always supplemented with fresh food. In the jungle along the roadside and less commonly in people's farms we would scavenge for banana, mango, papaya, tamarind, and coconut. At times, we would pick moringa and find shellfish if we were by the sea. My fabled fishing skills turned out to be just that, and so we'd stock up on fish along with other fruit, vegetables, nuts, eggs, tofu, and water whenever we went through a village market.

I developed a penchant for what became known as stink-fish. These are dried and salted small fish endemic in Asian food markets. These and a dangerously excessive appetite for boiled eggs were my dietary staples, and as such, the intake of these was relegated to outside the bus's five-metre green zone.

We traversed Bali, Lombok, Sumbawa, and Flores. Each island had its splendour and its troubles, but Flores was the one that we all agreed was the most impressive. Where we were parked that afternoon outside of Moni, had not been an unusual day.

Not long after we parked, the girls took off on a hike and forage. As they wandered off, Rocket declared she would cook that night. I nodded as my taste buds cowered back into their sockets. I stayed and sat with a view over the rice paddies and pretended to make progress with the ukulele.

As with most villages in those parts, parking such a vehicle within walking proximity has a gravitational effect on the locals like driving a giant fluorescent light into a dungeon full of moths.

And in the villages of eastern Flores, a white guy is rare, let alone a white guy driving a car with two blondes all living inside said car. It was often unfathomable to them, and they were not well rehearsed in hiding this fact. Not more than five minutes had passed before the swarm was upon me. I couldn't figure out where the heck they all came from, but I was happy for the ambush.

It was those kinds of interactions that I loved most about Flores. Bewildered villagers would scratch their heads only to snap out of their trance when they discovered that the strange creature speaks their language. In places such as that one, they speak no English, and only basic Indonesian, it being their second language after their tribal dialect and at best a bit worse than my own. We broke into the usual chatter about what type of creature I was, what the hell we were doing there, why we lived in our car, what was half the stuff in our car, did I want to marry one of their daughters, and finally would we be joining them for evening *mandi* (bath) and dinner?

"Mandi? Mandi where?" I asked the head moth.

"Air panas," he says as he points out across the rice paddy landscape.

As he uttered "hot water", I realised that together with his dinner invite he had simultaneously saved us all from having to search for the hot water springs and eating the child's inevitably gruesome dinner creation. We agreed to meet back at the bus just before sunset, and we would accompany them to the springs for the village mandi session and then join them for dinner up at the chief's house.

Perhaps an hour later the girls returned, flustered and competing to tell me about some incident with a pig. They'd stumbled across the village pigsty about fifteen minutes down the road. Rocket was nearly in tears as she recounted the horrible incident to me. Amongst half a dozen pigs was one that was tied to a stake with no more than a foot of rope. The rope tied around its ankle had disappeared under its flesh, no doubt having been there for a long time. Not only that, this unfortunate wretch could not move to avoid the rocks that two village children were throwing at it. Seeing this, Amber hurled a rock at the children, who fearfully scarpered. But that would not be the end of it.

Both of the girls were budding animal liberationists, and we had discussed their previous escapades in that industry. We agreed that their practice of buying caged animals and releasing them only made the problem worse, as it stimulates demand. I did not have all the answers, but since that input, I was invited as a probationary member into their inner sanctum when it came to animal welfare.

So, we hatched a plan to save the pig. We accepted it might die upon release into the wild, and we accepted it would likely be replaced, but in this macabre case, we all agreed this poor animal deserved some freedom even if it died of its wounds. Better to live one day as a free pig than a tortured life as pending bacon. We decided that ultimate stealth was required. It must be done in the middle of the night.

Just before dusk, as we were fine tuning our tools, roles, methods, and liberation plan, the villagers started drifting down the street towards the bus and veering off the road and down to the rice paddies. They walked along the paddy embankments like ants in single file. By the time the chief turned up at the bus, we had concealed any evidence that might incriminate us. I introduced the girls to the head man, and we followed him to the back of the queue.

Ahead of us, folks were disappearing into a depression, concealed by bushes that we had seen from the bus. We had thought it looked a bit odd, the only blight in an otherwise perfect patchwork of fluorescent green. Hidden there was the

Kolorongo Hot Springs, and it was to be an experience of so much more than a hot water bath.

We arrived at the depression. From the edge, we saw maybe twenty men, women, children, and babies semi-submerged in the steaming water. On rocks amongst the mud surrounding the pool, candles flickered. The men wore underwear or, like the women, a sarong around their waists. By that time rumour had spread that the aliens would be joining them for mandi. The looks on their faces when we appeared were thus less of surprise than that of excitement for the coming interaction. Each was soaping up another, washing each other's backs and washing the children from head to toe. Most were whispering and giggling as they no doubt poked fun at our unusual appearance.

The clean, hot water entered the pool from a spring above, collected soap and body grime, and then flowed out to an irrigation aqueduct below. We slipped our gear off in accordance with hot springs fashion, Rocket reluctantly, and climbed into the water with them. We joined in the cleaning with the communal soap bars, albeit within our own white tribe. They gossiped amongst themselves, mostly in dialect. Occasionally a bold villager would talk to me in Indonesian. Others close by would hush and listen to the dialogue.

We soaked for about an hour. The light was long gone, as was the soapy water as the springs moved into the rinse cycle. The stars began to prick through the darkening blanket above, and soon after the villagers began their evacuation, collecting probably as much mud on their feet and hands from the embankment as they had washed off in the first place. At least it was fresh mud.

The chief was the last to leave, reminding us that his wife would feed us soon and to head up to the village. After that, the only sound was the water slapping into the pool from the spring above. Aside from the candlelight reflection on our faces and ripples on the surface of the pool, there was only blackness. We lay on a shallow, sandy section quietly looking up the saturated star scene. We were mesmerised by the beauty of what had just and was still unfolding.

The family dinner up in the village was like many I had had until then and would have after that. I usually enjoy them when I am alone as I can communicate well with local people. With the girls, it was more rigid, and I'd say almost uncomfortable as they hadn't pursued the language. Aside from some pointing and smiling, this rendered them mostly spectators to my own conversation. It wasn't long before I could sense their unease.

That minor discomfort paled in comparison to the unease I felt about our plan to betray the villagers' open and innocent generosity by liberating their bacon. But it was like when you see an endangered animal eating an endangered plant. What do you do? You can only choose the least worst option. I was confident they did not notice our discomfort, but either way, we didn't stay longer than was polite, expressed our gratitude, and made off back down the hill to the bus.

We awoke at midnight after a few hours of restless sleep. We had decided to perpetrate the crime at precisely midnight, for mainly theatrical purposes but also as the moon would have lit up the crime scene by then. The excitement of the rescue was mixed with the kind of nervousness you get when you know you're doing the right thing, but no one else agrees with you, including the law.

With the headlights out, we rolled the bus down the hill and away from the village until we were alongside the pigsty. We went through the plan one more time. Rocket started asking nervous what-if questions, but it was too late for that. The three of us crept up on the moored pig in the middle of the sty, me with a straight edge knife in hand, Rocket with her bag of backup tools.

Amber leapt, catching us by surprise and rugby tackled the pig, presenting its bound front leg for my part in the escapade. The ear-splitting squeals demanded immediate action, but I still paused and admired how professional that tackle was. I hit the dirt with my knife, grabbed its leg, and tried to figure out where the hell the rope was entering its skin under its fur. This was going to get ugly.

"Cut it! Cut it, Bluey!" Rocket begged in a panic.

I found the entry point and tried at first delicately to cut as little skin as possible as the pig wriggled and reared, no doubt sensing something awful coming its way. It wouldn't cut!

"Cut it, Bluey," hissed Amber.

"It's not cutting! Hand me the serrated!"

Rocket handed me the recently sharpened serrated blade that I knew would make more of a mess, but we had no choice now; the clock was ticking.

She started sobbing as she handed me the blade. I grabbed it and without another option, cut through the flesh where I could see the bulge of the rope, outlined under the skin. As the skin spread open a terrible-smelling vanilla-and-strawberry custard spewed out, years of puss and infection and blood in various stages of decay. The moment I got through the rope was obvious as the whole loop around its ankle, if pigs can be said to have ankles, loosened. I felt the pig slump as it ceased to squeal. But it didn't slump to the ground, just in situ, as if reacting to the released pressure of the rope and the liquid build-up.

I cut the rope that tethered it to the stake at the ankle end. I couldn't dig out the rest of the rope as it was fused to its tendons and sinew under the skin all around the ankle, but this was a far better predicament than it was in five minutes earlier. The pig

232

was released and bolted into the surrounding forest. Gone. It was dripping a bit of blood but gone.

Our adrenaline was more pressurised than the puss sack on the pig's ankle as we made for the adjacent rice paddy aqueduct to wash off the more significant pieces of pig shit. We got in the bus, sweating, pumped, and proud, and drove off down the hill and away from town with the headlights off. The pig had made a lot of noise, but we saw no village lights go on. Still, we figured we better put half an hour between them and us before we slacked off and lit up the road. My initiation into the animal liberation gang was complete.

ESCAPEE LIFE

It's late February 2017, and I'm sitting on the wooden deck of a riverside restaurant in Huay Xai, northern Laos. The establishment leans dangerously over the river, and I can't figure out what stops it from collapsing into it and joining the rest of the construction scraps, tree branches, and other rubbish drifting by. As each additional foreigner adds their weight on the deck, my heart beats a little faster. Perhaps the local folks, who are all sitting inside on solid ground, know something we do not.

My newly assembled posse and I have just spent a few hours navigating the Thai–Laos border disorder, which turned out to be slightly different for an Australian, a Canadian, and a Pole. Law and order in that Golden Triangle outpost is as fluid and turbulent as the river below us. I've been travelling with Dan, a Canadian friend, for a bit more than a week. Agata, whom I met in India some time ago, joined us as we packed up and left Nokkie's two days ago. We are here with dozens of other foreigners buying up supplies to keep us fed on the slow boat from here to Luang Prabang two days downriver and the main city in the north of Laos.

I had been at Nokkie's place for about a month. A good deal of that time was spent lounging and writing in the balcony office with Denzo and occasionally other drifters. For a few hours of each day for the last two weeks there I went to a Qi Gong school on the other side of town. The classes were affordable and added more finesse and structure to that section of my wake-up ritual. It also got me out of the office. I'd walk a different route each day exploring the architecture, the street life, and the food of the old town. Some days I'd rent a scooter and head out into the surrounding villages, mountains, and waterways. It was slow living.

I'd fallen in with Carlos and Socrates, not through any deliberate intention, but more due to a kind of proximal osmosis that revolved around the daily lunch ceremony, which took about two hours all up. Those two gents had cornered the market in cheap meals. Each day at approximately eleven o'clock, the procedure would begin. Carlos would trek off on Nokkie's bicycle. He'd found a street vendor fifteen minutes' ride away that would part with stale noodles left over from the previous day's business for next to nothing, no doubt bound for the street dogs or trash can otherwise.

I would join Socrates on his missions to the local market on the other side of town, about an hour round-trip by foot. There, he'd found another vendor who would give him a large volume of soup in a plastic bag, which on account of foregoing the customary noodles, he would get for fifty cents. With me in on the deal, he'd get a litre of a usually fishy broth. It varied slightly each day.

We'd all meet back at Nokkie's and then merge the spoils in a large pot, add spices that had been leftover by other tourists to the mix and reheat the resultant concoction. We'd then sit down to dine in the common room where Carlos would find an international soccer game on the cable TV and proceed to abuse the players throughout our meal. Socrates and I, not so interested in the sport, would discuss domestic affairs, the last of which centred on the problem of the yowling cats.

One of Nokkie's feline femmes was in heat and flattering cats from not only Nokkie's but also the surrounding neighbourhood would assemble and caterwaul throughout the night. No one was around to keep them at bay with the slingshot usually meant for the miner birds, so they'd form a crescent-shaped choir and serenade the caged animal causing all the fuss. It was indeed the most significant issue we had to deal with that month. Uncharacteristically, Nokkie picked up on the unrest, and one afternoon, released the female so that one, some, or all of the suitors could satisfy the yearning in their loins. After that, the nights were peaceful, and we never saw the floozy again. I sure was living the life.

Or was I?

There is nothing at all wrong with slow living. But there is a difference between purposefully slow and languishing in the world of freedom from. In some ways being attached to freedom from can be quite negative. Whether it's work, government, money, or something else, not only are you still related to it by thinking you are free from it, but nothing pulls you forward once you're free, and you start getting excited about domestic cat reproduction.

After about a month in Chiang Mai, Qi Gong classes had finished, and a spell of self-reflection guiltlessly suggested I consider my options. By that time, the constant herbal haze at Nokkie's had left me somewhat lobotomised, so it took the arrival of Dan to set the wheels in motion. Dan was only visiting for three weeks, and if I inflicted my incumbent routine on him, I knew it might well have been the end of our friendship.

The initial impetus for leaving Sumatra was to ride a motorbike around Southeast Asia. Up until Dan's arrival, I'd only been riding Nokkie's leather couch. But it wasn't for nothing. That month I had spent very little money, perhaps ten dollars a day. Based on my budget, of around thirty dollars per day, I decided I had been paid twenty dollars a day to do some writing and complete a Qi Gong course. That's how my brain, when it does, works. It also meant I was well positioned to live the coming month a bit more extravagantly. With visitors, the pace is usually a bit faster and therefore more expensive, and the standard of luxury is usually a little higher than that to which I am accustomed.

We hired a couple of motorbikes and set off on a well-worn loop route through northern Thailand, passing through Pai, Mae Hong Son, Mae Cheam, and Doi Inthanon National Park. It was my first exposure to the joy of riding on winding mountain roads and through heavily forested river valleys. The flexibility of route and timing one gets with a motorbike is hard to beat. This was the start of what would be eight more months on two wheels.

Having a riding partner in Dan was hugely advantageous. He is a practical and mechanically minded person, being a rancher and logger from northern British Columbia. Any mechanical questions or issues I had were quickly sorted out. I was hungry for his knowledge. Dan was also something of a philosopher, though not anything like Socrates. Via his many hours cutting, raking, and baling hay in the summer and no doubt as many hours chopping trees in the winter ice with only his thoughts to harass him, he had come up with some simple truths about living. His two rules, which I found myself saying after a while, were 1) nothing really matters, and 2) see Rule 1. I couldn't help but think that I was living the book *Zen and the Art of Motorcycle Maintenance*, by Robert M. Pirsig.

Besides just general camaraderie, Dan was completely sober. I had been drinking more alcohol than I was comfortable with, and his influence had a partial sobering effect. I cannot say that he was completely straight, though. For good times, Dan had replaced alcohol with a veritable treasure trove of pharmaceuticals. And Thailand is to pharmaceuticals like Willy Wonka is to candy. He did express a valid reason for each remedy, but I questioned whether it were based on a genuine malady. I questioned them, that is, until I too started to contract these mysterious ailments. I began to feel general pain in the mornings before we would set off each day, for which I took Tramadol. This had a smoothing effect on the day's biking. In the evenings to prevent potential anxiety and stress, I took OxyContin or a no-name local morphine product. Not that anxiety and stress were ever a threat, but according to Dan, one can never be too safe. And the daily dosing certainly made me more receptive to his prophetic ramblings. The road trip took on something of a dreamy quality, so much so that upon meeting Agata back in Chiang Mai a week later, I was not able to clearly describe what exactly had transpired.

Agata had been on her own brief adventure up until we met. Hers was littered with a higher concentration of alcohol-inspired episodes, partying, and excess. Shorter trips and vacations tend to impress a sense of urgency in one's days. The last week on the road with Dan was devoid of any such urgency. It was mellower, and while there was the adventure of the road, there were also the adventures of the interior. There was plenty of conversation, contemplation, and philosophising.

Now, as we wait for the slow boat in Huay Xai, Agata's disappointment that my appetite for alcohol has disappeared is only eclipsed by my own. After all, alcohol was my customary go-to intoxicant and indeed the one over which we had met some months ago in India. I can't help but think that now is not the best time to quit alcohol as we watch the steady stream of tourists arrive, each purchasing their bottles of Lao Lao. This vicious local liquor is known to contain anywhere from 30–50 percent alcohol and retails for a dollar a litre. Its reputation in Laos for rendering even the hardiest of alcoholics temporarily insane is unrivalled.

Regardless, with Dan monitoring my efforts to resist temptation, and knowing that he probably has a pill to deal with that anyway, I let Agata go it alone with her Lao Lao. In so doing, I isolate myself from the majority of the boat passengers, who already were syphoning the first drops of this veritable poison into their gullets.

11. Travel and Accommodation

TRANSPORTATION AND TRAVEL

Getting from one point to another needn't be merely a functional process. Getting from Huay Xai to Pak Beng, an opium-producing outpost at the halfway point along the river to Luang Prabang, Laos, could not have been less functional. Why not treat transportation as just a side effect of a ridiculous adventure? Be it by bus, bike, boat, scooter, van, or foot and in the mode of narco-tourism, eco-tourism, death-list-tourism, or pharma-tourism, the destination only represents the very end of the experience. In everything that happens before that is the space in which the escapee expresses his freedom for travel.

The flat-bottom boat has been drifting down the Mekong River now for a few hours and the din coming from the now-half-drunk majority towards the front is so constant that it has ceased to irritate me. I listen to the waves lapping at the sides of the boat.

We pass small wooden villages on the riverbanks where inhabitants wave and children fool about at the water's edge. It seems paradisiacal.

Dan and I edge away from the mob, moving a few seats back and away from the increasingly rowdy drunkards. We're only a few hours into a full day on the boat, and I can see some Lao Lao bottles are half empty. They are rearranging the seating, which I can now see was not fixed to the boat, to the edges, and music has started up out of somewhere. Then Agata seems to launch at us out of the congealed horde and asks why we're not joining in the fun, to which I tell her that we are, but on a different frequency.

Dan, who by now seems to be landing somewhat from his morphine morning, suggests we should test something he bought in Chiang Mai, some tablets he was assured would be good for our general depression. We had not detected depression in ourselves until he mentioned it, but we both agree that prevention is better than a cure.

"Aww thanks, Tramadan," as she affectionately has started calling him.

She turns and is consumed by the thirsty mob like a planet being swallowed by the Death Star. I too eat whatever it is I am given, trusting in Dan's diagnostic abilities. Feeling a bit anxious soon afterwards, I ask Dan what was in the anti-depression tablets. He shrugs and says he understood them to be uppers. He hands me the foil packet and using my translation application, find out that we were not at all suffering from depression, but instead, had all inexplicably contracted asthma.

There's a lot to be said for slow travel. One can enjoy an experience that much more when there is no urgency to arrive anywhere. I wanted the boat to go even slower, even more inefficiently if it possibly could. There is no need for efficiency out here; efficiency would only paint a big ugly sign saying "destination" all over the beauty of the experience.

At dusk, we arrive at a steep, muddy dock void of any structure in Pak Beng. Dan and I hold our positions as we watch what seems like a poorly packed and drunken scrum push and shove their way off the boat. The pressure from the back of the melee creates such momentum that the front rowers only realise there is nowhere to gain purchase on the bank after it is too late. Several backpack-laden foreigners slip down the embankment into the water between the boat and the bank, much to the entertainment of the Laotian baggage handlers. After some flapping about, they eventually either fish themselves or are fished out of the reedy water, sopping wet and muddied.

We join Agata on the road above, who looks for us for guidance about what happens next. We don't need to know, as we are herded into jeeps and trundled up the hill to the village. It seems here that one family monopolises all of the services and efficiently controls the flow of our money towards transport, accommodation, booze and food. We are not even off the jeep at the village before all deals are done, and the mob seems to find renewed vigour with the promise of cold beer.

We could very easily have travelled all the way to Luang Prabang in one day. By bus or on a fast boat, it would have been around the same amount. But then, where is the fun in that? I would have missed the mellow boat ride, the debacle at the embankment and the night in Pak Beng listening to the nocturnal jungle life. When there is nowhere one needs to be, and the ultimate destination is death itself, why go directly there? Dally a while and enjoy even the most basic functions such as transport.

One obvious advantage of abstaining from alcohol is that I have a better chance of feeling sharp the next morning, although the benefit of this is not enjoyed as much as it could be when there are so few amongst whom to exhibit that sharpness. Maybe there is value in grazing with the herd.

It is the following morning and Dan is the only other person awake. We're in the kitchen of the hotel, which housed the drunken hoard last night, fetching ourselves a caffeine hit. Being sharp, with or without caffeine, means you're more likely to notice and further, be amenable to the adventures that surface throughout each day. If I am hung over, I tend not to notice opportunities, and when I do, I feel less than enthusiastic about them. The best experiences often come out of nowhere; they are unplanned, but you have to be on alert for them.

There's nothing wrong with planning a vacation or an expedition in infinite detail or knowing in advance every step that shall be taken while travelling. There's nothing wrong with package tours or high-end adventures with all the bells and whistles. There's nothing wrong with an experience where everything is done for you, and all the entertainment is provided. But your plan will be based on stuff you've already partially discovered before you even set foot on the road. The more you plan, the more you know what you are going to get and the less room there is for the unexpected and the stuff about which you don't yet know.

That's not me. I generate my daily excitement just by waking up each day and walking face first into whatever comes my way with yes on the tip of my tongue. It seems that for adventures and experiences, I am no minimalist. I do get into a bit of trouble; sometimes a minimalist's no would be more appropriate in retrospect, but retrospect is never around when it could be useful. And besides, it's not what happens to you that is important; it is how you deal with what happens to you. I don't need to buy my experiences in general because they are all just there, waiting for me to crash into them, as long as I am looking for and indeed expecting them.

Agata and the rest of the wounded souls drift in and out of the dining area, and I am not surprised to see some folks breakfasting on cold beer. It will be a long day for them. The jeeps' beeps announce it is time to go back to the boat. We drive back to the embankment. This time, with yesterday evening's desperate skid marks still serving as a warning in the mud, the transfer between land and boat is considerably more conservative.

Very quickly, the battle lines are drawn again with the folks intent on a relaxing experience gathering towards the back of the boat, the party people arranging furniture again at the front of the boat, and Dan and me somewhere in between. An hour into the journey, revelry returns to the front of the boat. By now I know they are mostly Australian and English with a few other breeds scattered amongst them for good measure.

Somewhat isolated midship, I try to ignore the racket at the bow and watch the riverbank glide by. I breathe thick and tasty lungs full of jungle air, almost collapsing the environment around me with inhalation, and then re-inflating with each exhalation. But I'm too close to the hoard; it's grating on the experience. I consider for the first time that all of the folks at the back of the boat must be unhappy about their noisy and belligerent co-passengers.

I get up and move to the back of the boat and sit next to a French woman, who is apparently not impressed.

"Enjoying the ride?" I ask

"No."

"Bit rowdy?"

"They're just doing what they're famous for."

She apparently recognises the provocateurs as Australians and English. As an Australian myself, her comment shamefully deflates my conversational aspirations. Any other day and that may well have been me upending bottles of Lao Lao, so I am no one to judge.

With the sparkling mood of my new neighbour, I realise that conversation might be a bit challenging. I gaze past her to the dreamy showreel playing out on the banks of the river as my mind drifts and slows down to about the same pace as the life happening there. Everything is so god damn vivid; life is happening at such intensity, human and otherwise. It seems so integrated. As I take in the world that is out there, I feel it is also in here and all part of one happening. *This is all me, all my perception*, I think. Out there and in here, it is all my world. I can still hear the constant ruckus from the front of the boat, but it bothers me not as that is me too. That is just another angle of the myriad of aspects of my world. I feel thankful for all of it. I feel grateful for this experience, for the mystery, complexity, and oneness that travel affords me.

The slow boat arrives at the dock in Luang Prabang, a city that can afford a structure for a port, so yesterday's mishaps of disembarkation do not repeat. Tuk-tuk drivers encircle the tourists within a few metres of the boat, herding them like sheep and jabbing guesthouse pamphlets at them. Once upon a time, I would have no problems being abrupt, even rude to vendors such as these. But they are local folks trying to make a living; they are not the enemy, and I appreciate them for that. I notice a few of the boat passengers speaking harshly and demanding this and that and think that they could probably get what they are after and do it in a friendlier manner.

I signal to Dan and Agata to follow me. We walk clear of the commotion, politely denying the touts, and go in search of somewhere to stay. Our luggage very much renders us targets, so I set a fast pace in the general direction of the centre of town.

As we walk I think still about the variety of life and lifestyles on this earth and that it is precisely that difference that makes it so beautiful. I think about the other tourists at the port, making demands through their Western lenses. Can one truly experience a place when one has conditions that it be at least somewhat like home? And do those conditions and expectations begin to change the place itself as the locals seek to please the tourists? Are we playing a role in homogenising the globe when we travel by wanting it to be the same as at home?

We walk through ancient market lanes in the historic centre looking for somewhere to sleep. The narrow alleys are lined on both sides by marketeers selling fruit and vegetables, many of them unknown to me, and all manner of animals. Various types of meat including amphibians, rodents, and insects, cooked and raw, splayed and skewered and some still alive and croaking are displayed. The lanes dense with chatter and bargaining are mud mixed with cobblestones from one era and cement from another. Two-story, narrow houses and guesthouses lean into the alleys. They are made of old, dark, and ornate timber with slate or terracotta tile roofs. Much of it is left over from French provincial times. Recent makeshift repairs using blue tarpaulins and corrugated iron blur the distinction between them and market stalls.

But then we come across something that jolts me; it is like being rudely awakened from a sublime dream. There on one corner is a brand new, polished, cement-and-glass building, a three-story guesthouse with a Western bar and restaurant on the street level. There are half a dozen staff milling about in slacks and polo shirt uniforms—very authentic. The glass front protects its preciousness from the bustling market. It reminds me of my days in Bali not so long ago. Many of the traditional

245

coastal areas are undergoing what some call gentrification. It is more like a "retailification." It is out with the old and the traditional and in with the Western-owned, operated, and styled. I later find out that this place is owned and run by an English couple.

I am not against the new and the modern, but I don't understand why foreigners who like a place so much that they decide to live there, want to change it. All the enchantment of these market lanes ends at this guesthouse. It is like a monument to its foreign owners, and besides contrasting with every other local building, it is too expensive for any Laotian to enter, as is evidenced by exclusively foreign guests inside dining on expensive Western breakfasts. I doubt even my co-passengers from the boat could swallow the price tag here.

Why escape from one place only to bring aspects of that place with you? Why impose your values and ideas on a place instead of leaving it alone? Let it be itself. If we insist on Westernising the globe, how will we continue to enjoy the different peoples and places of the world? As they say, don't leave your mark on a place; let that place leave its mark on you.

We eventually locate a locally run and frequented guesthouse outside the old town where prices seem less affected by the mass tourism. Luang Prabang is a beautiful historic city, and I did have an idea before I came here that I might stop here and make something of a home for a while. But it is undergoing a massive transformation that I am not interested in witnessing, and it is unexpectedly expensive. We agree to have it serve as a base only and not to linger. Exploring the countryside has more appeal at the moment. We persuade Agata that riding a motorcycle is as easy as peddling a bicycle and get about sourcing some wheels.

ACCOMMODATION

I often find myself stopping for a while in places that have a certain appeal for me. When I do so, I feel like I am feeding my innate human need for the experience of home. I say "innate" because the sensation of feeling at home is something that lies deep within us all. The feeling is not easy to pinpoint and perhaps is easier to describe by explaining what it feels like to not be home, or to be homesick. One suffers from a kind of longing or even loneliness. Our attachment to home is evidenced when we see our homeland threatened and we become protective of it. When our house or apartment is invaded, we feel violated and angry.

The idea of home is so important to us that our lives often revolve around it. Much of our time is spent in the buying, renting, renovating, moving, or otherwise adjusting of our physical abode to make it homier. We take great care of our homes not only for superficial and financial reasons but also because we are trying to fulfil our internal desire for home, the desire to alleviate the longing.

We tend to think about our country, our suburb, and our house or apartment as our home. We think of it as a physical thing. There is nothing wrong with thinking about home in this way but it is not just the physical things that give us our feeling of home. Like happiness, it is our emotional state that makes us feel at home. When you buy a new house, do you feel completely at home the moment you step through the front door? If you have ever moved countries or suburbs, did you feel at home on the first day that you moved? The chances are that you felt the opposite and were homesick for your previous circumstance. But eventually, your new physical situation will feel like home. It is an internal sensation that accumulates over time. It grows as you come to know a place and its people, as you are affected by it, and as your feelings about that physical place evolve.

I get this sensation when I stop somewhere for a while. When the streets become familiar, people who recognise me become more open and friendly, and I find my niche in that place. I begin to inhabit it. It doesn't only happen for me in Australia, and it doesn't only happen in a house. I feel at home wherever my soul seems happy. It's happy in a bus in the jungle in Sumatra. It's happy in a car park on the island of Nias. Home is a sensation of the soul as much as anything physical.

The soul is forever seeking to be home, but that doesn't mean it is only looking for a country or a house in which to live. In fact, it is often dissatisfied when only those criteria are used to quench its longing. Simply moving to a more luxurious house in a better suburb will not satisfy it. One must also consider other intangible ideas about home. It feels at home when it feels secure, welcome, and involved. It might be when family and friends are close by or when you're around folks who share your dreams and worldly ideas. It might be a place where your intellect is stimulated, and you are doing something you feel is worthwhile. I find it is anywhere that I am close to the natural world of rivers, mountains, and oceans. Put simply, it can be any place in which you are happy. When we are in these situations, we tend not to think about home as much because we have elements of it right there.

Increasingly, because I take my internal feelings about home wherever I go, I find that my physical home is becoming more expansive. At the risk of sounding clichéd, I often think of the earth as my home. It explains why it upsets and angers me to see it damaged wherever I go. The protective behaviour we experience when our countries and homes are invaded or damaged seems to flare up when I see any damage done to the world. I'm sure this is common. But I suspect that often in our daily lives we are insulated and remote from this damage and so our protective idea about home is usually within a tighter circumference and frequently a more urban setting.

Travel and experiencing the earth create a deeper connection to it, and from that stems a desire to protect it as our home. Perhaps travel is one of the keys to greater involvement and activism to stem the environmental damage that happens in our world.

Contrary to what you might think, travel and adventure are in themselves consistent with the idea of home. Whether in the specific situations you find yourself on the road where your soul is happy or just a deeper connection with the earth as a whole, both enhance the sensation of home.

We left Luang Prabang a few days ago, and it turns out that motorcycles are not as easy to ride as we thought, at least for some of us. Agata's first accident is long forgotten now, though; the scrapes have started to scab over, and it seems all are now able to remain mounted on their steeds while in motion. We ride in boy-girl-boy formation. This way Agata can be warned about obstacles in the road, potholes, gravel, humans, and water buffalo while being monitored from behind.

The Laotian rural landscape is dense with secondary forest and in some rare instances primary growth. It is scarred in many places from clear felling and timber extraction, and I feel fortunate that I am seeing it before it is all gone, which sadly is what the future holds for this cash-strapped country.

After riding south out of Luang Prabang, we turned east at Phou Choun out towards Phonsovan and the Vietnamese western border with Laos. Villages and villagers are mostly brown and muddy, grow mixed vegetables, and keep a variety of livestock. They have cattle, pigs, chickens and ducks. We see many dogs as well, which may or may not be livestock; one never knows. If we ride early in the morning as if to get the deed done before too many witnesses are out and about, we occasionally see a dog on a spike being cooked with a welding torch, fur and all.

At Phonsovan we turn south to follow a circuit we had mapped out that would take us to Vang Vieng, something of an institution on the Laos tourist trail. The town is renowned for its wild riverbank parties. They have been so wild that twenty-seven tourists died there in 2011, mostly in drunken accidents. The law has since intervened, and things are supposedly a lot quieter. Those who go there now, like ourselves, are drawn there by the reputation of its natural beauty. But as the road turns from asphalt to dirt about twenty-five kilometres south of Long Tien, we come across a military checkpoint. Three army personnel, who seem to have shared one uniform between them and are otherwise plainly dressed, tell us we cannot continue as the road is "not convenient" for us.

"Why not convenient?" I ask.

"Bad roads," their spokesman responds.

"That's fine, rental bikes."

"Wild animals," he tries again.

"Great, we're interested to see them."

"Bad people," is his final attempt, and with this we finally accept that we are unlikely to pass.

We guess that the area either has a problem with bandits or, like so many other areas around here, still has much unexploded ordinance on and around the roads and tracks.

We turn around and make a new plan. We decide to head north and chart a course for Muang Hiam, after which we will get up into the high range that runs parallel to the northern border with Vietnam. Up until now, it has been hot and sweaty riding. The quick ascent up to Muang Hiam exposes our lousy planning as we start to feel the cold. We stop at a local market and kit ourselves out in items of new but locally sized and styled clothing. It's all either too small, such as my new gloves that restrict independent finger movement, or utterly not fit for motorbike, riding such as my pair of after-dinner woolly slippers.

We continue north still cold, hoping to make it to Muang Hiam before dark. It continues to get colder, and with so many bends and so much road work our pace is slow. I wait on a rise for Agata and Dan who are trailing and discover as they approach that Agata's bike is painted in mud; she has taken another fall in a grader track. Dan has obviously worked his magic psychologically and pharmaceutically as she is smiling when she reports the incident to me.

The sun disappears behind the steeper mountains at times, making the cold quite unbearable. We are all shivering, and although my slippers might be warm in some circumstances, with open toes and no socks in my possession, my numb feet start to fumble with the gears. We stop and all agree that we just need to find any accommodation, anywhere, or risk being caught out in the dark and the cold. We continue slowly as I start to have problems managing the bike with frozen hands and feet. We cross the still visible and beautiful Nam Neum River, and I'm certain we let out a posse-wide breath of relief as we arrive in Sop Lao, which has several hotel signs on the roadside. If ever there were a sight for frozen eyeballs, this was it.

On a sunny day, this town may not have been anything special. We'll never know, but at this point it is nothing short of paradise. We choose the first guesthouse, and the friendly, smiling proprietors welcome us in. Detecting our climatic distress, they quickly inform us that the rooms have hot water. The rooms are simple and comfortable. The shower thaws my body, and the feeling comes back into my extremities. An overwhelming feeling of well-being overcomes me almost as if the hot water is warming my very soul.

I change into dry, dirty clothes, put my slippers back on, and walk through the heated guesthouse to the rendezvous in Dan's room. Agata joins us, and all three of us crack a cold beer, even Dan, who is deciding what medicine he requires right now. Perhaps it is just the contrast from the hellish ride today, but in this moment, I feel at home.

In the morning, I don't want to leave this place, partly on account of its homeliness but also because I fear the road ahead. We reluctantly say goodbye to our hosts, wear as many clothes as we can without losing limb mobility and set off. We have checked the maps and know that we need to go higher today and cross over to the northern side of the range and back again before we can start heading back downhill again. It's not long before we are in the clouds or fog. Who can tell? My hands have frozen around the handgrips, and my shivering is causing the bike to wobble. Are we still in tropical Laos? My teeth are chattering so much I worry about my enamel. But I remember that shivering and chattering are bodily functions designed to warm you up, so I let them continue unabated.

Soon, a cross-wind picks up that sends the fog buffeting against our bikes. I suspect we have crossed to the northern side. I realise that riding like this on narrow mountain roads with oncoming vehicles appearing out of the fog with only just enough time to veer is becoming dangerous, and I think about Wim Hoff. He's that guy who can survive sub-zero temperatures for long stretches of time just by using his mind and breathing techniques. I start practising my own version of the Wim Hoff technique. I have no idea what it is, but it seems to work. Slow, concentrated breathing almost as if in meditation stops the bike from wobbling as we persist through the cloud and wind.

We seem to level out, and I hope we have reached the highest point. We cross back from the northern to the southern side of the range, which makes me think we might be riding along its crest. Then the road turns down, and I know the worst is over. Sunny sections become more frequent, and after another five crawling kilometres we reach a shoulder in relatively permanent sunshine and pull over, frozen. Dan, who is the best equipped for this climate with his ice-logging experience and his superior score at the clothing shop, rubs us both down until we stop shivering. We sit on the roadside and wait for this welcome warmth to heat us through to our bones.

The road from there back to Luang Prabang over the course of the next week was as stunning as any section and thankfully relatively warm. Agata took one more spill on a gravelly corner, cracking some ribs, scraping her knees, and proclaiming, "I don't want to die," but otherwise the time passed pleasantly.

We arrive back in Luang Prabang and return to our out-of-town guesthouse. As much as I have said that home is about an internal sensation, I concede that it is easier to sleep in a bed than in a feeling. Sleeping in a bed in a house in this town that would unexpectedly grow on me over the next two weeks, I would again experience the feeling of home. During that time, a local doctor would confirm Agata's broken ribs and both her and Dan would leave for their respective homes. I would be left to plot the next adventure.

I don't care too much if the place that I sleep in each night does not feel like home, at least in the short term. For longer stays ideally it would, and such places are not always found where you might think. Some of the homiest situations I've stayed in were not houses, apartments, or even guesthouses, but were 'alternative accommodations'. They usually offer a lot more than just accommodations.

The first category of accommodation that I am drawn to is free, at least in money, not in effort. If someone offers me accommodation for which they no doubt have worked for, the least I can do is contribute in non-monetary terms. Whether it is cooking, cleaning, babysitting, or renovating a bathroom, it is satisfying to be able to contribute something more than my sparkling personality even when that is usually all being asked.

When I am visiting Australia, I tend to freeload on friends and family, surfing a couch, a piece of carpet, or in gold mine scenarios an actual bed. Folks think I'm kind when I wash dishes and clean, but this is selfish behaviour as I find this kind of work satisfying and meditative. Why wouldn't I want to babysit or look after kids? It gives me a chance to get to know some little humans with whom I am often not acquainted.

There are many online communities where you can do the same but with complete strangers. In Mexico City via couchsurfing.com, I stayed with a lovely girl who offered me her brother's bed for a week while he was away. I'm not sure how he felt about that, but my time there was outstanding. I couldn't have felt more at home. I inherited an instant social circle, an in-house city guide, and a friend to this day. While she was at work one day, I hastily renovated her bathroom. It was a filthy room, so I bleached, washed, and sanded the walls and then painted it for her, all at the cost of a tin of paint. She was almost brought to tears when she came home that night. I tell myself they were tears of joy not of horror at my colour selection.

And then there is house sitting, another free option of which I plan to do a lot more. My brother does this extensively and stays in amazing houses all over Europe. In his case, he uses a website trustedhousesitters.com, which focuses on house and pet sitting. Because he and his girlfriend love animals, it's a fantastic deal for both parties. Another one is mindmyhouse.com.

Doing a bit of work for your room and board is another option. I once used workaway.info to find secure a stint in an absinthe distillery with free food and board in exchange for learning how to make the wacky bohemian liquor. Win-win! I'll spend a month learning a new skill, and the money I'll save goes straight onto my balance sheet. There's also the Worldwide Opportunities on Organic Farms (wwoof.org). You can learn and then teach sustainable organic farming techniques in dozens of countries, including Turkey, New Zealand, Norway, and French Polynesia. And these options are usually centred on a community and a common goal or interest, increasing the likelihood of feeling right at home.

And finally, there are some more unusual options, such as living in a bus. In my bus, Rosie, in Sumatra I pay no rent and will eventually sell her to recoup my initial outlay. Life has never been cheaper or more interesting and adventurous. I've stayed in a hammock village in Malaysia, where one brings communal food, coffee, or some other contribution, and a local self-appointed landlord allocates two trees for your hammock and ensures security. I'm not sure security is needed, but it's a nice sentiment. Many years ago, in Colombia, I hung my hammock up in a decaying medium-rise building site along with many other travellers. It was urban roughing it at its best. Each squatter looked after other's belongings when sorties to the outside world were in order.

The options are limited only by creativity and flexibility. Experiment and be adaptable, and you'll find a great deal of adventure stems from your choice of where you lay your head at night. The contrast between accommodation and home options can help your appreciation of each as well. From Hiltons to hammocks, the wider the variety, the better it is. You never appreciate a five-star hotel like you do the night after staying in a burnt-out building site.

12. Growth and Education

"Knowledge is learning something every day.
Wisdom is letting go of something every day."

—Zen Proverb

EDUCATION

Dan's knowledge pharmacopoeia was not as inspiring as his general knowledge about all things practical. In addition to a slight morphine addiction, he left me interested in learning how to do more things for myself. Constant learning and growth are essential to well-being and learning how to become more self-reliant has great synergy with a frugal minimalist lifestyle. An escapee has the freedom and the time to learn about such things and anything that interests him.

Before I left Luang Prabang again, I purchased a low-calibre motorbike for $200. It was a 110CC Honda Win and a favourite bike for new riders in Indochina. They have the same engine as the endemic Honda scooters, and every mechanic from Laos to Cambodia knows how to repair one. Honda Wins are known to spend a good amount of time in workshops. This would be my mode of transport for the rest of this adventure and indeed my classroom as I set about learning how motorbikes work.

256

Fortunately, with this particular motorbike, a class would be in session roughly every three days, so it would be a steep and rapid learning curve as I forced my apprenticeship on bemused mechanics.

Throughout March and April of 2017, I rode throughout Laos and northern Vietnam while breaking and replacing almost every part of the bike. I wasn't looking for it to break down, but I was most happy when it did. I began to diagnose and repair issues myself as many problems would recur. The Chinese parts were extremely cheap because they lasted about as long as a tank of gas. Just as human cells regenerate and replace such that over a certain period of time you are not actually the same person as you were previously, Honda Wins can regenerate entirely in eight weeks. As a result, I arrived in Hanoi, Vietnam, where I am now, on a different bike from the one I bought and with some valuable knowledge that would keep me rolling through the rest of Vietnam and Cambodia.

Continual education and growth are integral parts of escapee life. It can be intellectual stuff like learning to play chess, learning languages, or figuring out a Rubik's cube. It can be spiritual such as my experiences with Ayahuasca or my current studies in Zen. It can be artistic or musical, where you're not only challenging the opposing side of your brain but you're adding something of beauty to the world. It can be physical such as learning new movements for the morning wake-up ritual, doing a free-diving course, or finally becoming a legend on the salsa floor.

How you find stuff to learn about can be planned or unplanned. I always have a list of things I want to learn. In addition to improving my Spanish and Indonesian, I want to learn Persian. I like how the letters look. I want to learn more Qi Gong and yoga. Inversely, I did not plan to become interested in Zen. I never imagined I would find myself reading the Sutras and meditating on the Koans.

257

Learning can even take the form of your part-time job, or you might find there's education in shortfall projects. Education seems never-ending out there for my shortfall projects of photography and writing. The gravy on the potatoes here is that you may be remunerated for your efforts.

I am sitting on a park bench alongside the Hoàn Kiếm Lake in Hanoi's Old Quarter. It's 6 a.m., but it's peak hour for the fitness folk. There's a free outdoor gym here, which I have been coming to some mornings just to add some variety to the morning routine. There seems to be a regular crew with me who attend from before sunrise, starting at about 5 a.m. They speak no English and I only minimal Vietnamese, but their body and facial languages are always welcoming. That is, except for the gym boss, an oriental Arnold Schwarzenegger, dressed in full army combat gear who still gives me the cold shoulder, ignoring my good morning nods. I remember that aside from his strongman roles, Arnold also starred in *Kindergarten Cop*, so I decide to persist with him. He must have a soft side.

There is a group of middle-aged ladies nearby practising Tai Chi augmented with their fluttering, decorative, fans. I can barely hear their tape-recorded Chinese chime music because Irene Cara's "Flashdance" is playing at full volume over by the Zumba class about twenty metres further along. People are jogging, many others are practising Dịch Cân Kinh arm-swinging exercises, and small groups are chatting on lakeside benches.

With all the active-wear on display at such an early hour, one could be fooled into thinking this is Ubud, LA's Venice Beach, or Sydney's Bondi Beach. There's a handful of Chihuahuas as well to add to the imagery. But unlike those beaches, the average age of the people exercising here is more like 65 than 25. I am surprised to see so few youngsters here. But I am not surprised that the next song that follows "Flashdance" is "Gangnam Style".

But not everyone is a fitness fanatic at 6 a.m. Right next to the outdoor gym is a pair of grey-haired and scantily toothed men drinking their first beers of the day. Their cigarette smoke drifts through the gym. Cans of Hanoi Beer being consumed so close to sunrise raise no more eyebrows than I did yesterday when I shimmied in at the back of the Tai Chi class with the ladies, sans fan. Anything goes in Hanoi.

Hanoi is turning out to be quite a fruitful health stop for me, so much so that I am considering making it an annual pilgrimage to get myself repaired. When I first arrived in Hanoi, I posted a request for treatment information on the Hanoi Facebook community. I figured I'd get my shoulder bursitis looked at. I was quickly answered with many suggestions for treatment by foreigners, usually cheaper than I would expect in Australia, though not much. Hanoi is no backwater. Why would I pay a foreigner many times the local price to be treated?

One response amongst the many stood out like a protruding collarbone. A Ukrainian chap, Igor, said his "Master" was a renowned acupuncturist and all but guaranteed me a swift resolution at a ridiculous $3 a treatment. Could it be? The address that Igor gave me took me to a Kung Fu dojo in a small village on the outskirts of Hanoi. I parked my motorbike just inside the gate. The venue was overgrown with trees with exposed roots and all manner of punching bags suspended from them. Vines were breaking into the premises from all directions. There were contraptions that would have been unremarkable in a torture chamber. Huge and ancient-looking vats containing carp and lily pads were dotted about, and carved stone and wooden symbols and insignias adorned the perimeter walls. I'd walked right into a scene from a Jean-Claude Van Damme film.

Igor arrived as I was contemplating the scene and took me to a large pond in the central garden alongside of which several Vietnamese boys were sitting around Master. He was holding court, speaking in fluent gibberish for all I could tell. Interrupted, Master had a discussion with Igor about my condition without consulting with me at all. How was there so much to say when I had given nothing more than the name of my ailment? Master huffed and grunted throughout the conversation and then nodded abruptly to declare the diagnosis over. He returned to his disciples.

Igor reported that Master could fix my ailment; it would take eight consecutive days of electro-acupuncture and acupressure. I was also given a liquid concoction of herbs and alcohol both to both drink before meals and massage into my shoulders. I was sceptical. How the heck could he be so final about it without so much as looking at me? In any case, at $3 a session plus another $3 for the acupressure, there was little to lose, and as a young man, I always wanted to go to the Kumite Mixed Martial Arts Tournament in Hong Kong, so this was close enough. Treatment would start that day.

Igor then asked if I were interested in Qi Gong. I said that I was as I remembered that one of the underlying skills in many Kung Fu schools is Qi Gong. I signed up for that as well. It was free. The students, who were also Master's helpers in the treatment section of the school, were the instructors. They would teach me when they were not running errands for Master.

After eight days, I had learned the twelve primary movements, noting that it was different from the Mantak Chia Qi Gong I had practised in Thailand. This would slide into my morning wake-up ritual somewhere. Additionally, to my astonishment, my shoulder was completely healed. It was difficult for me to accept that Master was able to succeed where many others had failed. It was a learning experience on many levels. Master, when I heaped praise on him with the help of Igor translating said only, "Of course," and nodded conclusively to dismiss me.

Later that day, I took a trip into my future to look back on my current self to see if there were anything that I would regret not having done in this unusual and beneficial situation. My future self said that I would be mad not to get my back looked at and to continue with the Qi Gong training. He said to my current self to make use of this opportunity. Finding treatments and training under the guidance of one of Southeast Asia's most well-known eastern healers was a windfall not to be dismissed. Also, he was a feared and respected Kung Fu practitioner. Master could push a four-wheel drive thirty metres from a stationary position using only a sharpened bamboo pole lodged in his windpipe. I am not sure under what circumstances that would be useful, but it was very impressive.

I arranged to have my back examined. I explained to Master, through Igor, about my condition. He wandered around me, prodding and knuckling my spine, and after much grunting, muttered his conclusion to Igor. Nodding, to confirm his diagnosis as fact, he would need thirty days with four hours of treatment each day. Treatment would consist of electro-acupuncture, Vietnamese hot herbal poultice, traction, and another round of poultice. I was to continue with Qi Gong, as it also, according to Master, would be beneficial.

None of this was something I planned, especially not the education. I set about preparing for a month of spending most of my days at the school. It would be quite a different month in Hanoi from what I had expected (i.e., partying myself stupid). In this case, my expectations' not being met would not make me unhappy. I took a rooftop apartment in a nearby neighbourhood that same day and stocked the kitchen with healthy food. I set myself up for a routine.

Every day for the next thirty days was fundamentally the same, except my familiarity with Master and his students grew. The comic aspect of our utter inability to understand each other's

261

language grew as well. Master assigned me a mentor named Tuan. He seemed to be the second in command at the school and was referred to as Tuan the Torturer or the Beast by the other students. His physical condition relegated Jean Claude Van-Damme towards the Michelin Man end of the body fat spectrum. He was a tangle of high-speed sinew. He would be responsible for my treatments and Qi Gong education and would eventually be castigated by the Master for trying to coax me away from my main work there and into his own breakaway Kung Fu sect within the school.

The series of treatments would start at a different time each morning. Everybody except me knew the formula for the start time, so I would arrive early every day, sit by the central carp pond, and drink green tea. The pond was the social gathering spot where all would meet before and between treatments and classes, drink tea and smoke cigarettes relentlessly. Smoking cigarettes and poor health do not seem to have been linked yet in Vietnam.

Tuan would arrive, drink tea, smoke, and poke fun at my physique. I never knew what they were saying, but I was happy to contribute to the comic atmosphere even if it were about my comparatively large, useless body. Even the children would challenge me to contests of skill at Tuan's insistence. Tuan would make particular fun of how weak and soft my hands were; if only they had seen them when I was an accountant, the place would have gone into meltdown.

I recall one brief conversation at the carp pool in which a young child was quizzing me about my hands.

"Why are your hands so soft?"

"Well, for twenty years I only typed."

"Ah, OK. For twenty years, Tuan only break bricks."

Eventually and simultaneously, as if internally wired to some extrasensory school bell I had yet to install, everyone would rise and begin their duties. I would follow Tuan to the torture rack where he would chat and laugh without pause as he stuck sixty needles into my back and had one of his helpers apply the electrodes. There was always one helper whom I feared as he was clumsy on the voltage and often turned the dial too fast and too far, causing me to convulse and Tuan to lead the chorus of laughter.

After that it was back to the carp pool, tea, and cigarettes, and then back to the rack for the hot poultice. The students brewed the poultice from a variety of plants and herbs, beat it to a pulp with a mortar and pestle the size of the smallest student there, and then boil it. They then would apply a great lump of scalding vegetable matter to my back and wrap me in cling wrap. I don't know whether after five minutes it actually felt good or it just comparatively felt good because it was no longer burning me.

After an hour, it would be more tea and cigarettes, and then the traction treatment. The traction bench was an old gym bench press that had been modified with a series of bicycle inner tubes. Students would secure my ankles to one end with inner tubes and ropes and arrange a complicated harness of tubing under my armpits and behind my neck. Then with their feet braced against the head end of the bench press Tuan and a student would yank the tubing harness as far as it would go and then fix it to a winch welded to the bench press. A student would wind the winch every ten minutes or so, lengthening my spine. I would force myself to think of other things because thinking about what was happening to my skeleton brought on a degree of panic, which worried me more than the mild physical pain. It seemed to also stretch everything inside me. My lungs felt tight and my breathing became shallow. It wasn't much fun. But nor was it shit.

After an hour I would be unable to sit up. With my back stretched and weak, I would be carried to the poultice rack

263

without tea or cigarettes, and I would lie through another hour of poultice treatment. While there was some pain in the traction, it dissipated when the subsequent poultice heated my spine and the vertebrate slowly contracted again. At the conclusion of each days' treatments, Tuan would point to one of the younger students and yell something, and that student would take me through my Qi Gong practice.

Throughout my time there, the ambience never lost its ancient mystique. The smell of incense, the sessions by the carp pond, the general joviality, the students who seemed to be there all day alternating between practice and chores, the weapons and contraptions lining the outer walls, the daily meditation, communal lunch, and nap time all left a permantent impression. The treatment and the learning were parts of it, but the experience as a whole was something more significant, and hopefully, should I develop new ailments, one I will repeat

Most education or learning I seek is to gain long-term benefits. But it is not always this way. During my last escape attempt, I was in Guatemala for a time. I decided it might be useful to study the local Mayan dialect, Kaqchikel. I would hear the old women in the markets using this language and thought it would be fantastic to join their discussions. I also thought it would be a way of respecting them by speaking their language rather than expecting them to speak Spanish. It took a while to find a teacher, but I tracked one down at a Spanish School. He was an older gentleman and confused as to why I would bother. But he didn't say no to my money, and we commenced daily Kaqchikel lessons.

Each day during lunch break I would go to the local market and show off my new words by ordering food in increasingly complete sentences. I could never understand what they would say back to me, but nobody seemed to notice. And I was always pleasantly surprised by what I was served even though nothing was near what I thought I had requested. It would only be a few days before a group of old women would be at my favourite food stand each day at the same time, waiting for me to turn up and request something in their local language. They seemed to enjoy it, and the whole lunchtime experience was a noisy and hilarious affair. I would always have at least a few of the women talking at me at once saying god only knows what. They seemed not to care that my answer to almost everything was, "Good afternoon. Toasted cheese sandwich, please."

The language has many sounds that are difficult to make. There is much clicking in the back of the throat, saliva-filled hissing, and other sounds that were new to me. My tutor went to great length to have me pronounce them correctly. One day he asked me why I wanted to learn the language. I said it was so that I could communicate with indigenous people in Guatemala, particularly around the lake where our coffee farms were.

This was when I discovered that learning this language would have a different kind of benefit. Apparently, the version of Kaqchikel I had been learning was only minimally used in a few villages on one side of the lake. Moreover, it was a dying language with almost everyone now speaking Spanish and with very few and only elderly people still speaking it. Oops. In that instant I thought about my market ladies and the joy it seemed to bring them each day. I decided to continue learning the dying language. When they smiled and laughed, even though it was at me not with me, I smiled and laughed. The benefit was in just that.

As I would I explain to the Spanish students at the school who asked me why on earth I was learning it: I would like you to imagine you are walking through the Sahara Desert with a girl you are trying to impress, but you are both about to die of thirst. You come across an elderly Guatemalan woman concealing some water. Your girlfriend recognises her outfit and says, "Oh, great. She only speaks Kaqchikel; now we're fucked."

But at that moment you respond, "Don't worry, darling, I speak Kaqchikel." Just imagine that!

SELF-RELIANCE

Learning almost any function or skill results in an element of utility and often will contribute to your level of self-reliance. I accept that studying Kaqchikel may prove to be of little use and learning the break dancing move the "helicopter" thirty years after it was fashionable may not provide many benefits, but these are exceptions to the rule.

There is no limit to the range of things you can learn about. Indeed, the more the better because learning in all its forms contributes to living a good life in terms of your health, prosperity, and happiness. Learning about biology, diet, and fitness lets you to take greater control of your health. When you learn to do things for yourself, you need to buy fewer services, so you use less money, which contributes to your prosperity. And when you study things that you find interesting and worthwhile, the sense of fulfilment makes you happy.

Even learning about the seemingly mundane, little, and obscure things will reap benefits. Learning how to service a carburettor, open a wine bottle with a shoe, and identify edible plants that grow in your local environment makes you just that more self-reliant. Learning how to do things yourself is more interesting and fun than outsourcing them.

This is not how our systems are set up, though. Our mainstream educational systems, at least in the developed West, and the world of work encourage us to become specialists. With the increase in the amount of knowledge available to be employable in your field, you must know a heck of a lot about it and so forego knowing about other stuff. It's unlikely that you will be proficient at all of vascular surgery, marine biology, and tax accounting. The modern system does not support or promote this. This is a good thing in that we need experts, such as in medicine. But it also means we are funnelled into knowing a lot about a little rather than a bit about everything.

From childhood throughout our studies and then in work, we become accustomed to outsourcing everything outside of our realm of knowledge. For this, we have to pay, so we need to work, and so we have no time to pursue additional learning. The service economy thus exists.

The service economy's omnipresence means we outsource the education of our children, the growing and distribution of our food, the making and mending of our clothes and houses, and the provision of entertainment. We outsource these to gadgets, appliances, machines, and other people. In the past, much of these tasks, if not taken care of personally or within a family, were handled within a local community. This is not a scenario that is easily achievable today. We are stuck in a feedback loop, working to afford the products and services we have to buy because we don't have time to learn about and do them ourselves because we are working.

With outsourcing comes the loss of the skills. We have watches and clocks to tell the time but cannot judge it by the sun. We have a compass and Google Maps but cannot navigate by the stars or other environmental features. We have the internet for all our answers, so we don't need to think and figure as much. We have appliances and machines that magically do as commanded without us having a clue how they work, and those same devices are slowly replacing the dexterity and the strength of muscle we once used to do the same task. There is a specialist job in society for an ever-increasing number of tasks.

The more specialised individuals of our modern technological society become, the less they know about how stuff works and even less about how the world itself works. This is a contributing factor that keeps consumer society alive and kicking, but is it dumbing us down? Bernard Shaw in *Maxims for Revolutionists* puts it bluntly, "No man can be a pure specialist without being in the strict sense an idiot."[26]

As an escapee, I understand that specialisation is not always a good thing. Being specialised to the point where I cannot function outside of my house, workplace, technology, or elsewhere is something I avoid at all costs. It is more desirable for me to seek self-reliance and to re-learn the things we as humans once knew how to do. I aim to be a generalist.

A generalist aims to operate outside of his speciality or vocation and strives to onboard as much as he can. He seeks to develop all sides of himself so that he can come up with creative solutions for all of his needs. He is continually learning new skills whether he sees an immediate application or merely out of interest.

As part of my education and former employment, I learned how to do my taxes, financial planning, and general money management. I no longer earn or spend money in this field. What I knew about before I escaped ended somewhere around about there, but I have been busy learning new skills relevant to my lifestyle since then.

I have learned by doing mechanical work on my motorbike and before that my bus. That journey is a never-ending one, but with each issue I encounter my reliance on a mechanic diminishes. I have learned to work with wood. The advancement in the quality of the work inside my bus Rosie, is clearly visible. The bed was obviously made by an accountant. For the bookshelf, that is less obvious, and the kitchen looks almost professional. My cooking skills have improved such that I am no

268

longer disgusted by my creations. I've learned what food from my environment I can eat, mainly fruit, but also leaves and berries. I don't rely on anyone for transport because I use my own or I walk. I think nothing of spending the entire day walking around a city to find dental floss, which I have been considering replacing with seaweed. As I do so much manually, my physical strength has changed. I can climb trees as I did as a kid, and my typist's hands, while not worthy of Tuan's respect, are not so singularly useful anymore. If I had to depend on my ukulele skills for entertainment, there could be some boredom, but I find that just by walking out into the world, entertainment usually finds me. As for health, the learning is endless but almost always beneficial.

I learn a lot in reading non-fiction, philosophy, and memoir-style books by those with whom I share interests, as I find much there off of which to leverage. From my reading about the history and practice of Zen, I am gaining much even though what I am learning, according to Bodhidharma, is only an illusion.

Many of the things I learn about have applicability across other disciplines. When I read about the benefits of grounding, that is, walking around with no shoes on to connect and inherit electron energy from the earth, I decided to practice it. Whether it works or not, from it I benefitted in other ways. My calloused soles give me much better purchase on coconut trees, and they will undoubtedly fare better on barnacles now. I also may not have to replace my flip-flops when they finally pass away because a rubbery sole is now inbuilt in my physiology. My practice of Zazen meditation has unexpectedly delivered me from insomnia, and daily yoga practice has bettered my surfing. With each new skill, the direct benefit is usually accompanied by unexpected advantages, and my ability to creatively solve problems increases.

As a frugal minimalist, my needs are few. Because I aim to solve problems myself, rather than buy solutions, I am further from consumer society and less dependent on money. Of course, I do still use money, but as I need so little of it, my options for work are many. I don't need to work in a full-time job with the remuneration a key consideration, and I will have a wider variety of options than previously because my skills are more varied. Here is where another feedback loop shows itself. The more I learn to do myself, the less I need to work, and the more time I have to learn to do more things myself. Which loop would you prefer?

I don't aspire to live like a caveman in exile from all the wonderful advancements in science, technology, and medicine. I don't know what I'd do without my laptop or my Kindle. But I do think there is a point where we need to do things for ourselves. The trajectory and the plans modern society has for you otherwise are to remain trapped in the work-consume-die cycle. I find it odd that we call this situation civilised. We call it advanced. We call the pre-historic man primitive. He could make his own tools, home, and clothes. He could manage heating and running water and find sufficient food in his environment to live. All of this he accomplished within a working day of around two to three hours. The rest of his day was his own. Maybe they were primitive, but who's got it backwards?

13. Contribution and Activism

CONTRIBUTION

The well-being that arises from learning and growth fertilises the pre-embryonic notions of contribution. The escapee knows the more that he takes care of his health, happiness, and prosperity the more freedom and inclination he has to contribute to others and the world. Just as with the market ladies in Guatemala, when one is free, otherwise wasted efforts in utility can turn out to be the undercover agents of contribution.

Being of service or doing something for others can take a great many forms. It can be small favours like lending someone a hand, an ear, or a shoulder on which to lean or cry. Trivial acts that break a smile on someone's face or just saying hello to the unsuspecting in the street all constitute acts of contribution. It can be offering your time and labour as a volunteer or teacher or being involved in organisations that seek to empower people to stand up for themselves. We don't always know what all of the collateral impacts are going to be, but if the intention is to make the world a better place, then that is contribution.

With the time I have to consider things and my general satisfaction with my lot, these days I contribute in ways that I never once would have. When I was living in the bus, wherever I was parked my blip would pop up on the radar of some village somewhere. Curious local folks would gather around and make me think that my mundane, daily chores were the acts of some kind of other-worldly sorcerer. Not aware of what I consider to be my personal space, they'd poke their heads into my home through any unsecured opening and scan the contents - myself being the least interesting of them. They'd lock on and become entranced by something specific and superficial. It might be an artisan bag that I use for food storage, a trinket hanging off my rear-view mirror, or even a can of sardines. Often, I'd offer it to them (the sardines reluctantly). They would not be expecting it, and almost always it left them dumbfounded with their face alight as if from the reflection off of a bar of pure gold.

When I was camping near such villages, I'd take a stroll into town to buy supplies as a decoy to start a conversation with the locals. I would get information about the lay of the land, secret spots like waterfalls and rivers, and the best places to have my chickens and goats butchered if I required it. I would invite them for a meal at the bus. I'd get a buzz from the looks on their faces when they ate daal for the first time. What a strange variety of rice. Lentils are not readily available in Indonesia.

I have given away more significant things, but the most valuable contribution that one can make is with one's time.

It is the start of July 2017, and after a successful health stop in Hanoi, I am back on the road again. Visas don't last in perpetuity, and there was a lot of ground to cover. I pass again through the Karst Mountains of north-western Vietnam. They are staggeringly beautiful. They look like the Earth's teeth after they've been filed back in preparation for crowns. The roads are smooth and windy – great motorcycling. In the outlying areas of the Karst Mountains and progressively creeping inwards, the mountains have been blown up to extract the limestone to make cement. There are dozens of cement plants, and they and their clouds of cement dust in places overwhelm the landscape. Their product will be used to build more and better roads and hotels and bring more tourists to see the very landscape that they are blowing up.

Further south, in the town of Dong Hoi, I stop on account of the suffocating wafts of seafood. I decide not to eat any when I hear about a recent Union Carbide chemical spill that left the water unfit for swimming. You can't swim here, but you can eat the seafood.

However, I like Dong Hoi for another reason. On my first night, a young local teacher comes to the hostel. He befriends a few of the foreigners and invites us to join him for a free dinner with a bunch of local children from his school. He explains that they want to practice their English. Now, you may be thinking that the free dinner was what caught my attention, but no.

I do find free food, but it is almost all meat. Vegetables in Vietnam are only the accessories or decoration for meat. About a dozen children from five to fifteen years old, a few teachers, and my two foreign compatriots Sam, an Englishman and Sophie, a young Austrian girl, climb into the feast like it will be their last. The conversation starts to flow naturally, and the lists of questions they had previously produced are folded away.

A few sets of eyes notice my abstinence, so I explain to the table about my vegetarianism. The restaurant goes silent, perhaps in sympathy for what they consider to be an eating

273

disorder. I think I even hear a chap at a separate table drop his cutlery. Mouths full of food hang open as if to ask, "You mean to say you don't eat this?" After much condolence and pity, the teacher we met at the hostel, almost in a panic at his unanticipated poor hospitality, looks about the restaurant for a solution. His line of sight crosses beams with my own, as they land on the beer fridge. An eyebrow raises here; a nod joins it there; and within an hour I am overstepping my socially acceptable conversational perimeter on account of about a dozen cans of cold beer and no food inside me. The food and beer were certainly very welcome, but it was not the motivation for nor the reward from that night. Both of these, were found in the act of contribution.

I ride south through the historic city of Huế, the modern metropolis of Da Nang, Hội An, and Qui Nhơn. All are beautiful cities, and in all I can see much modernisation and the retailification and pollution that come with it. In Qui Nhơn, I contemplate stopping for a while and starting a mission to educate folks about rubbish. But this contribution goes no further than the theoretical realm. It flies in and out of my mind like Vietnamese Death Riders fly in and out of traffic.

The Death Riders are the mostly female scooter riders who seem to have no fear of death and absolutely no visibility of its coming on account of their outfits. To keep their skin white, they wear full-body onesies with a hood that keeps the sun off every part of their body but also obstructs their view of anything not directly in front of them. They remind me of Ewoks in desert garb. Not only are they restricted to horse blinker visibility, but they also come screaming out of side streets from between buildings and cross two lanes of the highway before settling on the shoulder, where they carry on unaware of the chaos they cause behind them. The possibility of encountering one or more of them keeps me alert and my knuckles white while I'm riding.

By August, I am at the southernmost border crossing to Cambodia at Hà Tiên. It would be fair to say that on account of the rate at which I was moving and the lack of any stops that lasted more than a few days, I didn't contribute a heck of a lot in Vietnam. But in Cambodia, this would change.

For a month, I drift around the popular tourist destinations of Angkor Wat and the islands in the Gulf of Thailand, but it is the Cardamom Mountains in Cambodia's southwest that I will remember the most. This region is often referred to as the last wilderness in Cambodia, and I can confirm this seems to be the case. The road from Pursat at the northern edge of the region and the last proper town before entering "The Cardamoms" is challenging without a dirt bike, particularly in the wet season. I get a taste of what riding a motorcycle must have been like for Agata.

After months of almost entirely human affected landscape, this is the first real nature I have seen: no towns, farms, raised forests, hydroelectric plants, and almost no people. The jungle is thick and loud. When I stop the bike for a drink or a cigarette, the raucous objection of birds and insects intensifies and proclaims that I must keep moving. This is no place for my kind. After so many months without it, I return to bathing in rivers again. It reminds me of Sumatra and bus life, and I begin to think it might be time for me to return soon.

I arrive at the Osoam Community. This is one of the very few villages in the region and nothing more than a dozen buildings along a stretch of dirt road. The first building stands out from the rest, and this is where I park. It is part of a large compound with multiple buildings, and it's where Lim, a local man, is trying to set up a permaculture educational facility for both locals and tourists alike. When I meet Lim, I find he is unusual for a Cambodian in that he thinks about long-term solutions to his country's problems. He talks about sustainable farming, replacing logging with tourism, decontaminating the land, and how to reuse, repurpose, and recycle. I like him. We chat about his various projects and his struggles to get the local people to understand this way of thinking. Many people here live hand-to-mouth. Surviving is the priority for them, not thinking about the long-term.

I take a room in his lodging. It is a simple wooden room with unfinished sections of the walls that he calls windows. They look out onto his farm's papaya, pepper, dragon fruit, and pineapple plots. There is a desk and a chair. Paradise. I decide to stay a while and help out with the various projects he has on the go. I know he arranges work for food and board deals, but I don't want to be bound to any work schedule, so I don't mention it. I'll just help out when I feel like it.

In this beautiful part of the world, I stay for two weeks. I befriend Lim's neighbour, an Englishman, Nik, who fills his time running dirt bike tours and educating, or rather scolding, Lim, a newcomer to permaculture. Nik ran farms in Spain many years ago and has the wherewithal about such things. One of our main projects, under Nik's command and Lim's execution, was the building of an industrial-grade compost heap. This involved not only the construction using waste wood materials we could find around his property and the village in general, but also the precise and pedantic manner in which to layer the compost itself. Some days I would be on cow poo-finding missions, others on general weeding. The product of this would be meticulously applied to the growing heap, much like one would prepare a lasagne.

When I was not interested in working, I would read and write and improve my chess skills with Nik. He was indeed a master. Why wouldn't he be? He had plenty of time. In the two weeks I was there, I saw not a single customer.

He taught me a lot about bikes. He taught me how to recondition a carburettor. Of course, he taught me a lot about compost and permaculture. It didn't feel like I was labouring for nothing. It didn't feel like I was working at all. I was just helping out with no expectation of anything in return, but at the same time gaining much.

So, what am I saying about contribution? Do I contribute because even though I don't know if I will receive something return, I suspect that I will? Possibly I only help out because I subconsciously expect the recipient of my favour to feel obliged to repay it. Or do I think making deposits in the Karma bank will put me into credit? Maybe. Maybe I contribute because I believe I will receive a warm and fuzzy feeling of gratitude. Perhaps I want others to feel good and laugh because that makes me feel good. If so, is contribution selfish? On account of all of all of these possibilities, it probably is. But the result is usually a win-win all around.

I was in The Cardamoms when the final chapter concerning my old stone building in Croatia unfolded. Previously, the house had been listed for sale for some time, and it had generated little interest, except for a Bulgarian lady who came across my internet advertisement and could see the dream that I once saw in it. She wanted to buy it. This would not only deliver a sizeable balance sheet bonus but would also stop the leaking of $200 a month in corporate accounting fees.

We struck a deal, and as she was not financially in a position to buy it, we established a payment plan over three years. For the first few months, everything proceeded as planned. We increased our contact and developed something of a friendship even though I had never met her.

The payments soon became scarce and eventually stopped, but we remained in contact, and she remained apologetic, sending small amounts when she could. She regularly spoke of her dream of living by the Croatian seaside in an ancient stone building. This was my dream too, once, but not anymore. Why was I holding on to this liability when it could fulfil someone's dream?

One night there in the mountains, I got in touch with her and said she could have it. That's that. Do the paperwork, and it's yours. As a European citizen, she could put it in her name and avoid the accounting fees. We nullified our existing deal and commenced the transfer process. She was obviously elated and insisted that she would pay me every cent according to the original contract. Whether she does or not is up to her; it is no longer my concern, and I am content to forego any sale proceeds from an alternate buyer.

When I think about it even now, I feel mostly relief. That thing caused me no end of worry and cost, all for something I didn't even want. So, what exactly happened here? Did I forego an alternate sale and give it to her as a selfless act? On some levels, specifically the financial one, it might seem like that, but there was more to the transaction than dollars. It was not conscious or intentional at the time, but my act of contribution, giving someone their dream, was met with something in return. I was liberated from my monthly expenses and worries, and then I got to feel good about perpetrating a random act of kindness. Win-win, again! Perhaps there is something more to that feel-good factor than meets the eye. If one thinks back to an earlier topic about the falsehood of separation, and one considers that one is a part of the rest of the world, well no wonder being of service feels good.

I can tell you though, giving stuff away is not easy in this world. To give that house away I had to leave Cambodia, travel to Thailand to the Australian Embassy to witness a Croatian document to sell a house I bought from a Spanish fellow to a Bulgarian lady.

Contribution regardless of motive is about adding something to the world. This includes adding something to yourself, your friends and family, your community, and the world at large. If you ask yourself if in any act you have added value, then that is contribution. When I ask myself this question about the things I do in my day, I can see when I am not adding value and subsequently consider doing something else.

Adding value to yourself can take the form of education and even self-reflection and making yourself a more peaceful and energetic person to be around. When you are happier within yourself, adding value to others is a lot easier.

And like everything, with contribution, it's got to be fun and not shit. Why take anything seriously? Even with serious matters, why not enjoy the process within that? Contributing by helping to feed starving children in Africa is not in itself a hilarious thing but working within it does not need to be morbid. One can make it as entertaining as possible. I suspect the recipients of your contribution would prefer to deal with someone who uplifts them than with someone gloomy.

ACTIVISM

There are so many ways you can contribute to the world, so choose something in which you are interested. I live outside of the usual political and societal frameworks of my country, perhaps any country. But that does not mean I am not interested in them. I like to contribute by undermining social and political systems that I see as unjust, inequitable, or destructive through writing and activism. I want to contribute to change in those systems. I find myself involved in such a way in some of the countries I travel through.

Sometime back in 2013 during my last escape attempt, I was in San Cristobal de Las Casas, Chiapas, Mexico. Chiapas was and still is a hotbed of activism that centres around the rights, dignity and autonomy of indigenous people, particularly of that the state, but not exclusively. The rights of the people are championed by the Zapatista Army of National Liberation (Ejército Zapatista de Liberación Nacional, EZLN), often referred to as the Zapatistas. Since 1994 their struggle has been ongoing. Led by the charismatic and poetic Subcomandante Marcos (who has recently renamed himself), the Zapatistas wear ski masks so that they *can be seen but not seen*, according to one of their slogans, and nobody knows the real identity of Marcos, known as the "Sup."

Their struggle has inspired international support, largely on account of the words of the Subcomandante. His and the Zapatista's stories are fascinating, romantic, inspiring, and yet devastating and the topic of many books written by the Sup and others.

San Cristobal de las Casas is a Zapatista stronghold, the flash-point of the armed uprising of 1994 and the centre for modern foreign involvement. The city was still awash with Zapatista energy when I was there. It was difficult not to get absorbed into it. Their struggle is magnetic, and many foreigners empathise with it, including me. Through his inspirational writings and resolve, the Sup is something of a sex-symbol to boot, and not just for women. I developed quite a crush on him in the months I was in that town, decided that I was with him, and set about getting involved.

A Spanish girl who was staying at my hostel and an Australian lady I had met in a cafe were already heavily involved, so I leveraged their information and contacts. There were film nights, meetings, and talks, clandestine and otherwise. After a while, it seemed that this was the only show in town. Activists would head off to one of five possible Zapatista villages in Chiapas to act as human shields in so-called peace camps. After being vetted to ensure they were not a paramilitary or government infiltrator, volunteers would be shipped off for two-week stints in one of the villages as 'observers'.

Camping somewhere near the entrance to the village, the foreign volunteers had to keep their electronic equipment visible at all times, mainly when the village was visited by those intending to cause harm, usually at the instigation of the federal government. The idea was that if the visitors with malintent suspected they were being monitored, events would pass peacefully, and there would not be a repeat of such a massacre as happened at Acteal, another Zapatista village, where forty-five villagers were gruesomely slain in a church with machetes by government funded paramilitaries.

The Zapatistas, considering their resources, were an efficient operation and had much solidarity throughout the world. Their message was getting out and foreign involvement increasing. They were somewhat secretive for self-preservation reasons, but they opened up one of their villages, Oviedo, on New Year's Eve so that solidarity groups and individuals could spend some time in their communities, listen to talks, see how they lived, and learn how to be active.

It was cold and muddy. The building allocated to us for sleeping was jam-packed. The amount of interest was impressive. Now, being an alcohol-free zone, it may not have been the wildest New Year's celebration, but being involved, listening, empathising, and seeing their reality made it most impactful and memorable.

The Zapatista struggle continues today, and while my minor involvement is on read-only mode for now, I plan to up the ante at some point in the near future.

Contribution by activism can be active or passive. Passive activism can be in signing and forwarding petitions on social media, boycotting products, and contributing $5 to a campaign. None of it is for nothing. But with freedom, you can become a more active activist. You can physically attend protests, visit your local government representative, and chain yourself to a tree to take on a bulldozer. If you don't have to go to work, why not? As an escapee, you have the time to think about your position on matters, and as you are not sedated by the paradigm into inactivity, you can consider doing something about it. There is no limit to how far you can go. Well, there is the law, but I tend to find the law a bit greyish and would not be entirely clear when I am and am not operating within its porous boundaries. The name of the game is to get involved.

14. Creativity and Experiments

"The difficulty lies not so much in developing new ideas as in escaping from old ones."

—John Maynard Keynes

CREATIVITY

An escapee can use freedom to focus on health, travel, learning, growth, and contribution. But what impetus is there to use that liberated time and space for creativity? First, humans tend to gravitate towards it when the inertia of the various levels of the paradigm is removed or reduced. Second, it is an effective way to increase your well-being.

I'm talking primarily about happiness. When you embark upon creative projects, particularly those of your own inspiration and conception, you increase the potential for fulfilment through your accomplishments. Even if they are not successful in the end, happiness is often supported by the fun and figuring you go through along the way.

How does one become creative and devise creative projects? A recent escapee might have had the faculty drained out of him over many years, but it exists inside everyone somewhere. One needs to rummage around inside and find the creator. But how does one do that?

The same tools I discussed in the section on Envisaging A Good Life apply here. This is how you reveal the creator and the muse. It's how to find out what truly inspires you. You need that same blank canvas. Once you use those tools to clear the debris from the windscreen of your mind, the creative road ahead will appear.

That might all sound a bit esoteric so there are a few other practical things you can do to light up the so-called "right" side of your brain. The first thing is to go beyond thinking that some people are creative and others are not. That's baloney. Sure, some people's creations might have more general appeal than others, but I'm not talking about opening an art gallery and going toe-to-toe with Michelangelo. I'm talking about being creative in everyday life.

We need to remove the belief that we are not creative, and to do this we can dissect and demystify the creativity of others. I know that sounds negative. Maybe it is, but it will help you get over your creative block. Obviously don't go and tell them that their work is crap; that's not the point even if it is crap. I like to look at articles and books in a similar genre to mine and examine the individual paragraphs and sentences. Where the book I am dissecting might have been impressive to me, when I look at what makes it up, it's no big deal. I tell myself I can write that sentence or that paragraph. When I find particularly bad examples, while I am not aiming to gloat, I tell myself I can write better than that, and that gives me the creative confidence to write as I do, which also may well be crap.

You might look at an invention and break it down, see how basic it is, and say, *I could have invented that.* Look at the yoyo, the cat flap, and the shoe horn. None of these creations is particularly outstanding. And as for Pro Hart, who can't shoot a pile of paint on a canvas with a shotgun? All I'm saying is that such creative exploits are not as unreachable as one might think, and it's important to know this when you are contemplating your creative potential.

The next thing to consider is clarity and simplicity. When I say that genuine creativity needs to come from a space of nothingness, that implies that the space has both clarity and simplicity. While it is true that I often generate creative ideas when I have had a few drinks of an evening, 90 percent of these are edited into extinction by a clear head in the morning. Intoxicants can shift a headspace such that creativity reveals itself, but it's hardly a reliable or sustainable approach. According to Emerson:

> The spirit of the world, the great calm presence of the creator, comes not forth to the sorceries of opium or of wine. The sublime vision comes to the pure and simple soul in a clean and chaste body. That is not an inspiration which we owe to narcotics, but some counterfeit excitement and fury. Milton says that the lyric poet may drink wine and live generously, but the epic poet, he who shall sing of the gods and their descent unto men, must drink water out of a wooden bowl.[27]

So, in seeking this clarity and simplicity, it is a good idea to be in good physical and mental condition. The two times in my day when I am the most creative are in the morning just after I have finished meditating and throughout my morning wake-up ritual. I keep a notepad handy to jot down words, notes, and ideas that almost always flow forth during and after these times. I also get interesting ideas when I am walking alone in the jungle or on the beach and sitting out in the waves at sunrise when there are few

285

others about. In all of these situations, it takes a little time for my mundane internal chatter to quiet, leaving the space for creative ideas to bud.

Your creative muse in no way needs to be useful. The result of creation can merely be art or beauty. I recall one afternoon in Bajawa, Flores, not long after the incident with the pig. We had gone as far as geography would allow and were on our way back to Bali. We were taking a break from the bus, staying in a guesthouse under the shadow of Gunung Inerie, the dominant volcano in the area. Amber had just finished six hours of hand tattooing. She had doodled some meaningless but artful design which she was progressively applying to my shoulder and back. It was one of her creative outlets. I guess my role was simply to provide the skin—a bit less creative, but still, I played a role.

We sat on a daybed in the yard with Inerie in the background, painting cicada shells with nail polish and paint pens, then affixing them to a nearby tree trunk in a winding single file to make it look as if they were on the march somewhere. This entertained us for few hours and is an excellent example of creating something with absolutely no utility. We laughed our way through the process, and I hear that for many weeks those cicada shells formed the basis of an urban myth about the unique and colourful breed of cicadas to be found in the Bajawa area.

The object of your creation can be utterly meaningless. Experiment with it. Whittle a gear stick knob in the shape of a phallus, paint unicorns on your bumper bar, and add tie-died ribbons above the windows and doors of your car to give it a bohemian feel. If that fails, tell people they are to ward off the flies. It really doesn't matter. Once you get into the flow, it becomes addictive and progressive as you move from one thing to the next. Before you know it, you are a creation machine, and you see possibilities everywhere. Just make sure that whenever you create something, "It's got to be fun and not shit."

EXPERIMENTS

Some folks say that creativity shines most in dance, music, and the arts. Judging by my achievements thus far, namely, my underwhelming salsa skills, a ukulele sound that even I wince at, and a remote tree somewhere full of multi-coloured insects, should you reconsider listening to me? Please stay, those folks are missing a vital component in the creativity recipe. They forget about experiments.

I am far more interested in play than I am in work. I believe that life should be lived as a game, going from one experiment to the next. And in this sphere, I think the opportunities are far more plentiful. Life in Bessie the bus, in Indonesia with Amber and Rocket, two people who were almost strangers to begin with, was one such experiment. I even referred to it as such at the time. It was an experiment in being nomadic, living simply, living wild, and sharing this with the idea of family.

And thinking back to that experiment, perhaps you shouldn't be listening to me after all because after six months in that mobile laboratory, things had stopped being fun and were becoming shit. By Christmas 2015, the cracks were starting to show in more than just the bus's paintwork. The experiment results were not yet conclusive, but it had to be shut down regardless, citing the potential for animal cruelty - to the three animals, that is, who were inside the bus. I loved the lifestyle, but as had become apparent, I was alone in that. We returned to the compound in Ubud, Bali.

At the start of 2016, I found myself idle, pondering new experiments. It was then that I embarked upon *The Consumption Cleanse,* one of my most beneficial experiments to date. But it was hardly as though being on a diet was a full-time occupation. Sure, I was researching and writing, but I was unfulfilled, and I knew I needed something more. A few short trips to Southeast

Asia did not satisfy me. I required something more significant, more worthwhile

Throughout the first half of 2016, stagnating with the girls in Ubud slowly dampened both my spirit of adventure and my relationship with them. But in that fizzling, there would turn out to be just enough spark to light the wick of a new experiment that came across my mental desk one day. There was not sufficient spark to reignite the relationship, however. That flame extinguished.

Around the middle of 2016, I bought a former food bus off a government repossession agent. This bus was called Rosie. I would say good bye to Bessie, Amber and Rocket and travel the other way from that which I had gone with them. I would go west, through Java and to Sumatra.

I enjoyed bus life previously. I knew the autonomy of transport meant I could go almost anywhere. I planned to live as simply, cheaply, and close to nature as I knew how. I planned to become as self-reliant as possible by filling in the gaps as I went. I would cook my own food, mend my own clothes, provide my own shelter and transport, and be as healthy as I could be. That was the basis of the experiment.

But before all of that, the first act of creativity was to customise the interior of a food bus. The bus needed some minor bodywork, and I needed somewhere to sleep. The means to cook was not essential as road food would fill my belly. I had no master plan. This build would be incremental and freestyle by building bits as I needed them from what was available to me as I drifted along. I found some body workers on the outskirts of Ubud; their workshop was slowly being consumed by the surrounding forest. I struck a deal whereby I would pay them to do the necessary bodywork, and I would use their workshop, electricity, and tools to make myself somewhere to sleep.

It took me about two weeks to gut the bus, build the bed and storage, and give the old girl a few test drives. It took the jungle brothers the same time to fulfil their side of the bargain, but most of that time was spent idly watching the odd foreigner build his new home inside his car. The concept was incomprehensible to them.

Leaving Bali after I had completed the initial bare essentials fit-out was a glorious day; it was day one of the next experiment. It was the start of my simple life on the road. It was a long-time dream exploding into reality. The other thing that exploded in reality a mere two days after the ferry crossing from Bali to Java was a couple of decaying seals that served some enigmatic purpose within the engine. They did serve to render my home and transport immovable. I knew that much. At this rate, I would be seeing 183 mechanics each year. Luckily, while I would see my fair share of repairs, this weighty ratio would not hold.

A farmer who saw me stranded on the side of the road in the pouring rain applying mathematics to my likely future breakdown frequency gave me a ride on his *Flintstones*-esque scooter about a kilometre down the road to a scooter workshop. Unable to replace or even know what these seals did other than cause a noisy geyser of steam to drain the radiator, the motorbike mechanic went to work fashioning new seals from spare bits and pieces found around the workshop's earthen floor. The result was impressive and would last at least another year. Hopefully beyond. Creativity is everywhere.

I drove quickly through Java and most of Sumatra until I got to Medan. I planned to move slowly from there. The roads to the west of Bali aren't as bad as those to the east, but the drivers make up for it. My knuckles were so white at the end of each day that, they almost looked like bare bone. I managed to avoid any injuries from collisions but my body was wrecked nonetheless. The physical stress and the constant yanking on the steering wheel left me with shoulder injuries that I would later get treated in Hanoi.

After Medan, I slowed down and slipped into the kind of living I had imagined. The building work continued as I added more utility to the bus. A Dutch girl joined in those first few weeks, and it was with her that I built the kitchen, perhaps why it looked so professional, and Rosie got her name. People wonder why a blue bus is called Rosie. The truth is that's just her first name. On account of the relentlessly bumpy roads, and possibly the accelerated bowel movements that go hand in hand with newcomers to Indonesian food, my new Dutch friend contracted a minor case of haemorrhoids. At that point, we thought of the name Blood-fart, but subsequently thought it was a bit crass. So, while that remained her hyphenated surname, we would introduce her only as Rosie.

We drove through regions of Northern Sumatra where the ethnic Batak people live. There they practice many varieties of religion characterised mainly by Christian and Animist dogma and rituals. We got to talking about Paganism and, with the help of Google, discovered that we were, in fact, Pagans according to at least one dictionary definition. I remembered my days in South America and the joy we found in the worship of *Pachamama* there and decided that I must look into more Pagan rituals as a future social experiment. It could be fun.

About a month or two after leaving Bali, a surfer friend from Sydney joined us, and we drove south with the plan to go surfing in the Banyak Islands. After many promises of large and empty waves and much fuss to get there, particularly for him, we found not a ripple. After my Australian friend recovered from disappointment and we released him from suicide watch, we abandoned all hope of surfing and decided to head north to the jungle in the area of Bukit Lawang.

Along the way, we met a remarkable mechanic. Rosie was not happy with the rapid low-gear changes required to handle a route that was more pothole than tarmac. Sometimes we would be in one pothole long enough to go through more than one gear. Rosie was having none of it and blew a seal somewhere on her underbelly in protest. We were able to get her to the nearest town's mechanic's house. A mob of local people followed us there. I could tell by their excited yapping that this man was something of a local legend. This short, quiet man worked closely with his son. Both of them lay in the mud under Rosie examining the complaint. He would ask his son questions in local dialect so I could not understand. His son would answer. It seemed that his son did the fetching, while the mechanic stayed closer to the problem. He seemed to only work when his son was under the car as well. Almost an hour into the repair about twenty people had gathered, and those who spoke Indonesian told me short stories about the vehicular guru who was under my bus. Eventually, after having his son modify a spare part at his detailed instruction, they fitted it and declared the problem resolved. It was another example of Sumatran creativity. The crowd was patting themselves on their backs for possessing such a hero. But it was only when he slipped out from under the car and stood up to face us, that we realised their pride was mostly because this man was almost completely blind.

We drove on that night, humbled by that man and his son. Two days later we arrived in Bukit Lawang, a dot that had whined for attention on my radar for some time by then. It was dark, so we took refuge in the first available guesthouse. It wasn't possible to get Rosie down to the river, so we left her secure a few blocks away. We would explore the village the next day and find a better place to sleep.

In the morning we woke up and set off along the river that defines the shape of the one-path town. The path hugs the river

291

for about half a kilometre and is dotted with guesthouses, cafes, souvenir shops, and woodcarving workshops. As you walk along it, the jungle dominates the view on the other side. After the initial stretch of side-by-side tourist establishments, the buildings thin out and seem to blend in more with the forest. By this time, we still hadn't found anywhere suitable to stay. We wanted somewhere organic looking, on the river, and cheap.

As we got close to where the path finished, we did not see where we would stay; we heard it. We heard the punishing, yet strangely entertaining shouting of a woman. We rounded a bend and saw a woman with her arms aloft shouting at a man who was working on an inflated tyre tube raft. As she yelled, he smiled and nodded like a naughty child being scolded, but he didn't waver from his task. He was smiling way too much for a man who was in trouble. They both saw our troupe coming. The woman gruffly shouted at us to come hither; the man laughed at her and waved us over. That would be the first of many visits I would make to see Masa and Nor, and with each time the greeting would become no less cordial.

After a week of jungle fever, my Australian and Dutch friends departed, and I set off to behind the jungle wall with Masa. He and I spent just short of a week in the intensity of the Gunung Leuser eco-system, camping under black plastic sheets in the mud and rain. We walked for most of each day and spotted unusual wildlife not found in the jungle wall. Sometimes we followed the spoor of an Asian rhinoceros, but we would never see one. I am told one does not want to see a tiger, as almost certainly, it will have seen you first and will not be there just to roast marshmallows with you.

Aside from the crew at the Mboy Guesthouse, it would be this jungle that would call me back again and again. It was far from comfortable, but somehow it already felt like home, and I would not be long away from it for the rest of my days in Sumatra.

By September I was on the move again, driving through Aceh, the most north-westerly of the provinces of Sumatra. For about a month I mostly camped, read, wrote, and exercised. There was plenty of surfing and mostly empty waves.

After circumnavigating Aceh, I ended up back in Singkil, the jumping-off point for the Banyak Islands. It was also one of the ferry ports for the island of Nias. I knew close to nothing about Nias, but there was a car ferry, so I presumed there were roads. I waited for the overnight ferry and then with Rosie, hit the high seas for this surfing mecca of surfing meccas. I arrived in Gunungsitoli the following morning sick, grey-faced and unrested. It was the roughest ocean-going journey either of us had experienced.

At the dog-ridden market there I stocked up on food, not knowing what to expect in the south where I was heading. On the ferry, I read up about Sorake Beach and Lagundri Bay, the home of one of the most exceptional right-hand reef breaks in the world, apparently. A few hours later, after passing many small villages but mostly palm-lined beaches and more jungle, I pulled into Sorake Beach. There was some kind of festival on, so driving through the beachside village was slow. I like this because I get to soak up the local vibe. Locals like it less because they can't help but stare at me, and this sometimes causes human-to-human, human-to-electricity pole, and other minor collisions.

I inched through the main part of the village to the far end where it thinned out, and there were openings between the buildings where I could see the surf. Ordinarily, I would find accommodation first, but that time, looking at the perfect right hander breaking not too far offshore, I parked and embarked. In my naivety, and on account of the mostly sandy bottom breaks in recent Aceh, I didn't contemplate that epic waves such as these in Indonesia are usually caused by coral reefs. The very first wave I caught reminded me, though, as my first bottom turn scraped the reef and relieved my board of one of its fins. It was low tide. I left the water with my tail between my legs and went in search of accommodation.

Not far from where I was parked, which was close to the waves, I found a guesthouse that was sufficiently rundown to suggest it might be at the cheaper end of the spectrum. Not only that, there was a large gravel car park where, should I negotiate effectively, I could park without having to rent a room. I drove in and parked in a way that made the bus discreet to help with the negotiations.

I walked over to what was obviously the resident families abode, as it was of a higher standard than the guest quarters surrounding it.

"Selamat Pagi!" I hollered in the usual morning greeting.

"Apa?" came the annoyed reply from a diminutive and irritated-looking young woman who emerged gnawing on what looked to be about half a chicken carcass.

This woman immediately presented as someone not to be messed with. In the absence of paying any rent, I said I would eat her food and drink her beer hoping that would make my stay worthwhile for her. I needn't have offered though, as she seemed not all that bothered by me and far more interested in her meal. With that loose agreement and as she turned to walk away, I asked what her name was.

"Mamma Naya," she muttered, through a mouth full of masticated chicken.

15. Connection

---

*When people go within and connect with
themselves, they realize they are connected to
the universe, and they are connected to all*

living things.

— Armand DiMele

CONNECTING TO SELF

*I talk about connection, but the concept can be understood all
the way into redundancy. When the realisation hits home that
everything is already connected and that you are a part of
everything that you ordinarily consider not-self, then there is
nothing at all to connect to. You can say that your hand is
connected to your arm, but really, it is a part of it as much as it is
connected to it. Freedom from the paradigm gives you the freedom
for realising the different levels of connection such that the very
idea of connection disappears.*

I am often asked how I feel about spending so much of my time
alone. But unlike those lonely days back in Chile, while I am often
alone, I am rarely lonely. Back then I was missing the feeling of
connection. It is true that I would like to see my close friends and

family more frequently, but it is not often I think about it because I know I find connection everywhere, so I do not need to look for it. The most fundamental connection I found was the one I made with myself.

It's no secret that where we exist in space-time is here and now. We are not existing in any other time. The past no longer exists and the future does not yet exist. But how often do we live accordingly? It's one thing to read it; it's quite another to live it. Despite the common sense of it, in the chaos and commotion of modern life, it's not easy to live in this way. We spend so much of ourselves remembering and living in the past and planning for the future that we are rarely satisfied with right now. I realised, at least in theory, that I could not be satisfied and happy unless I lived outside of the dimension of time and just at the point of time that is now. Because that is the precise time and place when and where I exist, it is the only time and place to connect with myself. I have the "time," the space, and the notion and so I set about practising just that.

I had done some work in resolving my past through the transformational course I talked about earlier, and that structured approach was helpful in cleaning up some of my past distractions. Spending a lot of time in silence and solitude sent me on an inward trajectory where I could sweep up the litter of the past and the as-yet unrealised concerns of the future such that only here and now remain. When thoughts would pop up that were related to not-now, I'd just let them swim around until they exhausted themselves.

It was like a kind of waking meditation. After a few hours of wandering around like this in the jungle or on a lonely beach somewhere, the noise would stop, and a sense of peace would settle in. When that happens, it brought a deep satisfaction with everything, with right here and now and with myself and everything around me. I figured that this was probably the place to meet my real self, my true nature. There, it is not lonely at all.

When I experience that sensation, it is usually not something I have planned. However, there is also a planned department of that thought(less) experiment, and that is intentional meditation. It has the same effect, but it happens in much less time. When I'm not in a natural environment, I'll find a dark and quiet place somewhere and go about emptying my mind. I'll come out of the spell after about twenty minutes with that same inner and outer feeling of connection. It has taken some time and regular practice to get to this point, and I am not so Zen that I am connected to everything. Flies in my nose and ears and yowling cats can still break my trance, but they are a part of nature, and I'm working on that with them.

With man's noises, the traffic, construction, the noise of industry, and the sound of work, it's hard to find a peaceful situation. Nature's noise is different. The sound of waves and waterfalls, cicadas, birds, monkeys, and hopefully soon, even flies and cats seem to be conducive to connecting with our real self thus connecting with our awareness. It's no coincidence that it is referred to as our true "nature."

CONNECTION TO OTHER

When I say that connection is everywhere, I'm not suggesting that you can't manipulate the types and the quality of the connections in your life by putting yourself in their path.

It is mid-September of 2017. I have just decided after nine months here that my time in Indochina is over. I've been feeling the urge to return to the Sumatran jungle, the community there, and to Rosie. Something I did not at first understand about my jungle home was that it provides a density of connection at every level. With the solitude, the jungle noises, the jungle itself, and my community there, I'm surprised I don't overdose on it. It makes sense that I suffer withdrawal from it.

***

It's late afternoon as I turn the last bend on the riverside path and see the Mboy Guesthouse. I can see Masa's extended family milling around and blocking the path. Their family seems to have new members every time I come here. The guesthouse and its satellite shacks almost seem like they are their own suburb. Nor sees me, points, and yells, "Bung Toyib!" The commotion all turns at once as if watching a tennis ball that Nor has just served at me. When I reach them, the children grab for my hands to touch to their heads. Nor muscles through them and gives me a hug. She is followed by the other adults. I feel an embarrassing pride that I would deserve such a greeting.

Masa arrives a few minutes later on his motorbike; he had gone to the bus station to pick me up. I hadn't told him when I would be arriving and did not expect him to collect me. I wonder how long he was waiting. It does not surprise when I learn he had been gone for hours. We sit down in a new makeshift wooden and corrugated iron area that Masa says is their new café. It looks no different from any of the other shed-like buildings in their suburb.

It's not long before calm returns and river pace sets in. Cigarettes and storytelling set in as well as I fill them in on my adventures, and they tell me theirs. It feels good to be back. It feels good to see the jungle wall and the chocolate river that belies the fact that it has just been raining heavily. It feels good when each and every villager walks past and greets me, many not aware that I ever left.

In the morning after my wake-up ritual by the river, I wash in it, knowing that it is pointless with so much mud, but it still refreshes me. I find an eddy that isn't flowing fast and is clearer, brush my teeth in it, and think how long it has been since I have been able to do this. I sit in the whirlpool and watch the jungle for a while.

Before going back to Mboy, I walk the other way into the centre of the village. Many people I don't remember say hello and ask where I have been and when I came back. It's low season, so I'm more of an event than I would be in high season. I find a stall in the village whose owner I would often stop and chat with. She isn't there. But as I lean over her counter to see if she is sleeping behind it, a macaque jumps out of the stacked food as if he were just another thing for sale. He scampers past me and up a telephone pole on the other side of the path. It frightens me and wakes the stallholder, who was indeed asleep.

We skip the greetings as I point at the pole where the monkey is now trying to open a packet of Oreos it has stolen. The storekeeper is as agile as the monkey, and before I can say anything, she has come around to the front of the counter and thrown a can of red bull at the monkey. It misses and lands on the roof of the building opposite. The monkey drops the Oreos, which he had already opened, so they scatter all over the path. The stallholder laughs, and others from adjacent stalls come out to get her statement of the crime. Most of them laugh along with her; at least something happened today.

I usually eat with Masa and Nor, but this morning I walk to the far end of the village to a *Warung* where they serve pineapple rendang, one of my favourites. When I arrive, it is dark inside. There is a blackout. I repeat the same conversation I have had a dozen times already today, clear some cats to the edge of one of the tables, and order breakfast. The cats don't covet the curried

299

pineapple, but they can see I also have a generous pile of stink-fish, and as they are my dining partners, they will receive their allocation all in good time.

I arrive back at Mboy at the same time as Masa, again on his bike. I ask him where he has been.

"I take your battery to mechanic; it dead."

"Oh, OK thanks."

"Two hours and we go pick up."

"But there's a blackout isn't there."

"Maybe longer then."

I ask him if he can take me to where Rosie is parked so that I can check out her condition. When we get to the carport about a kilometre away, I see that she is covered in dust. I can also see that he has cut out a section of the cross-beam from the front of the carport to accommodate her height.

Before I open the door, I consider that everything inside her has been incubating there for nine months, including dirty bedding, clothes, possibly food scraps, and probably rodent droppings. Managing my expectations, I brace for the inevitable. I open the door expecting a stench like that from of a pile of spent tropical jock-straps. Instead, I'm hit by the same smell that I left there all those months ago. And riding on that familiar waft, transformed through my olfactory factory, are all the memories of the adventures gone by.

I look at Masa who is grinning at me like I'm about to sit on a planted whoopee cushion.

"Nor. She worry it smell, so she take all your clothes and bed and curtain and wash."

I sit inside the bus and survey my kingdom. Even as the current feelings of connection with Masa's clan are still fresh, the smell in the bus is at that moment joined by the taste of adventure, and I know I won't be here for long.

300

***

It's the fifth day at Mboy, and I'm having breakfast with Masa and Nor. She has cooked fresh stink-fish and rice. Masa is talking about one of his fellow guides who claimed to have seen a rhino only a two day walk from here.

"Buang, we go to jungle. Only four days, we see rhino."

He assumes that I will be keen, but I have already decided to leave. The look on their faces when I say that I am leaving tomorrow was the same as on mine when Trump got elected. I know they both thought my travels were done, at least for a while, and I'd be inhabiting my little room above the river, spending my days staring at the jungle, eating, and joking with their family. Silence. Nor breaks the impasse.

"Where you go?"

"Berastagi," I tell them the name of a volcano complex four hours from here.

Berastagi is a four-hour drive away, but it's further than either of them has been. Without wanting the quiet to return, Nor orders me to bring her all of my clothes, and even though they are still clean from her last efforts, she would wash them. She explains that I can't be going to the city, as she seems to think it is, with dirty clothes.

"And where you yesterday? You be here today for lunch?" she continues, avoiding a silence that none of us wants to return.

I realise only now that her brushing me off after each meal when I ask how much I owe is because I am eating with them as family, not as a guest. Feeling now doubly guilty about my decision to leave, I tell her I will be back for lunch, bring her my clean clothes, and set off on a planned hike to the wild Landak River for about a four-hour round trip.

301

I walk for about an hour along the jungle tracks crisscrossing shaded waterways, passing occasional bamboo huts, and exchanging greetings with groups of smiling plantation labourers. Normally, I would be entirely absorbed by such a jungle walk, but I'm unable to stop thinking about the reaction of Nor and Masa when I told them I was leaving. I feel a sadness that at first, I think is sadness for them. I feel like I am stripping them of some joy. By leaving I am taking away some excitement, some variation from their relatively uneventful lives. I let that feeling sit for a while, and then I realise that is not at all what it is. The sadness is my own. These people have opened their homes, their hearts, and indeed their entire lives to me. They have provided the connection that I am so often without, for which I am so often wanting. Now I am turning my back on it. It is this strength of connection that I will again be missing in my life. It is as if in a small way, this was paradise found only to lose it all over again.

When this truth dawns on me, I stop walking. I am connected to nature almost every day in Sumatra, but to people, not so much. I abandon the hike and walk back to the village and back to the Mboy. I will still leave this place, but I will spend the last day with Nor and Masa.

I turn the last bend and can see Masa sitting at their riverside café and Nor preparing lunch. It is stink fish by the smell of it. I can hear their loud banter. As I get near they draw me in and I sense that they have accepted that I am leaving. We smoke cigarettes and chat until Nor serves lunch. Family members sit with us, eat, and then leave again. With all of them, I chat and appreciate it all the more knowing it will be the last time I do that, maybe forever, who can tell?

I can't remember a louder and more joy-filled Nor, a Masa who has laughed so much, or myself so grateful for these people who I knew not even twelve months ago. We spend the rest of the day like this, living the life as it is lived by the river.

The next day, Rosie and I are gone.

# # #

Epilogue

After leaving the jungle at Bukit Lawang, Rosie and I travelled through western and southern Sumatra and later Java. We spent three months living even more simply than before and spending very little money. Diesel was the main expense.

These months were not just about driving. It wasn't just an experiment in simplicity and living without using much money. It was about living life. And in living life, I like to reflect, review, and revise the way I'm living it. This process is never-ending but does not need to be a bore. I keep in the back of my mind that it is all about health, prosperity, and happiness and fine tune it to converge with those ideals.

And then looking at those ingredients from one level deeper, I'll review my consumerism and minimalism. I'm always looking to eliminate the unnecessary in my life. My health regime is constantly in a state of improvement, and I'm ever mindful that what I'm doing gives me a sense of fulfilment. I want to ensure that I have enough "freedom for" pulling me forward, so I don't slip back into the life from which I escaped.

During those last three months, I experimented with not drinking. As I write it has been almost two months without any alcohol, and I do feel much more energetic and creative, and I have spent a lot less money per month than I ordinarily would. Addressing bad habits is always a candidate for experimentation. Smoking is next. I want to keep this mind-and-body thing alive! I have no intention of refraining from all vices, but I want to control them.

It is now just before Christmas, 2017, and we have just arrived in Bali. Rosie doesn't know this yet, but for a present, I'm getting

304

her a new owner. I plan to sell her. And I plan to plan some new experiments.

While I go through the process of publishing this book, I will conceive the next great plan(s). I'll be looking to use the tools and methods I mentioned in this book to come from a space of absolutely nothing, to create something ludicrous to do with my time. Nothing is safe from me; everything is an option at this stage. As long as those plans fit within my general life manifesto, they are candidates. I might even do some work! Calm down; it won't be for money.

The plans that have so far made it to the embryo stage and will incubate throughout January 2018 are a mixture of adventures, escapes, and contribution.

As for adventures, I am considering a repeat of the Indonesian experiment with a few modifications. First, the laboratory will be another bus in Latin America. Sub-plots within that theme are a) drive from Mexico to Southern Chili and back to b) live without money (net) c) establish a cult of Zen Frugal Minimalists somewhere d) become a Salsa legend in Cali, Columbia, and e) do something with the Guatemala coffee farms. These adventures are undeveloped as I write, but I assure you that one, more, or all of them will be underway next year.

What about experiments in escape? I feel that to at least some degree I have escaped from the physical and societal boundaries that I set out to escape from. In looking at different restrictions from which to be free. I now turn inward. I draw from my readings in Buddhism, particularly Zen, for this one. Buddhists say that all suffering stems from craving, and craving comes from not living in the present. So, I plan to continue my education in this philosophical realm without a particular target in mind, but broadly to escape from cravings and to become enlightened. How hard can it be?

Something I have enjoyed thoroughly in Southeast Asia over the last few years have been teaching kids English. It happens that this is a viable shortfall project. So, I plan to earn the necessary qualifications such that wherever I am, and in whatever experiment I am involved, I will also be able to teach English. This shortfall income will also go some way toward funding all the yurts, magic carpets, mandalas, gongs, and dream catchers we will need at the Zen Frugal Minimalist compound.

About the Author

Michael Blue, the author of *The Consumption Cleanse*, was born and educated (indoctrinated) in Brisbane, Australia. He is formally trained as an accountant and information technology specialist. Initially, his career was based in Australia, but from his mid-twenties, he spent as much time travelling and working abroad as he did in Australia. Throughout that time, he was self-educated as an escape artist.

He has been on the road living a simple, minimal life since June 2015 and until very recently called a big blue bus named Rosie his home. That bus, which provided transport, a place to sleep, cook, contemplate, and write, would most commonly be found adrift somewhere in Sumatra, Indonesia. There is no plan and no map, but a driving desire to live outside of the consumption society and live in a way that prioritises physical and mental well-being, integration with the natural world, and human community and creativity.

You can connect with Michael at:

Website: https://thelifeadrift.com/
Facebook: https://www.facebook.com/thelifeadrift/
Instagram: https://www.instagram.com/blueyadrift/
Twitter: https://twitter.com/MikeBlue111

Other Titles

Winner of the 2017 International Writers Inspiring Change
"Most Inspiring Author Award"

THE CONSUMPTION CLEANSE

Giving up 13 consumption habits in 13 weeks
for a better life and a healthier planet

Michael Blue

The Consumption Cleanse is a no-nonsense, research-referenced and achievable roadmap to the mindful consumption of food and beverages. The author has peeled back the marketing spin and corporate hogwash that is wrapped around many of our common foods to reveal the truth about what we eat.

Get it on Amazon now: http://a.co/h3Mvpbz

Acknowledgments

During the preparation of this book I have greatly benefited from the suggestions, criticisms, and corrections offered to me by those who have reviewed it as it was being written and revised. For this I thank Claude Forthomme, Moris Steiner, Lea Frei and Paul B. I also extend much appreciation to Julia from Edit911 for her invaluable advice and corrections throughout the editing process.

Reviews are Gold to Authors!

If you enjoyed this book and would like to help, then you could think about leaving a review on Amazon, Goodreads, or anywhere else that readers visit. The most important part of how well a book sells is how many positive reviews it has, so if you leave me one then you are directly helping me to continue on this journey as a writer. It will only take a few minutes of your time. Thanks in advance to anyone who does. It means a lot.

If you would like to find out more about my other publications then please visit my website for more details. You can find it at:

www.thelifeadrift.com

Notes

---

1   http://www.nytimes.com/1998/01/29/us/fossil-shows-ants-evolved-much-earlier-than-thought.html, retrieved 6/3/2018

2   https://en.wikipedia.org/wiki/Extinction, retrieved 6/3/2018

3   Michael A. Hoffman II. "The Forgotten Slaves: Whites in Servitude in Early America and Industrial Britain", http://www.hoffman-info.com/forgottenslaves.html, retrieved 3/2/2017

4   George Monbiot. *"Feral: Rewilding the Land, the Sea and Human Life"*. Chicago: The University of Chicago Press, 2014.

5   http://www.smh.com.au/business/workplace-relations/the-38hour-week-a-rarity-among-fulltime-workers-new-data-shows-20151027-gkk1r6.html, retrieved 21/11/2017

6   https://permanent.access.gpo.gov/gpo73386/Africa-Center-Special-Report-No.-3-EN.pdf, retrieved 6/3/2018

7   http://www.bbc.com/news/magazine-33133712, retrieved 27/5/2017

8   http://www.dictionary.com/browse/well-being, retrieved 27/5/2017

9   Michael Blue. *"The Consumption Cleanse: Giving up 13 consumption habits in 13 weeks for a better life and a healthier planet"*. Self-Published. Amazon Kindle Edition, 2016.

10   John C. Bogle. *"Enough: True Measures of Money, Business, and Life"*. Hoboken, New Jersey: John Wiley & Sons, Inc.,2009.

11   Seneca, Lucius Annaeus. *"Letters from a Stoic"*. New York: Penguin Books, Inc., 1996.

12   Maslow, A.H. (1943). "A theory of human motivation". *Psychological Review*. 50 (4): 370–96. doi:10.1037/h0054346 – via psychclassics.yorku.ca.

13   Danilo Garcia and Sverker Sikström. Cyberpsychology, Behavior, and Social Networking. June 2013, 16(6): 469-472. https://doi.org/10.1089/cyber.2012.0535

14 Native American Traditional proclamation.

15 Thomas Moore. *"The Re-Enchantment of Everyday Life"*. New York: HarperCollins, 1996.

16 https://thelifeadrift.com/2018/04/29/fitness-for-drifters/, retrieved 6/3/2018

17 http://onlinelibrary.wiley.com/doi/10.1002/ejsp.674/abstract, retrieved 6/3/2018

18 https://en.wikipedia.org/wiki/Frugality, retrieved 6/3/2018

19 https://thelifeadrift.com/2017/04/03/less-is-more/ retrieved 6/3/2018

20 http://www.cowspiracy.com/facts/, retrieved 23/11/2017

21 https://thelifeadrift.com/2017/11/17/nett-giving-at-christmas/ retrieved 6/3/2018

22 https://www.reinventingparking.org/2013/02/cars-are-parked-95-of-time-lets-check.html, retrieved 31/3/2018

23 https://melbourneinstitute.unimelb.edu.au/assets/documents/poverty-lines/2013/Poverty-Lines-Australia-December-Quarter-2013.pdf retrieved 6/3/2018

24 http://thelifeadrift.com/2017/12/06/**living-with-40-things**/ retrieved 6/3/2018

25 Check virtualtourist.com and gridskipper.com for unbiased travel content about candidate countries.

26 Bernard Shaw. *"Maxims for Revolutionists"*. Amazon Kindle Edition. HardPress, 2006.

27 Emerson, Ralph Waldo. Self-Reliance and Other Essays (Dover Thrift Editions). Amazon Kindle Edition: Seahorse Publishing, 2013